REHEARSAL

The Masque of Beauty and the Beast by Michael Elliott Brill. Presented by Eastern Michigan University. Virginia Glasgow Koste, director.

PRENTICE-HALL, Inc., Englewood Cliffs, New Jersey 07632

Sixth Edition

REHEARSAL

The Principles and Practice of Acting for the Stage

MIRIAM A. FRANKLIN • JAMES G. DIXON III

Library of Congress Cataloging in Publication Data

FRANKLIN, MIRIAM ANNA.
  Rehearsal: the principles and practice of acting for the stage.

  Includes index.
  1. Acting. 2. Drama—Collections. I. Dixon, James G. II. Title.
PN2061.F7 1983   792'.028   82–9833
ISBN 0–13–771550–1   AACR2

Printed in the United States of America

10 9 8 7 6 5 4 3 2 1

Editorial-production supervision and interior design by Paul Spencer
Cover design by Diane Saxe
Manufacturing buyer: Ron Chapman

ISBN 0-13-771550-1

Prentice-Hall International, Inc., *London*
Prentice-Hall of Australia Pty. Limited, *Sydney*
Prentice-Hall Canada Inc., *Toronto*
Prentice-Hall of India Private Limited, *New Delhi*
Prentice-Hall of Japan, Inc., *Tokyo*
Prentice-Hall of Southeast Asia Pte. Ltd., *Singapore*
Whitehall Books Limited, *Wellington, New Zealand*

Acknowledgments

Appreciation is extended to those who gave permission to reprint the following:

From *The Pajama Game*, by George Abbott and Richard Bissell. Copyright 1954 by George Abbott an⦁
    Richard Bissell. Reprinted by permission of Random House, Inc.
From *The Star Wagon*, by Maxwell Anderson. Copyright 1937 by Maxwell Anderson. Copyright renewe⦁
    1965 by Gilda Anderson. All rights reserved. Reprinted by permission of Anderson House.
From *I Never Sang for My Father*, by Robert Anderson. Reprinted by permission of International Creativ⦁
    Management. Copyright © 1966, as an unpublished work, by Robert Anderson; copyright © , 1968, b⦁
    Robert Anderson.
From *Antigone*, by Jean Anouilh, translated and adapted by Lewis Galantiere. Used by permission o⦁
    Dr. Jan Van Loewen Ltd.

Contents

PART TWO

Preparing Your Acting Instrument

CHAPTER 4

Your Body   29

CHAPTER 5

Your Voice and Speech   57

CHAPTER 6

Your Mind   80

CHAPTER 7

Build Your Emotions   107

CHAPTER **8**

Character Study

135

PART THREE
Preparing for Performance

CHAPTER **9**

Learning the Language

161

CHAPTER **10**

Blocking Stage Action

172

CHAPTER **11**

The Director and the Cast

205

Preface

The sixth edition of *Rehearsal* has a new look and contains fresh material, but it fulfills the same purpose as its predecessors: to offer basic helps to students of acting. As before, it includes both a study of the principles of acting and scenes from worthy plays for practice.

Because acting is an art, it demands both a knowledge of principles and excellence of performance. You can move toward that excellence by working with the play scenes offered here, as you cultivate your native talent in expressing mentally, physically, and emotionally the finest in dramatic literature.

Students' goals differ. Many of you expect to enjoy occasional participation in a play. Others hope that theater work will be a continuing avocation. Some plan to make acting a life profession, and to these we say yes, you can become a professional—*if*, in addition to talent, you have the perseverance to accept hardships, disappointments, and discouragements without losing the will to keep striving toward your goal. *Rehearsal* has been written to help all who wish to be part of the world of theater, in whatever capacity.

We wish to express sincere gratitude to the publishers, authors, and agents who control the rights to many of the plays represented here. They have been notably gracious in granting permission to quote excerpts which make it possible for you, the student, to profit from the best in theater. Without these excerpts, *Rehearsal* could not be the learning tool that it has been and remains.

Miriam A. Franklin
James G. Dixon III

REHEARSAL

PART ONE
Introduction to Theater

CHAPTER 1

Loosen Up for Acting

Imagine, if you will, a person wandering through the stage door of a theater thinking it is the bus depot. Bewildered? Yes. He or she sees the prop crew arranging stage furnishings, actresses touching up each other's hairdos and makeup, a fellow crouched in a corner snatching a last look at the script, the director moving here and there with words of encouragement and caution. Everybody is astir, excited.

You will soon be a part of this backstage nerve-tingling First-Nighter. You will always be exhilarated on a First Night.

There is a universal urge in us to view the lives of other people. Theater helps to satisfy this urge. Perhaps you have imagined yourself behind the footlights or on the screen, playing those roles that look so easy. From your seat in the auditorium, while you are "looking through rose-colored glasses," acting looks like real life—just being natural. However, when *you* begin that "easy" job, you are likely to find there is much more to it than you supposed.

This book gives you the ABCs of acting, but also explains the principles and practices used by players who have reached the XYZ perfection stage. Though few become *great* actors, by using your talent in accordance with the pointers given here, you can become a *good* actor.

To begin with, if you feel a bit timid or ill at ease about getting up to perform, there are loosening-up exercises to help you. Most of us have had the experience of trying to communicate without vocal speech when attempting to talk to someone who doesn't speak English. When we try to communicate with such a person we use hand gestures, exaggerated facial expressions, or even broad arm movements. A very good game to help people communicate without voice is *charades.*

Charades uses two groups of players that compete against each other. Each side, A and B, has a leader. Together they decide the number of minutes for guessing a title before having to forfeit a player to the opponents. They also decide on the number of words permitted in a title. Each player on both sides writes the title of a well-known song, book, magazine, play, or poem on a slip of paper and hands it to his or her leader, who places the slips upside down nearby for drawing. The leader of group B picks a slip written by someone in group A. First, group B leader answers by shake or nod of head as members of group B guess which kind of literature the title is from. Group B leader then acts out words or syllables to help group B guess the title. If they fail within an alloted time, they forfeit a player.

Choose titles that are simple to enact, for example, *Harper's.* You might pretend to play a large harp, then, stretching your imagination, point to your ears. Or *Gone With the Wind:* wave goodbye to all, leave, then return blowing and puffing while you wave your arms wildly to represent wind. Charades is a good game to help anyone use bodily expression, and it is good adult fun.

In *pantomime,* a person's body speaks what the voice does not, or possibly could not. The muscles in arms, neck, hands, the whole body show action, reaction, and emotions. Suppose you pantomime lifting a heavy stone from the ground and laying it on a wall. Your actions tell the audience that it is heavy and give an idea of its size; your effort shows in the tension of your hands, in your face, eyes, mouth, neck, even legs. Imagine you are arranging prickly-stemmed flowers into a bouquet. Your facial muscles and your eyes, mouth, and arm and leg muscles show your concentration and your fear of the prickles. An occasional jab makes you jump; perhaps you shake your injured hand.

The following exercises give practice in pantomiming simple daily actions. Show your thoughts and feelings as you would if performing the real actions.

Pantomimes

1. Pack your suitcase for a weekend with friends.
2. Clean imaginary spectacles. Shine them.

3. Select fruits and vegetables at a market.

4. You are hot, tired, discouraged. Drop into a chair, fan yourself with a newspaper, then see an item in the paper that surprises you.

5. It is a cold, blizzardy day; you come into the house thoroughly chilled. Try to get warm.

6. Find mending materials and mend a tear in the lining of your coat.

7. Practice tossing a basketball into a basket.

8. Toss and catch a softball against the side of a building.

9. Build a snowman.

10. You are wakened by alarm for an early class. Get up terribly sleepy.

11. Give yourself a shampoo. Comb and set your hair.

12. Your rear tire is flat. Change it.

13. Your car engine has stopped, you don't know why. Try several ways to start the motor. Nothing works.

14. Set the dining table for twelve guests.

15. Play a game of solitaire. Become puzzled. Talk about it.

16. Pick a bouquet of garden flowers and arrange them in a bowl. (Keep in mind the kinds of flowers.)

17. Through your binoculars, watch a blue jay which chases other birds away from the feeder.

18. Polish your shoes and talk to your friend about a recent game.

19. You are mowing the lawn. A bee keeps buzzing around, bothering you.

20. You are watching a football game. Show your feelings as your opponents keep winning points.

Mimes are an effective introduction to acting because they demonstrate very clearly that acting begins with *actions*. Too often beginning actors think that acting begins with feelings. They jump right into the words and try to conjure up the complex emotions of a character without first becoming familiar with the basic actions of that character. Mimes are similar to pantomimes but are usually on a smaller scale.

Mime is acting without words. You act only with actions. As you play with these mime exercises, do not try to express deep psychological motivations or difficult emotions. Simply enact the actions. You may wish to attempt some of these as impromptu exercises. You may wish to rehearse others before presenting them to the class. In either case, take some time to plan a list of specific actions that you will enact, one after the other. Plan a beginning, a middle, and an end for the mime.

One more word about mime: do not use set pieces or props. You may wish to use them in rehearsal to get the feel of them, but in performance your actions should be clear enough to spark the imagination of those watching. They should know what you are doing without props. But remember: prepare a list of actions, and do not forget the seemingly minor details.

In all, be careful to *place* the imaginary objects involved. Handle them and relate to them as though they were real. When you place an object down, be sure you pick it up later from the same location. When you are holding an imaginary glass of water, do not suddenly swat a fly with that hand unless you then intend to pick up imaginary bits of broken glass. And when you close an imaginary door, do not later walk through it! Attention to such details requires excellent concentration. Your classmates will be quick to spot any slips.

Solo Mimes:

1. Go through the simple actions of one of your daily routines:
   a. brushing your teeth (and flossing them)—start with entering and end with leaving the bathroom—and don't forget to open the door before walking through!
   b. taking a shower
   c. preparing and eating your breakfast
   d. washing the dishes
2. Set the table for the following situations:
   a. a special dinner with a special friend you want very much to impress
   b. you are a ten-year-old wanting very much to go out and play a few more minutes before supper
   c. you are a waiter or waitress in an elegant hotel
   d. you are a waiter or waitress in a greasy diner
3. Prepare and enact the following routines:
   a. mowing the grass
   b. digging a hole
   c. painting a wall
   d. walking a dog
4. Create your own mime and enact it before the class. Be creative!

Duo Mimes:

5. Mime some actions from any two-person sport:
   a. playing catch (using a tennis ball; a beach ball; a baseball; a football)
   b. tennis
   c. badminton
   d. ping-pong
   e. tug-of-war

6. With a partner,
   a. lay stones for a wall
   b. pick up bales of hay and toss them on a truck
   c. cut down a tree with a two-person saw
   d. tie a bow (each use one hand; this is difficult even with the prop)

7. In the following, feelings should show through your face and body.
   a. You are reading a book. Your dog tries to get your attention by barking at you, jumping up to pull at your sleeve, and licking your hand.
   b. A service-station attendant is waiting on a customer.
   c. An adult is getting settled to read the daily paper.
   d. A parent is calling a nine-year-old son who has sneaked off to a neighbor's home to play and refuses to answer the call.
   e. You are hunting everyplace in the room for your keys.
   f. The mail is pushed through the mail slot at your home. You pick it up, look it over, see a letter that puzzles you.
   g. You are rushing off to catch a train to the city. Your travel case pops open, spilling all the contents on the floor.

8. Direct a tourist to the best place to eat and then back to his highway by a shortcut.

9. Saw boards and nail a box together. As you work, explain to a small boy what you are doing.

10. Get ready for a cozy evening with a good book. The phone rings. You try to be civil but are annoyed because of the disturbance.

ABANDONED ACTION

In all acting your fingers, arms, and feet should be free, uninhibited, ready to help express meanings of words. Some people are inclined to hold their elbows close to their sides when gesturing, using only the forearm, which is not natural. Use your arm from your shoulder even if a gesture is not broad.

Exercises for Abandoned Action

1. Pantomime hitting golf balls.
2. Pantomime driving a golf ball toward a distant hole.
3. Lay heavy flat stones in place for a patio floor.
4. Wave signals to somebody a block away.
5. Catch butterflies in a net.
6. Practice boxing with your younger brother.
7. Catch a pile of books falling from a high shelf.

Sly Fox by Larry Gelbart. Harold Dixon, director. Presented by University of Arizona. Jeff Warburton, photographer. Several small groups of characters develop a single theme.

The Servant of Two Masters by Larry Gelbart and Carlo Goldoni. Presented by New York University. Dunay Suleiman, director. Steve Friedman, photographer. Complete freedom of action.

8. Use a hoe to dig up hard ground for a garden.
9. Bathe a wiggly puppy.
10. Place dishes on a high cupboard shelf.
11. Make up a bed with fresh sheets.
12. Shovel deep snow from a sidewalk.
13. Bridle and saddle a horse.
14. Dust a floor under a bed, dresser, and table.
15. Catch lightning bugs.

Use your full arm, not just your forearm, to mime these sentences. Gestures can be small, but elbows must not hug ribs.

1. Let me see your book.
2. It's there on the kitchen table.
3. See this football. It's covered with initials.
4. You need to use your cane more.
5. Let me put this rose in your lapel.
6. I like your ring. Is it something special?
7. Our club meets here in this room.
8. Try that chair. It's better.
9. Here's a letter you'll enjoy.
10. The mail is there on the table.

In number 11, you will show several different feelings. Show these through physical action. (No lines!)

11. You, as a student, are not accustomed to receiving telegrams. When the maid hands you the message at the door of your room, you are somewhat frightened. You hastily open it and reveal the contents through your facial or bodily expression.

First, show pleasure as a friend wires you congratulations and good wishes before the contest which you are soon to enter.

Next, show your feeling toward acquaintances who wire that, since they are to be near, they will plan to spend a few days with you.

Then, portray your feelings as you read the announcement of the death of a very close friend.

IMPROVISATION

Improvisations are miniature impromptu scenes. You make up your lines as you act a scene. Given a situation and one of a few characters in a scene, you speak impromptu what seems to be appropriate for your character to carry forward the suggested situation. Other characters in the scene also speak lines, all creating a plausible dialogue for the story.

Improvisations are good for training your mind to think quickly and logically. In these impromptu acts, you must keep in mind the size, weight, and shape of any imaginary object you use. Practice them using your fingers, feet, head, and hands.

Group Improvisations

These should be performed as mimes (without props), but this time feel free to create some ad lib conversation to accompany your actions. The word "improvisation" suggests that these exercises should be impromptu: performed with little or no rehearsal. The fun of an "improv" is give-and-take, playing off of one another.

1. Play tug-of-war with two teams. Be sure that you do not allow the imaginary rope to stretch. When one team gains a bit, the other must give an equal amount.
2. Play a few minutes of volleyball. Take turns getting the ball. Shout clues to place the ball: "I've got it!" "Here's a set-up, Joe!" "Spike it, Tina!" etc.
3. Do the same with touch football, baseball, basketball, or any other team sport.
4. Using teamwork with a group of five or six,
    a. build a simple bridge over a creek
    b. move a piano from a 12-inch platform to the floor, then to a 36-inch platform
    c. put up a six-person tent
    d. change a tire

After playing these loosening-up games, you may wonder if players throughout history had stage qualms when they began acting. In the next chapters, you will get a brief mental glimpse of actors in the present and in historical times. After you have studied about acting in our time, let your imagination wander about the beginnings of acting and visualize players of the past.

CHAPTER 2

What Is Theater?

The single word *theater* carries different meanings. Is it that backstage atmosphere, a building with stage and seats, a game of make-believe, a picture of life, showing joys and sorrows of human beings? It is all of these. Theater comes in many forms: television, cinema, radio, variety show, and live stage plays. It is all these and more.

Theater is a tool to help people understand human nature, study and learn about themselves, and meet and attempt to solve human problems—all these combined with giving pleasure. It involves personality, activity, sociology, and psychology, along with music, graphic arts, dance, sculpture, and writing, blending them all into a single art.

In educational theater leadership, business training, advertising, set and costume design, and stage lighting are also taught. In this course, your primary study will be of people, in order to depict character through stage acting.

THEATER COMPARED TO OTHER ARTS

Theater is an art with some of the characteristics of the other arts and with some that are unique. Like all arts, acting appeals to the emotions, requires skill to produce, and demands genius and talent to create it in its highest form. The creative aspects of the theater must be mastered through training and discipline and, as in any art form, cannot be reduced to rules.

There are distinguishing characteristics. Acting seeks to stir spectators' emotions and to quicken imagination and intellect. The audience absorbs what they see and hear as if it were real life; their emotions are stirred and they willingly disbelieve that they are watching a play.

The art of the theater provides insights through which people understand themselves and others. Imagination is utilized in acting the experiences of others, even though the actor may not have had that experience. Actors use the tools of life: speech, gesture, movement, and human situations, motivations, and relationships. An audience learns to know a character's life, problems, inner thoughts, and emotions in a way different from any other art.

Another difference is that acting ties together the actions of all the players. An orchestra or chorus uses notes simultaneously, but in the theater each player brings out new thoughts and slants on experience, to which the other players respond.

One advantage theater has over and above all other arts is that in a theatrical production painting, music, dance, and other arts are incorporated.

The several forms of acting also differ from each other. In radio, actors read lines from a script. They rehearse scenes to give the best oral interpretation, using sound effects as needed to make voices, and volume seem at a distance.

Both television and motion picture productions require very different techniques from acting on the stage. Much of the action in those forms is filmed over and over many times to get just the right effect. The best *takes* are chosen to be used. In television, the director—out of range of camera sight lines—rehearses scenes, talks back and forth with actors, asks questions, and gives directions throughout.

Bits of sound are recorded elsewhere on tapes: running water, the clatter of hoofs or their dusty muffled thuds, the patter of rain, thunder, dogs barking, for example, are preserved in small segments and added later by staff to video tape or film.

WHAT MAKES GOOD THEATER?

The Play Itself. The playwright is first in line when we consider what makes good theater. The playwright, or dramatist, has a germ of an idea, then adds to it, shifts it, and alters it into an alluring plot which has a universal problem or appeal. He or she decides on an appropriate setting and finds characters of worth to carry out the plot and give truth to the situation.

Then comes the momentous task of composing the play in fine literary style with interesting dialogue. Throughout the composition, the dramatist appeals to characteristics found in human nature. Following the writing there are repeated changes: rewording, adding, and eliminating, while always working toward perfection.

Factors of a Production. Good theater results largely from workers behind the production. Very important is a director who plans a unified entertainment. The amateur *director* selects—sometimes with the advice of a committee—designers, actors, crews, production staff, and rehearsal schedules, and also maps out stage action.

Production crews soon begin publicizing the play; devising a stage set or sets; working on financial management; finding stage properties and visualizing, then creating, costumes. These theater crews cooperate with and advise each other under the guidance of the director to plan a unified production.

Attitudes. Crews and cast work together for orderliness by planning carefully to develop a smooth production. When a group of individuals works as closely together as do the production staff and cast, kindness and consideration for one another are foremost in developing a commendable production and in creating lasting friendships. If everybody works for the good of the production, there will be fewer distractions and more top-grade productions.

The *audience* has a powerful psychological influence on both amateur and professional actors. Actors respond positively or negatively to that indescribable something which penetrates the space between audience and actors. This feeling gives the audience an active role in every theater production. There is a continuous give and take between audience and performers which is absent from TV and the motion picture.

Laughter at appropriate moments is only a part of this contagion of feeling. A play may be very serious—no reason for laughter—but emotions expressed by the actors may or may not be felt by spectators. A lack of empathy on the part of the audience is telegraphed back to actors, perhaps by coughing or the creaking of seats. Some players work the harder to overcome this lack of response, while others are numbed; they find that their acting is muted and their enthusiasm deadened, even when they try to bring it up. On the other hand, an audience's hush of intense interest can encourage actors to do their best.

Remember this about laughter: sometimes an audience which laughs most heartily does not appreciate the play as much as an audience that accepts humor quietly but expresses appreciation with high compliments following the play. Be careful. Don't cheat people or fail to give your highest grade of acting because the audience is less demonstrative.

Acting on a stage is what people want to see, hear, and enjoy. They appreciate the director's and staff's contributions, but the story and the acting are their special interests and pleasures.

The overall objective is always the same. It is to help an actor develop his capacities—intellectual, physical, spiritual, emotion—with power to move the public to laughter, to tears, to unforgettable emotions.*

STAGE ACTING AND DAILY LIFE ACTING ARE RELATED

Shakespeare's Jaques, in *As You Like It,* reminds us that we are all actors in our daily lives.

All the world's a stage
And all the men and women merely players
They have their exits and their entrances
And one man in his time plays many parts,
His acts being seven ages.

We are all actors, and we pride ourselves on our little daily deceptions. The guest smiles and thanks her hostess for a delightful evening after listening to a boring account of a recent operation. A hostess, in agony with a headache, smiles as she converses with friends. Tom shakes hands with promoter Hank as he thanks him for the very helpful advice, which Tom believes is planned to lead him into a trap. At the same time, Hank prides himself on successfully building Tom's ego enough to entangle him.

We use theatrical devices to gain approval. At halftime a group of students forms a large human letter representing the name of its school, while pompom girls dance in flashy outfits. We all devise theatrical gimmicks like these.

Because the artistic enactment of roles is very important, each player should examine his or her part with infinite care. Many questions come to mind and should be answered as conclusively as possible. A sort of checklist will help: Why did the dramatist place my character in this play? What part do I play in the conflict? What is my objective? Where did I "come from" on each entrance?

What is my age, disposition, purpose, background? What is my relationship to others in each scene and in the play as a whole? When I exit,

* Aleksiev (pseudonym of Constantin Stanislavski), *Building a Character*, trans. Elizabeth Reynolds Hapgood (New York: Theater Arts, 1949).

where am I going, and why? What do I look like? How do I walk, speak, move? What kind of relationship do I have to other characters? Check all aspects of your character's attitudes and actions so that you feel as thoroughly acquainted with your character as you are with members of your family.

Know what emotions your character feels and how he or she expresses them. Viewers want to experience, to a degree, each character's emotions. As you act, depict emotions so that they carry to viewers—empathy is a strong requirement of good drama.

There is audience appreciation of the appeal to the heroic in a play. A sensitive audience is glad when actors recognize that it appreciates a compelling plot which is ethically appealing and artistically presented. These are some of the qualities that actors help contribute.

HOW DOES THEATER WORK TODAY?

After the playwright, the *producer* takes over. The producer is responsible for financing the play, engaging a director and theater, and finding enough money to see the play through rehearsals or until it is on sound financial footing from box office receipts. Few small theaters need a play producer.

A *director*, responsible for the entire play, selects the actors and helps them with characterization and stage deportment, and works with the many technical crews and with publicity people. After discussions with the playwright, when feasible, the director decides on the interpretation the play should have, and is responsible for any decisions to be made which will unify all elements into an artistic production.

A *designer* works primarily with the director. The designer learns what the special requirements of a particular play are, then sketches possible settings that will accomodate the action and provide atmosphere, as well as make possible rapid scene shifts.

The *stage manager* holds a very important position, so he or she should be chosen very carefully by the director. The stage manager is in charge of the *technical staffs* (scenery, costumes, lights, etc.), and attends rehearsals throughout the early weeks. The stage manager records all changes in production, and keeps a prompt book with cues for lights, special effects, scene curtain, and property shifts. From that prompt book he or she makes cue sheets for lights, scenery, props, sounds, and effects.

The directors of *music* and *dance* have combined their arts with that of the theater so beautifully that they have brought many people to the theater who previously had taken little interest. Music establishes a mood and style and, because it is delightful in itself, the audience is doubly entertained. Music and dance both lend variety to a production. Each can be used effectively for characterization, to create dramatic spectacle, to develop the story, and to make dramatic art even more enjoyable.

But what has helped us discover the pleasures and artistry of today's many and varied theatricals? We may think of it as the appeasing of an inner urge to act. However, much has come to us from the past. Through research, from ancient hieroglyphics to the latest computers, we have pieced together the evolution of public performances. The gradual development from earliest pantomimes to present-day extravaganzas makes even a limited study of theater interesting.

CHAPTER 3

Where Has Theater Been?

Theater in some form has provided thoughtful entertainment for many centuries. It has spread from religious festival to raw burlesque. Theater, of some forgotten form, began in ancient times; few historical fragments were left behind for us to study.

RITUALS

Rituals were the germ from which live theater as we know it today developed. Far back before any records were left for posterity, religious rituals were performed to heathen gods. Songs and dances were performed in search of blessings from the gods who controlled weather, sickness, death, pestilences, and other evils from which humankind suffered.

Depictions of Egyptian pageants, probably prior to 4000 B.C., are being found in modern times on murals, pyramid tombs, and ancient temple walls. These rituals were probably used in religious festivals to honor the sun god Atum-Ra. However, we know little about these ancient Egyptian festivals.

ORIENTAL THEATER

Chinese theater beginnings must also have existed many centuries before Christ, but scholars have been unable to find much proof. In China, there has traditionally been a lively interest in spectacle, a love of music and drama. In about the eighth century B.C., groups of players were organized. The Emperor called the comedians of his private acting group "Students of the Pear Tree Garden."

Chinese theater held to certain conventions of the stage. Costumes, properties, makeup, and gestures were symbolic only. All was utterly unrealistic, resembling a ritual. A screen, some stools, a bamboo pole, and some strips of cloth could be used to represent anything. A property man, clothed in black, sat on stage in sight of the audience. He put these symbols in place to represent whatever piece of property was called for—a door, a mountain, or a river.

Japanese theater, even though it was an offshoot of the Chinese theater, had two distinguishing characteristics. The *Noh* drama came into existence in the fourteenth century. Themes for these plays were taken from religious literature and presented with aesthetic excellence. Some of the words were chanted by a chorus and some were recited by dancers. These *No-gaku* Japanese dramas used only three or four actors, all of them men. Women's roles were played by men wearing masks. Because these plays were very short, five or six of them were presented on a single occasion. They were both serious in nature and very fanciful.

Kabuki, the other popular type of Japanese play, was more elaborate. The early Kabukis began at daybreak and lasted until sunset. Kabuki added very fine puppetry, an idea borrowed from Noh plays, to some of its acts.

GREEK AND ROMAN THEATER

Modern actors may thank the Greeks for recording the first chapter of theater history. Their festivals were held in honor of Dionysus, the god of wine, drama, and fertility. For centuries, forms of theatrical productions grew, died, were resurrected, changed, and developed, until 510 B.C. About that time contests were instituted to select the best tragedians. Thespis was the first contest winner, and his name has given modern players the title of Thespians.

The first Greek plays involved only one actor and a men's chorus. Between spoken scenes, while the chorus of twenty-four men chanted verses, the one actor slipped behind the *skene* to change mask and costume so that he could appear as a different character and recite that character's lines. Festivals lasted four or five days, with different poets as contributors. Each poet was allotted one full day for the presentation of his written works.

Try to get an imaginary picture of a great amphitheater and the religious festivals taking place there. Visualize a man named Lycon and his wife Penelope, who have looked forward for days to this great outing. They and a group of friends have ridden their faithful donkeys or walked for all of one day and one night before they arrive in Athens early in the morning. They have come to see and hear the dramatic poems of the great Aeschylus. Already the *theatron* has nearly been filled, but Lycon and Penelope find seats on the 65th tier, far up from the *orchestra*, which is a large circular terrace at the lowest level of the bowl-shaped hill where actors and chorus will present their poetry.

Remains of many amphitheaters can still be seen in Greece; tourist favorite is the great Temple of Dionysus in Athens. Locations for these structures were carefully chosen. They were always built on the side of a bowl-shaped mountain with a steep slope and acoustical qualities. Some of the largest amphitheaters could seat thousands, much like one of America's great stadiums.

The actor or actors often wore great masks and elaborately embroidered costumes. Some masks were grotesque, boldly painted to represent the type of character the actor enacted. Tragic characters often wore masks with scowls, vicious-looking mouths drawn down at the corners, and deep frowns in their foreheads. Comic characters often had corners of mouths turned up into a smile and twinkling lines about the eyes. Sometimes the masks were built with enormous lips which acted as a small megaphone-like structure so that voices could carry far out and up to the audience.

Aeschylus (c.525–456 B.C.) wrote tragedy, as did Sophocles (c.497–405 B.C.) and Euripides (c.485–406 B.C.). Changes in acting came with comedy poems. When dramatists of comedy, Aristophanes (c.450–380 B.C.) and Menander (c.342–291 B.C.), began writing, the actors began to wear comic masks. Comedians were loud and boisterous with horseplay, song and dance, and much vulgarity. The spectators knew the ancient myths, and enjoyed the effectively modulated voices and sonorous tones. They understood the wails of Thespis, the chants of the chorus, the broad sweeping features of the actors and the bright colors of the flowing draperies.

Rome followed Greece in its general theater plan, and both ancient countries enjoyed this form of theater for several centuries. However, the Romans did not develop a theater of lasting quality, although they excelled in the art of pantomime. Terence, a philosopher and playwright, had great influence on the Roman theater in the years before Christ. Seneca, a great tradegian, arrived soon afterward.

MEDIEVAL THEATER

As centuries came and went, life in the theater changed. Acting became sub-dued in form, and was even forbidden. But throughout these ancient days the theatrical instinct was never destroyed. In the Roman period, when women had begun to take part in plays, standards had been lowered, acting had become vulgar and obscene, and the newly founded Christian church objected. As the church rose in power, the pagan theater disappeared and the professional actor passed into disrepute. Many centuries went by before the theater again gained a respected place in society. Although the Christian church could not accept forms of drama which it saw as degrading, neverthe-less it came to embrace the theater as a teaching device and wholesome enter-tainment.

Miracle plays, dating back to the thirteenth century, came from the church in England. These were dramatic adaptations of the lives of saints. *Mystery plays* also developed. These were cycles of plays depicting Biblical stories from the Creation to the Last Judgment, climaxing with the Passion of Christ. These appeared after the institution of the festival of Corpus Christi, and were given by the town craftsmen. Each scene was presented by a par-ticular guild, or trade union as we think of them today. Cooks depicted the scene of the Last Supper, shipwrights presented the story of Noah and the Ark, goldsmiths took the parts of Wise Men bringing their gifts, bakers presented a scene showing the Feeding of the Five Thousand and, with grisly irony, the butchers presented the Crucifixion.

At first, Mystery plays were presented only in the actors' home towns. Later, however, about the time of the fourteenth century, certain groups began taking their plays from village to village in processional cycles. These religious plays were in vogue for about two hundred years. They were in-stituted by the church, and later banished by the church because the plays had deviated from their original purpose. Secular material had been inserted to amuse the people, and the plays became coarse and sacrilegious. Four complete Mystery Cycles have survived to the present day.

While allegory crept into Mystery plays, a third class of religious drama called the *Morality play* sprang up. Virtues and vices were personified in these, which remained in fashion until the time of Elizabeth I. *Everyman*, a good example of a Morality play, is often enacted by college and little theater groups in modern times.

Commedia dell' arte made its appearance in Italy around 1500 A.D. It spread to France and Spain, helping to develop a new kind of theater, and a little later became popular in England. Commedia dell' arte centered about a company of comedians. Each actor spoke with a particular accent or dialect and moved in a characteristic manner. Actors were given only a scenario of action, which someone often had merely scribbled out on his knee on the morning of the performance. Players improvised their own dialogue on the spot. However, dialogue was not all-important in Commedia dell' arte; the pantomine was brilliant, the dancing was robust, and the acrobatics were exciting. Although Commedia dell' arte appeared cheap and tawdry, it was a type of theater exceedingly popular throughout Europe for two centuries.

The French theater came into its own with Molière (1622–1673), whose brilliant wit brought new life into the art. Actors began to be trained in naturalness, and became skilful in depicting daily life with truth and sincerity.

THE ELIZABETHAN THEATER

In Renaissance England there was a revival of classical art and learning, as was true over much of Europe. The *Renaissance* boosted drama to a high level so that it became a vital force in the lives of the people. Three remarkable dramatists arose during this period: Christopher Marlowe (1564–1593), Ben Jonson (1573–1637), and William Shakespeare (1564–1616). These three great writers were all short lived: Jonson lived to be 64 years old, Shakespeare 52, and Marlowe only 29.

Shakespeare wrote about all classes of life in England and nearby European countries. He included historic plays to satisfy the historically minded and portrayed both ruling and serving classes of society. Jonson wrote good English humor, and Marlowe was the first to use blank verse and to center a play about one strong character.

The plays were given in every conceivable place—streets, courtyards, and woods—so that every Englishman began to see, hear, and enjoy theatrical performances. A number of playhouses were built, among them the Globe, where many Shakespearean plays were performed. Many plays were given in broad daylight, theaters often had no roofs, and all roles were played by men. Actors carried torches to suggest nighttime. Acting was of high grade, even though there were many disturbances by drunks and uncurbed rowdies. Costumes and background scenery were of little importance.

THE EIGHTEENTH AND NINETEENTH CENTURIES—TOWARD REALISM

Many changes improved the theater in the eighteenth and nineteenth centuries. Plays began to be performed at night. Lamps, candles, and limelight all became useful; acting was more realistic; stages with aprons, proscenium arches, and more comfortable seats helped spectators.

The Braggart Soldier by Plautus. Presented by Brandeis University. James H. Clay, director. Ralph Norman, photographer. Costuming suggests this is an ancient play.

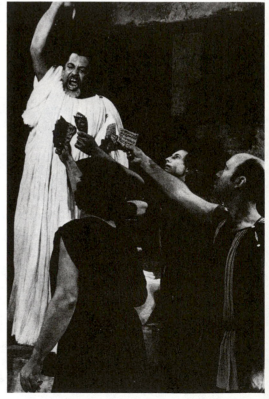

Timon of Athens by William Shakespeare. Presented by Yale Repertory Theatre. Lloyd Richards, director. Gerry Goodstein, photographer. Timon, the hater of humanity, looks his part; other actors appear somewhat indifferent.

Henrik Ibsen of Norway (1828–1906) has been called the "father of modern drama." His characters represented real people meeting great problems which they tried to solve—often with agony. Many theatergoers scorned the new realism. Some plays were staged as elaborate spectacles with which dramatists hoped to please critics. However, stories continued to be built around problems and places that the writers knew. Ibsen continued to speak out on the social problems of his day, which caused him to be known as a radical thinker.

Realism in dramatic literature soon spread all over the world. Great English dramatists came to the fore: Arthur Wing Pinero, John Galsworthy, and George Bernard Shaw. Their plays are still valuable contributions to American theater.

Russian Art Theater has been acclaimed as one of the finest. Constantin Stanislavski, one of its founders, taught acting by a new method. In the early years of the twentieth century, he promoted a theory that acting must first come from the heart, from inside the actor, then radiate to outer actions and emotional expression. Stanislavski devised the "Magic If." He asked his students to think: What if these events were happening now?

Many authorities do not agree with this "inside-outside" method. They feel that the opposite approach is right, that if an actor goes through a character's movements, gestures, and facial expressions, the inner feeling will follow. Both approaches have been highly successful.

Some see the two approaches as compatible rather than contradictory. They advocate that an actor start with the outer method "to tap the resources of his unconscious," and then let the inner feelings take over to develop the role. With practice, the actor will create a live thinking, feeling, and acting character.

Stanislavski said that "the inner and physical apparatus of an actor must be trained simultaneously. . . . The physical technique will become responsive to inner impulses."*

> Theater is a pulpit which is the most powerful means of influence. . . . With the same power with which theater can ennoble spectators, it may corrupt them, degrade them, spoil their taste, lower their passions, offend beauty. . . . My task is to elevate the family of artists from the ignorant, the half educated and the profiteers, and to convey to the younger generation that an artist is the priest of beauty and truth.†

In *Stanislavski and America*, Manyukov of the Moscow Art Theater describes an exercise beneficial to actors that is similar to the child's game of

---

* Sonia Moore, *The Stanislavski System* (New York: The Viking Press, 1965), p. 67.
† Ibid., p. 4.

"Hot and Cold." Somebody hides an object and a student is asked to find it. When he or she gets close, other students may say *good, better, very good.* When the student moves away from it they say, *bad, worse, very bad.* After the student has found the object, he again leaves the room, then returns and repeats the search, now knowing exactly where the object is. Notice how different the hunt is.

Stanislavski's concepts of acting are fundamental to our modern theater. He felt that no play should be presented until it is as nearly perfect as possible; that stage settings should be simple, often consisting of only a bare stage or plaform in a large room; and that there should be no applause at performances, no music filling time between acts, and that even the smallest roles should receive meticulous attention by directors and actors.

Anton Chekhov, who wrote in the late nineteenth century, is probably the Russian dramatist that Americans know best. *The Sea Gull, The Cherry Orchard,* and *The Three Sisters* are among his best-known plays. All his plays were presented by the Moscow Art Theater.

During the 1920s, as Stalin came to full power, Russian dramatists were gradually required to write plays which upheld, or even praised, communism. A leading hero was required to boost communism as the ideal way of life.

THEATER IN AMERICA IN THE TWENTIETH CENTURY

The twentieth century in the United States has been an age of varied theatrical innovation. Placed at the head of any discussion of American theater must be *Broadway,* in New York City. New York City is the top spot for theater-minded people to see legitimate plays.

Vaudeville became popular about 1900 and provided a variety-type show for many years, even up to the Great Depression. In vaudeville, several short acts filled a two-hour show with spice and flavor. Dance, songs, monologues, sleight-of-hand, and many other varieties of entertainment began there. The acts also traveled from city to city.

Stock companies, featuring a different play every week, sprang up in every fair-sized town. They were the beginnings of the *Little Theater* movement as we know it today. In 1915, three influential New York playing groups began as Little Theaters. They were the Neighborhood Playhouse, Washington Square Players, and Provincetown Players. The Little Theater movement still thrives across America. Many theaters have become dinner theaters, where the highest grade off-Broadway plays are presented in professional style with amateur actors.

During the first thirty years of this century, a popular kind of entertainment was the *Circuit Chautauquas.* It was an off-shoot of the series of programs given in Chautauqua, New York. About 1910, summertime Circuit Chautauquas began operating. They went into thousands of county-seat towns and small towns, even rural school districts. A large tent was erected, and each day for four or five days a new group of entertainers arrived to present the program. The backbone of Circuit Chautauquas was inspirational lectures, just as was the case in Chautauqua. Musical and novelty entertainments, as well as full-length plays, were presented.

The end of the First World War in 1918 marked the beginning of a new zest for the theater. Boys came home from "over there" bubbling with enthusiasm that they gladly gave vent to in amateur theatricals. There were acting groups in every town, with residents offering their support.

In the 1930s the depression, in general a destructive force, stimulated still further the growth of amateur theatricals. Every wide-awake community organized a group of players. Churches, schools, and clubs began to produce plays. *Colleges, universities,* and *high schools* began to give credit for courses in theater. Barns, warehouses, and garages were converted into playhouses; businessmen and housewives became actors and stage mechanics, all for the fun of working in the theater.

Social welfare recognized the therapeutic value of this new activity. *Barter Theater* became popular with groups of young people who worked up one or more plays, went to nearby towns, found an indoor or outdoor playing space, then traded tickets for whatever they could use: potatoes, bread and butter, fruit, a chicken, garden vegetables, or lodging.

Radio plays came into every home during the 1930s. While sitting in their own homes, discouraged adults and youth could endure privations and financial worries by listening to a gripping radio play. When the economy became stronger, television was instituted, which entertained with color, sound, and spectacle.

But hearing and watching others perform does not satisfy the inner urge in many people to participate in some aspect of theatrical production. The joy, the therapy, the honest fun in working on a play make theater an ever-stimulating activity that Americans continue to encourage.

The history of theater is interesting, but your purpose as students is to learn the *how,* the *why,* and the *when* of putting on a well-developed play. With that as our goal, we will now discuss the part your physical body plays in acting. Sample scenes are waiting for you in the next chapter.

PART TWO
Preparing Your Acting Instrument

CHAPTER 4

Your Body

THE MOST BASIC TOOL OF ACTING

Good acting results from simultaneous responses of your entire body. Your bones, nerves, muscles, and inner organs combine to form a complex human instrument. As an actor, you work to train your heart and mind, to tune your instrument to its greatest artistic potential.

In learning, tune the strings of your instrument, your movements, sounds, sights, and emotions, by using outer action to stimulate inner action. As you learn you will empathize with, and eventually think like, the person whose "mask" you wear.

DISCOVERING ACTION

To help train your body to respond, practice physical actions that demand control such as gymnastics, dancing, and fencing. Train your facial expressions also because, throughout a performance, your lines and actions must appear unpremeditated, as if you are sensing something for the first time, to present to the audience the illusion of reality. However, not every action must be realistic or seem natural to you. Use your imagination and an abundance of observation.

Become acquainted with your character—you'll enjoy making the acquaintance. Search the play for the locale of his or her background, for age, social status, and personality traits. Discover *how* the character adds to the play. You'll learn quite a bit from the way other characters think about and act toward her or him. Then incorporate your ideas about the character into physical movements.

Mimes and Pantomimes. Early mimes were farcical and short, and might have employed a number of actors who improvised actions to fit a situation. In mimes, actors mimic people and things. Enact these pantomimes; speak in some of them.

1. Walk like an elderly arthritic person. Reach for a copy of a book on a high shelf.
2. Sneak into a room. Listen, then search for valuables to steal.
3. You accidentally drop and break a piece of your mother's bric-a-brac. Pick up the pieces; show relief that they can be mended. Hear someone coming. Hunt for a place to hide the pieces.
4. As a high school boy in your grandmother's kitchen, prepare lunch. You can't find utensils, buns, catsup. Become frustrated. Pinch your finger in a door.
5. You are on your way to keep an appointment with your dentist. The car won't start. Search for the trouble. Discover you have the wrong set of keys.
6. Near midnight, you are reading a book near a window, you hear a noise, then realize that somebody is watching you through a window.
7. While picknicking with friends, you agree to start the fire. You search for fuel in vain. Try to light some dead leaves and grass to start the fire.
8. You are watching a football game. Near the end of the game, the opposing side is ahead, but your team has the ball. Help them from your position. As they are about to make a touchdown, they lose the ball.

Relaxation. Relaxation is primary, and a must for acting neophytes. Being relaxed doesn't mean droopy inactivity, but it does mean freedom from all bodily tensions and inhibitions. One should be completely at ease but alert, ready to act and react convincingly in every scene, and keenly interested in plot, lines, actions, and the other players.

Not only neophytes but experienced actors become overly nervous, keyed up, with strained muscles, tensed nerves, and addled minds. You can't think accurately when you are overly nervous. Remember this: we are talking about being *overly* nervous, not just nervous! Nervousness can stimulate your thinking and movements, but *stage fright* can stiffen your body and stifle your thinking. Your nervousness should disappear within the first thirty seconds on stage; it will seem to dissolve, but you will still be alert.

Your physical body should be trained, toughened, and made obedient, much as athletes train theirs. Exercises will help you relax and lessen nervous tension.

Exercises

1. Droop all over; neck, head, arms, legs, fingers, eyelids, shoulders. Suddenly straighten, stiffen. Rise to an upright position. Be sure to stand tall. Repeat this several times.

2. Stand feet apart for a good base. Stretch your arms to the sides as far as you can. Swing your torso as far as you can to the right, then to the left. Repeat ten times.

3. Yawn, mouth wide open, filling your lungs from deep down. Stretch arms, legs, shoulders, back. Now suddenly relax, droop. Yawn again, repeating all the elements of a good yawn, and stretch several times, until the yawn comes naturally. (It will.)

4. Run in place until you are tired. Droop, as if in complete exhaustion. Let your head fall down on your chest, arms limp, legs inert. Rotate head to one side and back, as far as possible. Your mouth will fall open; keep rotating. When you are completely relaxed, your jaw will be loose, and your head heavy. Feel the muscles of your neck pull. Repeat five times.

5. Limber joints. Stand, lean over deeply from waist, all body parts limp. Shake fingers, arms. Straighten up. Shake shoulders loosely. Bend from waist around and around, up and down. Continue long enough to feel limber. Again, run in place, fast enough to make your heart beat rapidly and your breath come short.

Excerpt for Practice

In Shakespeare's A MIDSUMMER NIGHT'S DREAM, a rough group of workmen prepare a play to be presented at a wedding. The men move here and there as they express their opinions.

SUGGESTIONS AND STAGE DIRECTIONS

QUINCE. Robin Starveling, you must play Thisby's mother. (*Calling*) Tom Snout, the tinker! 1.

1. QUINCE speaks with a loud voice as he moves from one to another.

SNOUT. Here, Peter Quince.

QUINCE. You, Pyramus' father; myself, Thisby's father. Snug, the joiner, you, the lion's part; and, I hope, here is a play fitted.

SNUG.   Have you the lion's part written? Pray you, if it be, give it me for I am slow of study.

QUINCE.   You may do it extempore, for it is nothing but roaring. 2.

2. There is general disorder. Only SNUG moseys to one side.

BOTTOM.   Let me play the lion too. (3) I will roar, that I will do any man's heart good to hear me. I will roar, that I will make the duke say, "Let him roar again, Let him roar again."

3. BOTTOM is loud-mouthed, moving here and there importantly.

QUINCE.   And you should do it too terribly, you would fright the duchess and the ladies, that they would shriek; and that were enough to hang us all.

ALL.   That would hang us, every mother's son.

BOTTOM.   I grant you friends, if that you should fright the ladies out of their wits, they would have no more discretion but to hang us; (4) but I will aggravate my voice so that I will roar you as gently as a suckling dove; I will roar you an't were any nightingale.

4. There is general confusion, even through this long speech of BOTTOM's.

QUINCE.   You can play no part but Pyramus; for Pyramus is a sweet-faced man; a proper man; as any shall see in a summer's day; a most lovely, gentleman-like man; therefore you must needs play Pyramus.

BOTTOM.   Well, I will undertake it. What beard were I best to play it in?

QUINCE.   Why, what you will.

BOTTOM.   I will discharge it in either your straw-coloured beard, or your French-crown-colour beard, your perfect yellow. 5.

5. BOTTOM, with his great ego, might go to and from QUINCE, pulling him about to speak directly into his face.

QUINCE.   Some of your French crowns have no hair at all, and then you will play barefaced. But masters, here are your parts; and I am to entreat you, request you, and desire you, to con them by to-morrow night, and meet me in the palace wood, a mile without the town, by moonlight. There will we rehearse, for if we meet in the city, we shall be dogged with company, and our devices known. In the meantime I will draw a bill of properties, such as our play wants. I pray you fail me not.

Using *abandoned action* and an excessive amount of facial and bodily expression will help you if you have not learned to feel free and easy on stage.

Trying to communicate ideas without the use of voice will show how much you can loosen up to put an idea across. Every one of us has tried at some time to talk with another who does not speak or understand our language. In trying to communicate with this person, we use a great deal of lip movement, broad gestures, and exaggerated facial expression. In the following exercise, "Transformation," you will have an opportunity to free yourself of inhibitions.

Transformations

This exercise is designed to break down your bodily inhibitions and to help you enjoy using your entire body in expressive ways.

1. Form a circle of ten or twelve people, at arm's length to each other and facing center.
2. The instructor will appoint one person as leader to begin.
3. The leader will begin moving his or her entire body in some unusual way (whirling the arms, taking heavy giant steps, undulating the body, etc.) while making some nonsense sounds with the voice (whining, growling, hissing, etc.). The leader moves into the center of the circle, while the sound and movement continue there for ten or fifteen seconds. The leader then takes the sound and movement to someone else in the circle. While this is happening, everyone should be *covertly* imitating the leader, ready to imitate *overtly* if chosen next.
4. The leader approaches someone, who becomes the new leader and must take up the same sound and movement, go to the center of the circle, and then *gradually* transform it into a new pattern. The key word is gradually: do not stop to think about what to do next. Let your *body* respond to immediate impulse as others continue their covert imitation of new sound and movement.
5. Each leader takes this new pattern to someone else. Repeat the process until everyone has had at least one turn. Do not repeat leaders until all have had one turn.

You may feel silly at first—but that is the whole point! We restrict our bodies because we feel silly. On stage your bodies must be free to do whatever the part requires—the more outlandish and exaggerated the better!

Also, do not get stuck doing realistic patterns (an airplane, a bear, etc.). Extend actions beyond realism; make them ridiculous, bizarre. Become as uninhibited as a little child, and enjoy it.

One final note: it is important that your movements are repeatable by everyone in the group. Do not stand on your head or walk on your hands; and no violence. The goal of the exercise is freedom of movement, not exhibition.

BODY LANGUAGE

Your whole body communicates to your audience. Even when you stand quietly, you are saying something. Body language may telegraph negative messages: "That actor must be dreaming," or "He is thinking of other things," or "She is going through only the physical motions of acting." On the other hand, if your body is in tune and is properly controlled, even the way you stand or walk will add something to your character and to the play.

First, think of *posture* as it is associated with poise. One of the *musts* for a good actor of straight parts is erect posture. Actors need to get the feel of *standing tall*, but many have lazy spines; they slump. A player learns to keep head and shoulders up, and to step lithely, with the length of steps in keeping with his height. Keep thinking "stand tall": stand with one foot slightly in advance of the other, weight on the forward foot.

Men need to be careful about elaborately pulling up their trouser legs as they sit down; while seated, they should seldom—and never without being so directed—rest one foot across the other knee.

To rise from a seat gracefully, an actor may place one foot back, the other forward, then rise with his weight on the rear foot. Deep-seated chairs and settees are the hardest to cope with. It is better to sit forward or lean against a plump cushion to keep from sitting too far back.

Walk in keeping with your character's personality and the mood and tempo of the scene. Don't saunter, unless your character would. In general, walk briskly and hold your head erect and your shoulders back. A slump on stage looks more sloppy than it does on the street. However, when you are playing an elderly person, you may walk flat-footed, be stiff-kneed, and rise from seats with difficulty.

Gesture is the backbone of dramatic action. Stage gestures are larger than those in real life. Your muscles and emotions can be trained to respond in countless ways as you enact the emotions, moods, attitudes of various parts. Action is truly the language of the actor as much as is speech. Gesture involves more than the hands; your whole body gestures when you shake your head, shrug, or kick.

Hands sometimes need to be overworked with exercise to train them to respond to your needs. In real life you express your own feelings but on stage you are a character, not yourself. If you have trouble with gestures, the cure is to *use your hands more than enough.* Don't wait for rehearsals to exercise them; gesture often just to train them.

Even when you are only listening to others on stage, if you are a part of a scene your hands should seldom hang at your sides. Watch people about the streets, on television, and at home, and you will see that their hands take various positions: in a pocket, in front of the body, behind someone's back, or

Romeo and Juliet by William Shakespeare. The play was presented at University of Kansas. Jack Wright, director. Notice body positions of most minor characters.

A Streetcar Named Desire by Tennessee Williams. Presented by Eastern Michigan University. P. George Bird, director. This shows natural pictorial body positions.

Man of La Mancha by Dale Wasserman, Mitch Leigh, Joe Darion. Presented in Grove City College. William Kennedy and James Dixon, directors. Excellent body control.

holding a prop. When other actors have a scene, even if you are merely listening you are definitely in the scene. Avoid the tendency some actors have to clutch their hands in front of them or to cross their arms too often.

Covert and Overt Action. There are two kinds of possible muscular actions: *covert* and *overt*. *Covert* action is small, almost imperceptible muscular movement, and *overt* action is, in effect, gesture.

The bones of our bodies are covered with threads of muscles whose tiny, almost invisible movements tell far more about us than we realize. The hands alone have dozens of these tiny muscles that are constantly reacting to give hints about our feelings through covert action.

Overt action includes all expressive bodily action of the large muscles of the body: a nod of the head, a kick, a shrug, a flip of the hand, or a bow. When speaking about some object on the stage it is usually best to follow this order in gesturing: *thought, look, action, words*. Keep these suggestions in mind:

1. Arm gestures should come from the shoulder. Guard against action by forearm only, elbows hugging sides.

2. A hand gesture should seldom cross the body. If you are facing front and wish to point toward the piano at left, use your left hand.

3. Gestures on stage are broader than in real life. In your own home, a finger might direct attention to a book on a chair, but an audience reacts to larger gestures.

4. Always gesture in keeping with your character.

5. Do not slow action with excessive gesturing, except in limbering-up exercises.

The illusion of the first time is the feeling that all actors hope to project to the audience throughout a play. It is akin to surprise—players try to react to lines or events as though they have never heard or seen them before, as if discovering them.

Repeated performances of the same play may grow stale unless actors can bolster themselves to bring new life into their parts. They want the scene to appear spontaneous, as if happening here and now for the first and only time. George Arliss, a great actor, said, "The art of the actor is to learn how not to be natural on stage without being found out by the audience." You must work to keep your sense of spontaneity, the illusion of the first time.

The James-Lange Theory. Actors can get great help from the James-Lange theory. According to this, we human beings often build our inner reactions as we take on the outer expressions of the emotion. For example, someone had had his new car struck by a careless driver. The two men look over the damage together. As the injured party gets angry he gives vent to his anger through words and actions. Expressing the emotion physically increases it. Take another example; suppose the Junior Prom comes just at the end of a series of mid-semester examinations. Helen has studied hard night after night until, when the last exam is finished, she feels exhausted. She wishes she didn't have to go to the dance. While dressing, she tries to pull herself together so that she can be civil to her date. However, when she arrives at the hall and begins dancing, she loses her tired feeling and is convinced that this orchestra is really the best ever. When she leaves the ballroom, she feels that she has had the best time of her college life. The reason? Helen put on the outer attributes of gaiety—dress, companions, music, movement, and atmosphere. These combined to buoy up her inner feelings and thoroughly reinvigorate her.

The James-Lange theory works in the same way for the actor. He puts on the outward muscle movements with words, smiles, scowls, muscle tension, dress, actions, and atmosphere. The inner feeling is induced as a result.

Business. *Stage business* includes all that the audience sees actors doing on stage. Gesture is a part of it. Movements of hands, feet, head, or shoulders are a part of stage business. There are two general divisions to be understood and used.

Definite business is suggested by the lines themselves. John may say, "Are you cold, Elinor?" He goes to close the window. Such business (action) may come before the line: he may look at her, get the idea, move to close the window. Or he may speak simultaneously with the line. Or he may get the thought, ask the question, then follow with action. However, the order is *thought* (seems chilly), *look* (at Elinor, then window), *action* (start toward window), *words* (speak as he goes toward window).

Indefinite business is planned by the director or by the actor to help build characterization and enhance the play. You may make use of objects on stage, such as tracing a design on a vase, rolling a newspaper and tapping a table with it, handling a hat you have been wearing, or twirling a cane you have with you. Costumes and accessories can help provide ideas for indefinite action: a pair of spectacles, ruffles on a cuff, a scarf, a magazine.

Hand props and costumes should be used in early rehearsals so that the actors can get used to them: beads, gloves, mirrors, dishes, food, floor-length dresses, men's cutaways, or Prince Albert coats.

Byplay may be mannerisms which blend into the scene. Byplay helps in developing unusual characters such as a man who often rolls the tips of his mustache; an absent-minded person taking off and putting on his or her spectacles, rubbing them, looking through them to see if they are clean; or an impatient person tapping a foot or snapping fingers.

Ensemble business is that which gives a play a total, general effect. Some of it may be business by all performed in unison, as in the chorus of a musical play; or business of individuals may be very diverse but blend into a total effect. An example which most people know is in the play *Pygmalion,* which was converted into the musical *My Fair Lady*. The opening scene shows a dozen or more London people stranded beneath an overpass, waiting for the rain to stop. The different characters perform varied pieces of actions expressing boredom, but all blend into a total effect.

FACIAL EXPRESSION

Everybody's *face* has tiny *muscles* covering it that make possible thousands of facial expressions. Eyes tell most of one's feelings and thoughts. Try facial expressions to communicate these feelings: cross, happy, worried, afraid, angry, loving, puzzled, bored, disgusted, and hopeful.

When you become thoroughly absorbed in your role, your character's feelings will be revealed involuntarily in the fine muscles of your brow, eyes, and mouth. Learn to *smile with your eyes;* cultivate the muscles around your mouth. Your eyes are most important in all expressions.

Eyes are of the greatest importance in paying attention—or in seeming to. After hearing the same stage dialogue a hundred times, it may be difficult to keep your mind on a thought. Nevertheless, your eyes visibly tell the audience that you are listening. An occasional smile, frown, or movement of head in keeping with the action of the play at the moment, even though you are in the background, is helpful.

The eyebrows reveal thoughts and emotions as well. Observe how you would be able to use your eyebrows to express these sentences:

I don't care.	You don't say!
So, he's stepping out, is he?	I resent that!
Oh, well!	That is not true.
I see through the scheme.	I'm delighted!
He's lost everything he had.	I love you.

Your eyes are the windows of your character's thoughts; you need to learn how to express varied meanings. This order of acting is usually natural: *thought, focus, move, speak.* For example:

Somebody says, "You'll find the car keys on the table." You look toward the table, take a step, and say "I did hunt there."

The conference is over. Look toward the door, rise from your chair, and say, "I'll see you at the next meeting."

Lunchtime is near. Look at the dining table, rise from your chair, and say, "I'll set the table for you."

A gas station attendant is trying to open you car's hood; you see his problem, start toward him, saying "There's a hook."

Indians by Arthur Kopit was presented by South Dakota State University. C. E. Denton, director. Notice the apparent disinterest on faces—characteristic of many American Indians.

Waiting for Godot by Samuel Beckett. Presented by New York University. Andrew Wood, director. Steve Friedman, photographer. Posture, faces, even feet, tell of characters' feelings.

Use of the eyes is helpful in trying to express hearing a noise. You may tighten your eyes, shift them right and left, focus on nothing, or tilt your head in the direction of the sound.

In onstage dialogue, you seldom always keep your eyes on those speaking. Except when lines are very important, you may look away, toy with a small object, or glance at the speaker often to indicate your interest. Watch television to observe actors' use of eyes.

Counter-focus. For mood, characterization, pictorial and other reasons, *counter-focus* is often a part of the business. Instead of all characters looking at the speaker or center of attention, even in an important part of the story, some may have eyes and head turned away. In a large group, there may be several with eyes looking away but assuming an attitude of thoughtfully listening.

When your character—whether as speaker or listener—appears to be in deep thought, your eyes may take on a faraway look. In enacting this, look out *above* the audience, or gaze up high, or on a level across stage, but don't cast eyes down for more than a moment at a time. Never look into the audience.

Reaction is as important onstage as is action. If characters have been chosen to occupy the scenes, they certainly should pay their rent with action and reaction. It is this blending that makes the play.

Background reaction should be unobtrusive. If the dialogue centers on two players, those listening can smile, scowl, shake heads, and make undertone remarks about what is being said, but they must be sure to *hear with the mind* and react accordingly. Characters should all react differently but appropriately. If the dialogue is commonplace, or if a character is a disinterested individual, reaction toward those in conversation will be limited.

Secrecy and Listening. Do you realize that we seem to listen with our eyes? Sometimes a person will close his eyes when listening to soft music, and will hold them wide open when listening to a lively band. You may be surprised to know what eyes do when you are intently listening. A character's eyes can suggest to the audience better than any other way that he is listening to or for some far-off sound.

Try this: while facing front, seem to hear something off L. Turn your eyes far left, squinting a little at the same time and "cocking your ear" in that direction. Your eyes may roll to the opposite direction while your head is still cocked in the direction of the far-off sound.

Don't overact when listening. You don't want to attract attention by hanging on every word, nudging your neighbor, smiling, shaking your head, or scowling during scenes in which you have no special communicating part. Effective reaction is invaluable in building a production of high quality. The following suggestions may help you to use your body as a whole in acting.

Locating. To *locate* an object, the eyes often focus on one thing, then another, when a person is trying to find something. For instance, you may be standing still while your eyes hunt. The attention of the audience can be drawn to a particular spot on stage, or an item of importance to the plot can be made to stand out by this emphasis. Suppose that, while an offstage car waits, a girl dashes back to pick up her purse. She looks at the chair where she was sitting, then at a small table, then at the piano bench. She sees the purse on the floor beside the chair. Her *eyes focus* there for a split second. Then she goes there, picks up the purse, and is off. Remember, on stage you *look before you move or speak*.

Exercises in Improvisation

1. DEATH OF A SALESMAN, by Arthur Miller:
   WILLY's wife LINDA is telling her two sons about their father's breakdown in health because of his lack of success as a salesman. They are astonished. She chokes back the tears as she tells them of certain things she has found that point to his plans for committing suicide.

2. TINY ALICE, by Edward Albee:
   This play opens with a scene in which the LAWYER is talking baby-talk to birds in a cage. The CARDINAL enters quietly, hears him, and calls him St. Francis. The LAWYER is embarrassed by being discovered by so great a person, but he kneels and kisses the ring of the CARDINAL.

3. OKLAHOMA, by Rodgers and Hammerstein:
   CURLY arrives to invite AUNT ELLER and LAUREY to ride with him to the box supper. But LAUREY, to spite CURLY, has accepted a ride with JUD, the belligerent and dangerous farmhand. She did so expecting AUNT ELLER to ride with them, and now is frightened to go with JUD alone.

4. A family is packing a car, preparing for a trip. *Mother* wants the lunch basket easily accessible, but out of 14-year-old *Phil's* reach. *Father*, packing things in, doesn't want luggage covering his tools. *Grandmother* brings practical items to make all comfortable, while *Grandfather* advises everybody. Seventeen-year-old *Maggie* brings paraphernalia peculiar to her wants.

5. Silverware and food have been disappearing night after night from the Zeta Zeta sorority kitchen. Three actives, *Janice, Mary*, and *Beverly*, are determined to catch the thieves. They are asleep on the dining-room floor at two o'clock in the morning. Somebody stealthily opens the kitchen window. The frightened girls arm themselves with chairs, pins, and rulers, ready for attack. They stand flat against the wall either side the window. *Stan* and *Orville*, pledges of Theta Chi fraternity, climb through. The girls strike with their weapons as the boys utter smothered yells. The girls recognize them, and the boys explain their pledge assignment. In the end, the girls

help the boys "steal" silverware and food, with the understanding that the secret must be kept from all.

6. Five people are limbering up. All keep talking, trying to prove to the others the advantages of his or her own choice of exercise: hula hoop, jump rope, dumbbell exercise, golf club swings, basketball tosses.

You have now studied a few of the many principles governing the use of the body in acting. You have yet to practice them to fit your acting, though you have a good start. The next learning step, which we will discuss in the following chapter, is a natural one: to study your voice and speech. You can develop a voice that can do many things for you on stage. Compete with one of your classmates to find out who can develop the larger number of acceptable voices, but *don't* strain your vocal organs.

Excerpts for Practice

In THE GLASS MENAGERIE, by Tennessee Williams, AMANDA *and her two grown children,* TOM *and* LAURA, *live in a small tenement apartment in St. Louis. The father left home long ago and has not been heard from since.* AMANDA *is constantly harking back to her past and her "gentlemen callers."* LAURA *is an extremely shy, slightly crippled girl who finds refuge in her menagerie of little glass animals.* TOM *wants desperately to escape his job and his domineering mother. This scene begins in the middle of a typical argument between* AMANDA *and* TOM.

TOM WINGFIELD

AMANDA WINGFIELD
*LAURA WINGFIELD

SUGGESTIONS AND STAGE DIRECTIONS

This scene provides an excellent opportunity to explore the emotions of an intense argument: anger, frustration, bitterness, spite, and then hurt and sorrow. Body and voice can be quite expressive in exploring these.

AMANDA.   What is the matter with you, you—big—big—IDIOT! 1.

TOM.   Look!—I've got *no thing*, no single thing—

AMANDA.   Lower your voice!

TOM.   —in my life here that I can call my OWN! Everything is—

1. LAURA is present throughout this scene. Her silent presence and movements say a great deal and are essential to the scene. Effective listening and silent acting require excellent concentration.

* Asterisks indicate small roles.

AMANDA. Stop that shouting!

TOM. Yesterday you confiscated my books! You had the nerve to—

AMANDA. I took that horrible novel back to the library —yes! That hideous book by that insane Mr. Lawrence.

(*Tom laughs wildly.*)

I cannot control the output of diseased minds or people who cater to them—

(*Tom laughs still more wildly.*)

BUT I WON'T ALLOW SUCH FILTH BROUGHT INTO MY HOUSE! No, no, no, no, no!

TOM. House, house! Who pays rent on it, who makes a slave of himself to—

AMANDA (*fairly screeching*). Don't you DARE to—

TOM. No, no, *I* mustn't say things! *I've* got to just—

AMANDA. Let me tell you—

TOM. I don't want to hear any more!

AMANDA. You *will* hear more, you—

TOM. No, I won't hear more, I'm going out!

AMANDA. You come right back in—

TOM. Out, out, out! Because I'm—

AMANDA. Come back here, Tom Wingfield! I'm not through talking to you!

TOM. Oh, go—

LAURA (*desperately*). —Tom!

AMANDA. You're going to listen, and no more insolence from you! I'm at the end of my patience!

(*He comes back toward her.*)

TOM. What do you think I'm at? Aren't I supposed to have any patience to reach the end of, Mother? I know, I know. It seems unimportant to you, what I'm *doing*—what I *want* to do—having a little *difference* between them! You don't think that—

AMANDA. I think you've been doing things that you're ashamed of. That's why you act like this. (2) I don't believe that you go every night to the movies. Nobody

2. Early in this speech, TOM should sit frustrated, and AMANDA should move about the stage as the speech gains momentum.

goes to the movies night after night. Nobody in their right minds goes to the movies as often as you pretend to. People don't go to the movies at nearly midnight, and movies don't let out at two A.M. Come in stumbling. Muttering to yourself like a maniac! You get three hours' sleep and then go to work. Oh, I can picture the way you're doing down there. Moping, doping, because you're in no condition.

TOM (*wildly*).   No, I'm in no condition!

AMANDA.   What right have you got to jeopardize your job? Jeopardize the security of us all? How do you think we'd manage if you were—

TOM.   Listen! (3) You think I'm crazy about the *warehouse?* (*He bends fiercely toward her slight figure.*) You think I'm in love with the Continental Shoemakers? You think I want to spend fifty-five *years* down there in that—*celotex interior!* with—*fluorescent—tubes!* Look! I'd rather somebody picked up a crowbar and battered out my brains—than go back mornings! I *go!* Every time you come in yelling that bloody *"Rise and Shine!" "Rise and Shine!"* I say to myself, "How *lucky dead* people are!" But I get up. I *go!* For sixty-five dollars a month I give up all that I dream of doing and being *ever!* And you say self— *self's* all I ever think of. Why, listen, if self is what I thought of, Mother, I'd be where he (4) is—GONE! (*He points to his father's picture.*) As far as the system of transportation reaches! (*He starts past her. She grabs his arm.*) Don't grab at me, Mother!

AMANDA.   Where are you going?

TOM.   I'm going to the *movies!*

AMANDA.   I don't believe that lie!

(*Tom crouches toward her, overtowering her tiny figure. She backs away, gasping.*)

TOM.   I'm going to opium dens! (5) Yes, opium dens, dens of vice and criminals' hangouts, Mother. I've joined the Hogan Gang, I'm a hired assassin, I carry a tommy gun in a violin case! I run a string of cat houses in the Valley! They call me Killer, Killer Wingfield, I'm leading a double-life, a simple, honest warehouse

3. TOM should jump up from his seated position.

4. "He" refers to TOM's father. For clarity, you might substitute "my father" for "he" in this scene.

5. Out of anger and frustration, TOM goes into an exaggerated performance designed to mock and shock his mother. He must use all his expressive powers to achieve this.

worker by day, by night a dynamic *czar* of the *under-world, Mother.* I go to gambling casinos, I spin away fortunes on the roulette table! I wear a patch over one eye and a false mustache, sometimes I put on green whiskers. On those occasions they call me—*El Diablo!* Oh, I could tell you many things to make you sleepless! My enemies plan to dynamite this place. They're going to blow us all sky-high some night! I'll be glad, very happy, and so will you! You'll go up, up on a broomstick, over Blue Mountain with seventeen gentlemen callers! You ugly—babbling old—witch. . . . (*He goes through a series of violent, clumsy movements, seizing his overcoat, lunging to the door, pulling it fiercely open. The women watch him, aghast. His arm catches in the sleeve of the coat as he struggles to pull it on. For a moment he is pinioned by the bulky garment. With an outraged groan he tears the coat off again, splitting the shoulder of it, and hurls it across the room. It strikes against the shelf of Laura's glass collection, and there is a tinkle of shattering glass. Laura cries out as if wounded.*)

LAURA (*shrilly*). *My glass!*—menagerie. . . . (*She covers her face and turns away.*)

(*But Amanda is still stunned and stupefied by the "ugly witch" so that she barely notices this occurrence. Now she recovers her speech.*)

AMANDA (*in an awful voice*). I won't speak to you—until you apologize!

(*She crosses through the portieres and draws them together behind her. Tom is left with Laura. Laura clings weakly to the mantel with her face averted. Tom stares at her stupidly for a moment. Then he crosses to the shelf. He drops awkwardly on his knees to collect the fallen glass, glancing at Laura as if he would speak but couldn't.*) 6.

6. Be careful to play these pantomimes for all their emotional worth, especially the last one.

In Maeterlinck's THE BLUE BIRD, the children MYTYL *and* TYLTYL *have been wandering through the great forest searching for the Blue-bird. When they come into The Land of Memory, they find themselves to be again in the home of* GAFFER TYL *and* GRANNY TYL.

TYLTYL   *MYTYL
GAFFER TYL   *GRANNY TYL

TYLTYL (*looking first at his* GRANDMOTHER *and then at his* GRANDFATHER). You haven't changed Grandad, not a bit ... And Granny hasn't changed either ... But you're better looking. ... 1.

When a player's eyes actually focus on something, the audience is conscious of it.

1. TYLTYL pointedly looks at the countenance of each grandparent.

GAFFER TYL. Well, we feel all right ... We have stopped growing older ... But you, how tall you're growing! ... Yes, you're shooting up finely ... Look, over there, on the door, is the mark of last time ... That was on All-hallows ... Now then, stand up straight. (TYLTYL *stands up against the door*.) Four fingers! ... That's immense! (2) (MYTYL *also stands against the door*.) And Mytyl, four and a half! ... Aha, ill weeds wax apace! ... How they've grown, how they've grown!

2. MYTYL has few lines, but she probably runs about after TYLTYL seeing what he calls attention to, clapping hands and dancing in her delight.

TYLTYL (*looking around him with delight*). Nothing is changed, everything is in its old place! ... Only everything is prettier! (3) There is the clock with the big hand which I broke the point off ...

3. TYLTYL first looks at, then speaks, then moves to the object of interest. Both children keep running about and looking with wonder.

GAFFER TYL. And here is the soup-tureen you chipped a corner off. 4.

4. GRANNY TYL must have great interest in all that the others see, but she probably remains at one side, smiling.

TYLTYL. And here is the hole which I made in the door, the day I found the gimlet.

GAFFER TYL. Yes, you've done some damage in your time ... And here is the plum-tree in which you were so fond of climbing, when I wasn't looking ... It still has those fine plums.

TYLTYL. Why they're finer than ever!

MYTYL. And here is the old blackbird! ... Does he still sing? ... (*The blackbird wakes and begins to sing at the top of his voice*.)

GRANNY TYL. You see ... As soon as one thinks of him.

5. TYLTYL looks, stops, then speaks in amazement and delight. A pause could precede the important idea.

TYLTYL (*observing with amazement that the blackbird is quite blue*). But he's blue ... (5) Why, that's the bird, the Blue Bird which I am to take back to the Fairy ... And you never told us that you had him here! ... Oh, he's blue, blue, blue as a blue glass marble! (*Entreatingly*.) Grandad, Granny, will you give him to me?

GAFFER TYL. Yes, perhaps ... What do you think, Granny Tyl?

GRANNY TYL. Certainly, certainly ... What use is he to us? ... He does nothing but sleep ... We never hear him sing. ...

TYLTYL. I will put him in my cage ... I say, where is my cage?) (6) Oh, I know, left it behind the big tree ... (*He runs to the tree, fetches the cage, and puts the blackbird into it.*) So, really, you've really given him to me? ... How pleased the fairy will be! ... And Light too! 7.

GAFFER TYL. Mind you, I won't answer for the bird. I'm afraid that he will never get used again to the restless life up there and that he'll come back here by the first wind that blows ... However, we shall see ... Leave him there, for the present, and come and look at the cow.

TYLTYL (*noticing the hives*). And how are the bees getting on?

GAFFER TYL. Oh, pretty well ... They are no longer alive, as you call it up there, but they work steadily ...

TYLTYL (*going up to the hives*). Oh, yes! ... I can smell the honey! ... How heavy the hives must be! And the flowers are so beautiful! ... And my little dead sisters, are they here too?

6. Remember the order: first look, then the movement, then the words, TYLTYL glances about for the cage.

7. MYLTYL will stay alert to everything that is said or done. She could ad-lib "Ohs" and "Ahs" and other brief exclamations.

Shakespeare's THE TAMING OF THE SHREW is the classic confrontation between the proud, strong-willed man (PETRUCHIO) and the sharp-tongued, hot-tempered woman (KATHARINA). Before her younger sister can be married, KATHARINA must be wedded. No one has had the courage to attempt this until PETRUCHIO arrives in town.

PETRUCHIO   KATHARINA

PETRUCHIO. I will attend her here,
And woo her with some spirit when she comes.
Say, that she rail; why, then I'll tell her plain,
She sings as sweetly as a nightingale:
Say, that she frown; I'll say, she looks as clear
As morning roses newly wash'd with dew:
Say, she be mute, and will not speak a word;

SUGGESTIONS AND STAGE DIRECTIONS

This scene provides opportunity for a great deal of physical action: grabbing, kneeling, slapping, etc. The action needs to be timed carefully so that no lines are missed. Rehearse the actions carefully, but make them appear spontaneous.

Then I'll commend her volubility,
And say, she uttereth piercing eloquence:
If she do bid me pack, I'll give her thanks,
As though she bid me stay by her a week:
If she deny to wed, I'll crave the day
When I shall ask the banns, and when be married.—
But here she comes; and now, Petruchio, speak.

(*Enter* KATHARINA.)

Good-morrow, Kate, for that's your name, I hear.

KATHARINA.   Well have you heard, but something hard
of hearing:
They call me Katharine, that do talk of me.

PETRUCHIO.   You lie, in faith; for you are call'd plain
Kate,
And bonny Kate, and sometimes Kate the curst;
But Kate, the prettiest Kate in Christendom;
Kate of Kate-Hall, my super-dainty Kate,
For dainties are all cates: and therefore, Kate, 1.

1. Perhaps moving towards her and around her through this speech.

Take this of me, Kate of my consolation:—
Hearing thy mildness prais'd in every town,
Thy virtues spoke of, and thy beauty sounded,
Yet not so deeply as to thee belongs,
Myself am mov'd to woo thee for my wife.

KATHARINA.   Mov'd! in good time: let him that mov'd
you hither,
Remove you hence. I knew you at the first,
You were a moveable.

PETRUCHIO.   Why, what's a moveable?

KATHARINA.   A joint-stool.

PETRUCHIO.   Thou has hit it: come, sit
on me. 2.

2. He kneels on one knee and extends his arm to her; may try grabbing her and forcing her to sit on his knee.

KATHARINA.   Asses are made to bear, and so are you.

PETRUCHIO.   Women are made to bear, and so are you.

KATHARINA.   No such jade as to bear you, if me you
mean. 3.

3. Frees himself and pushes her over.

PETRUCHIO.   Alas, good Kate! I will not burden thee:
For, knowing thee to be but young and light.— 4.

4. Getting up.

KATHARINA.   Too light for such a swain as you to catch,
And yet as heavy as my weight should be.

48   *Your Body*

PETRUCHIO.   Should be? Should buz.

KATHARINA.   Well ta'en, and like a
   buzzard.

PETRUCHIO.   O slow-wing'd turtle! shall a buzzard take
   thee?

KATHARINA.   Ay, for a turtle, as he takes a buzzard.

PETRUCHIO.   Come, come, you wasp; i'faith, you are too
   angry.

KATHARINA.   If I be waspish, best beware my sting.

PETRUCHIO.   My remedy is, then, to pluck it out.

KATHARINA.   Ay, if the fool could find it where it lies.

PETRUCHIO.   Who knows not where a wasp does wear his
   sting?
   In his tail.

KATHARINA.   In his tongue.

PETRUCHIO.   Whose tongue?

KATHARINA.   Yours, if you talk of tails; and so farewell. 5.

PETRUCHIO.   What! with my tongue in your tail? nay,
   come again.
   (*Detaining her.*) 6.
   Good Kate, I am a gentleman.

KATHARINA.   That I'll try. (*Striking
   him.*) 7.

PETRUCHIO.   I swear I'll cuff you, if you strike again.

KATHARINA.   So may you lose your arms:
   If you strike me you are no gentleman,
   And if no gentleman, why, then no arms.

PETRUCHIO.   A herald, Kate? O! put me in thy books.

KATHARINA.   What is your crest? a coxcomb?

PETRUCHIO.   A combless cock, so Kate will be my hen.

KATHARINA.   No cock of mine; you crow too like a
   craven.

PETRUCHIO.   Nay, come, Kate, come; you must not look
   so sour.

KATHARINA.   It is my fashion when I see a crab.

5. She starts to leave, crossing downstage of PETRUCHIO.

6. Grabbing her left arm.

7. If she slaps him, be sure she cups her hand and lets Petruchio move his head to exaggerate the force of the blow; or she can strike his chest with the bottom of her hand.

PETRUCHIO.   Why, here's no crab, and therefore look not sour.

KATHARINA.   There is, there is.

PETRUCHIO.   Then show it me.

KATHARINA.   Had I a glass, I would.

PETRUCHIO.   What, you mean my face?

KATHARINA.   Well aim'd of such a young one.

PETRUCHIO.   Now, by Saint George, I am too young for you.

KATHARINA.   Yet you are wither'd.

PETRUCHIO.   'Tis with cares.

KATHARINA.   I care not. 8.

PETRUCHIO.   Nay, hear you, Kate: in sooth, you 'scape not so. (*Holding her.*)

KATHARINA.   I chafe you, if I tarry: let me go. 9.

PETRUCHIO.   No, not a whit: I find you passing gentle.
'Twas told me, you were rough, and coy, and sullen,
And now I find report a very liar;
For thou art pleasant, gamesome, passing courteous,
But slow in speech, yet sweet as spring-time flowers.
Thou canst not frown, thou canst not look askance,
Nor bite the lip, as angry wenches will;
Nor hast thou pleasure to be cross in talk;
But thou with mildness entertain'st thy wooers,
With gentle conference, soft and affable.
Why does the world report that Kate doth limp?
O, slanderous world! Kate, like the hazel-twig,
Is straight, and slender; and as brown in hue
As hazel nuts, and sweeter than the kernels.
O! let me see thee walk: thou dost not halt. 10.

KATHARINA.   Go, fool, and whom thou keep'st command.

8. He immediately grabs both her wrists. The next several lines are delivered face to face.

9. She attempts to break free. On the second attempt the struggle can find them in a different position, such as with her arms back.

10. He lets her go. She limps away with emphasis.

THE DARK OF THE MOON, by Howard Richardson and William Berney, is a folk play based on the mountain ballad "Barbara Allen." In this scene, two mountain witches make a deal with the CONJUR MAN *concerning the fates of* BARBARA ALLEN *and* JOHN, *the witch-boy who turned mortal because he loved her.*

CONJUR MAN   DARK WITCH
              FAIR WITCH

The DARK WITCH *is sitting atop the rock and calls down. 1.*

DARK WITCH.   Conjur Man. Conjur Man.

(*The* CONJUR MAN *appears.*)

CONJUR MAN.   What that?

DARK WITCH.   I got some news fer you.

CONJUR MAN.   What are you?

DARK WITCH.   I'm here. Heard about the revival meetin' at the church to-night?

(*The* FAIR WITCH *appears on the rock.*)

CONJUR MAN.   What you mean?

DARK WITCH.   Witch boy gonna lost he bargain— bargain he made with you.

CONJUR MAN.   Hit warn't no bargain a mine. Had nothin' to do with hit.

FAIR WITCH.   He gonna lose he bargain and he be a witch agin. 2.

CONJUR MAN.   I reckon that'd please you.

DARK WITCH.   I reckon.

CONJUR MAN.   That don't mean you'll ever git him back. He'll still be in love with Barbara Allen.

DARK WITCH.   Not after she untrue to him. Not after she been faithless with another man.

FAIR WITCH.   She break the bargain, and he be a witch agin.

CONJUR MAN.   But he still love Barbara. He still love Barbara Allen.

DARK WITCH.   Not after she leave him. You fergit that he a human.

FAIR WITCH.   He still a human till he turn back to a witch. And humans, they is different. Thar love can turn to hatin' when the gal untrue. 3.

CONJUR MAN.   And Barbara gonna leave him?

DARK WITCH.   Hit the will a heaven.

Eccentric characters like these require eccentric use of the body. Experiment with sinuous gestures and movements. Find ways of distinguishing between the two witches through body and gesture.

1. Note that some higher elevation is needed here. Be sure to place it so that the CONJUR MAN does not have to turn his back to the audience.

2. Keep the witches distinct in body and voice. Establish different gesture patterns and pitch ranges for each.

3. All the characters speak the backwoods American dialect. Practice until it is uniform and comfortable.

FAIR WITCH.   Yes, sir. Hit the will a heaven.

CONJUR MAN.   (4) I know hit ain't my business, but I do feel right sorry fer the boy, right sorry.

4. Turning away.

DARK WITCH.   Well, hit'll be the best thing fer him.

FAIR WITCH.   He better off with us.

CONJUR MAN.   (5) You ain't got him yit, witch gals.

5. Turning towards them again.

FAIR WITCH.   But we git what we goes after.

DARK WITCH.   We never lose wunst we make up our mind.

CONJUR MAN.   You seem mighty sartin.

FAIR WITCH.   We are. (6) Have you seen him sinst he been changed to a human?

6. FAIR WITCH can begin to climb down toward CONJUR MAN

CONJUR MAN.   No, I ain't.

FAIR WITCH.   Well, I reckon you'll git a chanst to soon enough. After church to-night you'll see him.

DARK WITCH.   Shore. (7) He be up here a-beggin' to git outen he bargain. He be up here to ast to stay down thar in the valley.

7. DARK WITCH can climb down from the rock.

CONJUR MAN.   No he won't neither. He made a bargain and he be true to he word.

DARK WITCH.   You mighty shore a yer opinion.

CONJUR MAN.   I reckon.

FAIR WITCH.   How would you like a little bet that you wrong? 8.

8. Closing in on him, one on each side.

CONJUR MAN.   I ain't averse to hit.

FAIR WITCH.   If we lose, we promise to give up the witch boy.

CONJUR MAN.   You won't git him anyway, but hit a bet.

DARK WITCH.   And if we win, you got to promise to do somethin' fer us.

CONJUR MAN.   What is hit you want?

DARK WITCH.   The life a Barbara Allen.

CONJUR MAN.   You plenty jealous, ain't you.

FAIR WITCH.   We ain't got nothin' agin her, but we jes' as soon she dead.

CONJUR MAN.   She live a long time, witch gals. 9.

9. He crosses down-stage, away from them and the rock.

BOTH WITCHES.   You backin' outen the bargain?

FAIR WITCH.   Thought you said you was mighty shore what John boy would do.

CONJUR MAN.   I am shore.

DARK WITCH.   Then the bet still on?

CONJUR MAN.   Hit still on.

FAIR WITCH (*running up on to the rock again*).   Then you better git ready to change a man back to a witch!

CONJUR MAN.   That ain't none a my doin's. I didn't change him, and hit ain't up to me to change him back. Asides, he ain't lost yit.

DARK WITCH (*as church bells begin ringing in the distance*).   (10) Hear the bells a-ringin'? They startin' the revival. Barbara git redemption, and John'll be a witch agin to-night!

10. She comes down center, backing off into the audience, ending with posture and gestures of triumph.

THE PAJAMA GAME is a musical play by Abbot and Bissell, with lyrics and music by Adler and Ross. The scene is the Sleep Tite Pajama Factory where girls work feverishly to please MAJOR HINES. "PREZ" heads the group of workers and advises them as to the best strategy. The elevator entrance is at one side. PREZ, JOE, and FACTORY GIRL are just entering. Lyrics: "I'm Not At All in Love."

JOE	POOPSIE
PREZ	BABE
	BRENDA
	* FACTORY GIRL
	* MARTHA
	* VIRGINIA
	* MAE
	EXTRAS

SUGGESTIONS AND STAGE DIRECTIONS

Facial expression, small movements of heads, hands, shoulders, differing with each character, all creating the ensemble atmosphere.

PREZ.   You elected me President, you've got to have confidence in me. 1.

1. PREZ probably enters first, speaking as he comes.

JOE.   Sure.

FACTORY GIRL.   We only said . . .

PREZ.   Listen, this is no time to be talking about no ultimatum and no strikes. 2.

2. PREZ may turn on the others sharply.

JOE.   Yes, but that seven and a half cents . . .

PREZ.   Wait a minute. . . . There ain't no question but we're gonna get that seven and a half cents' raise, other companies are paying it and we're entitled to it, but we got to be smart. Wait till old Hasler's got so many orders in he can't afford to shut the factory down. Then we got him. 3.

3. PREZ moves with an air of importance. Others step toward him trying to get a word in.

JOE.   You bet!

(JOE *exits*. MAE, BRENDA, POOPSIE *and* MARTHA *enter*.)

POOPSIE.   Yeah!

MAE.   Well, I wouldn't want no super to try and shove me around.

4. The FACTORY GIRLS ad lib talk, and laugh with one another. Guard your group arrangements GIRLS languish by doors, steps, or bench.

POOPSIE.   Hiya, Prez.

(BABE *and other* FACTORY GIRLS *enter*.) 4.

PREZ.   Hello. Say Babe, what about that kid that got hit? What'd the super have to say for himself?

BABE.   That's one for the birds, Prez. That kid hasn't even got a bruise on his arm. He's a faker.

PREZ.   You think so, huh, Babe?

BABE.   Sure, he's a phony. If that guy Sorokin ever really hit him he'd break him in two.

PREZ.   Okay.

(*Music begins.* PREZ *exits*.)

5. GIRLS begin to kid BABE with significant winks, glances, and actions. Individualize GIRLS by primping, chewing gum, sipping coffee, etc.

POOPSIE.   Mr. Sorokin is soooo strong . . . 5.

MARTHA.   He's so wonderful.

BABE (*looking from one to the other*).   What's this?

POOPSIE.   I think the new super is simply woo woo, don't you?

BABE.   I didn't notice.

POOPSIE.   *I* noticed.

MARTHA.   I thought Babe was noticin' too.

BRENDA.   Yeah . . . she lit up.

BABE.   You girls are getting . . .

BRENDA.   Love comes at last to Babe Williams!

BABE.   Oh, get off it! I hardly looked at the man. I'm the Grievance Committee. *Love*— are you nuts?

POOPSIE.   Some people can't tell when it hits them. . . .

BABE.   Bah!
    I'm not at all in love, not at all in love, not I,

Not a bit! Not a mite!
Tho' I'll admit he's quite a hunk o' guy.
But he's not my cup of tea,
Not my cup of tea, not he.
Not an ounce, not a pinch!
He's just an inch too sure of himself for me! 6.

BRENDA. (*sings*).　Well of course you've noticed that manly physique and that look in his eyes.
And I'm sure he can cut most any man down to size. 7.

VIRGINIA (*sings*).　He must be as fierce as a tiger when he's mad.

POOPSIE (*sings*).　And I'll bet he cries like a little boy when he's sad.

BABE (*sings*).　But I'm not at all in love, not at all in love, not I,
Not a straw, not a hair!
I don't care if he's as strong as a lion,
Or if he has the rest of you sighin',
You may be sold, but this girl ain't buyin',
I'm not at all in love!　8.

6. As background for BABE, girls may begin a dance routine. Perhaps BABE moves about as she sings. She directs the song toward the house. GIRLS might sway, snap fingers, or eye each other. They must not distract audience attention from BABE.

7. As each sings, she is probably somewhat apart from the group.

8. Keep the whole scene light, happy, gay. BABE's importance on one side of the stage can be balanced with a group on the other side.

"I'm Not At All In Love"

From the Broadway Production "The Pajama Game"

Words and Music by
RICHARD ADLER
and JERRY ROSS

CHAPTER 5

Your Voice and Speech

There are two basic reasons why people go to the theater: They want to *see* the play, and they want to *hear* the play. The hearing of a play depends on a theater's acoustical qualities and on the actors' voices and speech.

Voice is sound as it comes from the vocal cords; *speech* is that sound formed into words. Both pleasant and unpleasant voices belong in the theater, according to the character being enacted, but speech must always be clear and distinct.

VOICE

Vocal Quality. Your head has a number of cavities which amplify sound and help create vocal quality. The cavity's size, shape, and surroundings provide each of us with a distinctive voice. When nasal chambers are clogged by a bad cold, speech is bad. *Physical defects* will also cause a voice to be unpleasant, but most unpleasant voices result from poor use of one's voice. Different kinds of voices seem to belong to different localities. Southern people, as a rule, have pleasing soft voices; others could have, through practice.

Vocal Abuses. Most of us follow the vocal patterns of our associates, good or bad. If each person listens to his or her own voice, compares it with others' voices, and listens critically, that person can then take steps to improve vocal habits. Think of yor own speech and voice as you think about the bad habits listed here.

Nasality is caused by too much nasal resonance in certain sounds. *M*, *N*, and *NG* sounds are dependent on nasal resonance. All speech needs some, but bad speech habits can be formed by using too much resonance with the wrong sounds.

Tight Throat produces harsh, buzz saw-like speech.

Immovable Jaw creates muffled sounds, indistinct speech. You should drop your jaw for words such as *hay, can, long, mine, now*.

Lazy Lips. Lips should be rounded to form words such as *who, use, lose.* Use two jaw positions for some diphthongs: *boy, out, oil, use.* Stretch lips and drop jaw for some diphthongs: *ate, ice*.

Flabby Tongue. When tongue is flat in the mouth, sloppy speech results.

Throatiness. If throat is open, voice coming from back of throat, a hollow tone is made.

Breathiness, caused by using too much breath, can be heard.

Wallowing Words means too much mouth cavity, sometimes puffed cheeks, resulting in speech "mushiness."

Vocal Energy and Intensity. Acting is much like life, only bigger. That means bigger voice, bigger clarity, more careful ("bigger") articulation, bigger action. Use full voice to speak your lines, and articulate clearly for those in backrows and balcony. The *volume* must be bigger too. You are in an unnatural situation because you are speaking *to* a character who is near you, but you are speaking *for* those farthest from you. When they can't hear you, sometimes people tell you to "speak louder." Yes, you should speak loudly so that people can hear, but other methods project speech more effectively.

To project the thought, make two or three words *top* those of your cue, and use more force and careful articulation with the last few words. The last words and the start of a speech are often the most important but are habitually dropped by many unskilled players, and so are lost. Start each speech with a *push* and end it with another *push* to project both words and meanings.

Focus, that is, direct your lines, toward the back of the house. Don't yell. Speak as you would to a friend who is some distance from you out of doors. Purity of tone, distinctness, and focus, rather than volume alone, are agents that project lines. Use a calling tone but one that is subdued, with careful articulation.

Breath Control. Breathe deeply from your diaphragm instead of using a shallow lung intake. You need power for ease in speaking. The *diaphragm* is made of muscle and membrane, and separates the chest and abdomen. It lowers to give the lungs more room for air, then contracts to push the air out, energizing your voice rather than causing you to shout. Good breathing will keep your throat from tiring.

Exercises

1. Inhale slowly and gradually fill the lower parts of your lungs. Hold. Your abdomen should be pushing out as you start your intake. Exhale very slowly; keep pushing the air out of your lungs until your lungs are deflated.
2. Breathe rapidly, in and out, in and out. Your abdomen should push in and out with each inhalation and exhalation. Work fast to exercise the diaphragm.
3. Repeat a phrase or paragraph over and over again, as much as is possible on a single breath. Then vocalize "ah" as long as possible on one breath.

A *stage whisper* is half voice, half whisper. You need to use extra force to project your whisper far from the stage. A stage whisper carries well and is useful in many situations. Period plays often use *asides.* They are directed away from other characters, who seem not to hear. It was also considered good theater in old plays to use *soliloquies* for the leading characters. In some the actor talks to the audience and in others he talks to himself, seeming to be thinking aloud.

SPEECH

Speech involves organs that are used in voice formation. A baby uses voice to express need, but has not learned how to turn these sounds into verbal language.

Diction. Diction is the first consideration in studying speech. Clear distinct speech, careful articulation, meaningful rhythm, choice of words, correct pronunciation, expressive voice—all these and other qualities are important. Good diction is not overly precise and does not sound affected or pedantic. Even though a tone of voice may be beautiful and expressive, the speaker's diction may be bad. The quality of diction results from either voice or speech, or both; from vocal quality, pronunciation, speech quality and word arrangement.

Articulation. Americans are in the habit of doing things in a hurry, with the result that their actions are often only half done or are poorly executed. Our speech is an example. Final *t*'s, *d*'s, *f*'s and other consonants sound indistinct and blurred. *I can't do it* becomes *I cand do ud; A great disappointment* becomes *a grad dizappoin men. Eleven of us came* sounds like *leben ovuz cum.* Consonants within words are also mutilated. The word *little* becomes *lil; something* becomes *somthun; perhaps* becomes *praps.*

Vowels are often given wrong values as *get* becomes *git, no* becomes *naw,* and *piano* sounds like *piana.* There are endless examples of careless articulation—work to clean up your speech.

Articulate carefully to help your audience understand the words. Speak in *phrases,* with slight breaks between phrases. *Clip your words,* not in an objectional way, but to make thoughts clear. *Speak from the front of your mouth,* on the very tip of your tongue, and with limber lips. Repeat this and feel it: "The tip of the tongue, the tip of the tongue, the tip of the tongue."

Enunciate carefully the *last four words* of every speech. Many actors, even professionals, drop their voices at the ends of speeches. Those last four words are the "hinges"—the cue—for the speech that follows.

Hamlet's Advice to the Players. William Shakespeare had Hamlet present his thoughts about good acting and the presentation of lines. Hamlet advises the players on the use of voice, diction, and bodily gesture.

> Speak the speech, I pray you, as I pronounced it to you, trippingly on the tongue; but if you mouth it, as many of your players do, I had as lief the towncrier spoke my lines.

Then he turns his attention to accompanying action.

> Nor do not saw the air too much with your hand, thus; but use all gently: for in the very torrent, tempest, and—as I may say—the whirlwind of passion, you must acquire and beget a temperance that may give it smoothness . . .

He reminds them of the reason for acting. Shakespeare evidently had trouble with the acting of some of his players, just as some directors today have similar difficulties.

> Be not too tame neither, but let your own discretion be your tutor: suit the action to the word, the word to the action; with this special observance, that you o'erstep not the modesty of nature; for anything so overdone is from the purpose of playing, whose end, both at the first and now, was and is, to hold, as 'twere, the mirror up to nature; to show virtue her own feature, scorn her own image, and the very age and body of the time his form and pressure.

Laughter that is the result of burlesque is less to be desired than approval of an audience that sees artistry in the acting—the aim of the player.

Now, this overdone, or come tardy off, though it make the unskilful laugh, cannot but make the judicious grieve; the censure of which one must in your allowance o'erweigh a whole theater of others.

Diction Usage. Good diction uses *contractions,* unless each of the two words needs to be emphasized. We say "he's not in this room," instead of "he is not in this room." We also use *weak forms* of words in good diction: adverbs, adjectives, pronouns, conjunctions, and others. "He ate 'is breakfast," "I'll go 'ith you," "This 's th' place."

Melody. You can develop a pleasing and expressive voice. Although it is rare to develop a beautiful voice, a melodic voice is an attribute that all can attain. Melody—the tune of language—consists of varying *pitch* changes and *inflections* which constantly change from rising to falling to circumflex. Meaning and emotion induce melody.

Inflection. Nuances of thought and emotion defy description or instruction. *Rising inflection* indicates that a thought is unfinished, suspended. *Falling inflection* is used to express finality or for emphasis. "Downreading" is often overused; an actor needs to keep his audience expectant through use of rising inflections. *Circumflex inflection* says, in effect, *yes* and *no.* The voice wavers to suggest a waver in thought. You say, "I think I'll go," but your voice wavers on the word *think.* Or you may say just one word, "yesss," with a *yes* and *no* waver that indicates doubt. All inflections help to create the melody of each speech.

Tone. "Tone" is a general word for the depth and quality of voice which gives individual character to the sound of speech: "Her tone indicates that she is not pleased." It includes modulation of voice, which changes to give meaning to every word and thought. The following are some simple but helpful terms to describe tone.

Domestic tone is used with family and friends.

Social tone "has curves," is soft and courteous, unhurried.

Business tone is straightforward, often forceful, businesslike.

Solemn tone has a soft manner, expresses deep feelings.

In cultivating your voice to be pleasant, with a melody that is varied to make speech interesting and meaningful, avoid any vocal expression that becomes monotonous.

Pace (Tempo and Rhythm). *Tempo* is a factor of rhythm, but is not the whole of it. Tempo is the speed of a line, a scene, or a play and has great effect on the emotional experience of its audience. *Pace*—the term used in theater language—should be meaningful and so appropriate that the audience takes no notice of it, but accepts it as fitting the mood and character of the situation.

Tempo changes often, from line to line or scene to scene, but *rhythm* is an overall characteristic of a play. All of us move and talk at different tempos, which gives each individual his or her own characteristics.

Let's consider some sounds that affect tempo. The English language has *alphabetical stops:* b, d, g, j, k, p, and t. Their sounds cannot be lengthened. The *liquid* sounds are l, m, n, r, and all the vowels, which can be lengthened, as in *right hand, mound of money.*

Phrasing is the punctuation of speech. Do not confuse phrasing of speech with phrasing in grammar. In speech, phrasing is the brief bits of time left between small groups of words. The frequent short pauses allow time for breathing and help to make the meaning clear and to defeat monotony. You should express thoughts in groups of words so that listeners can catch them by thinking in groups of words. People neglect to phrase when reading aloud; this creates monotony more than any other speech factor.

Rhythm relates to every living thing; all living animals and persons, even countries, have their characteristic rhythms. A quiet little town seems to have a languid rhythm, whereas New York City has a bustling rhythm. In thinking about plays, a dramatist has written a rhythm into his creation through his characters, the plot and situation.

Rhythm results from sound, inflection, force, cadence, pitch, and tone variations, blended with bodily attitudes, characteristics, and movement. Rhythm is tied closely to emotions and muscle tension. We take short breaths when angry, and the muscles of our legs, arms, diaphragm, and jaw tighten as anger grows, all resulting from our emotional state.

In *Julius Caesar*, Marullus speaks before a Roman crowd. Note the inflection, emphasis, and phrase marks through the first part. You may complete the passage.

(*It is a day of great excitement in Rome.* MARULLUS *is rebuking the crowds for forgetting Pompey so soon.*)

MARULLUS.   *Wherefore* rejoice? / What conquest / brings *he* home?

What tributaries follow *him* / to Rome, /

To grace in captive bonds *his* chariot wheels? /

You *blocks*, / you *stones*, / you *worse* than senseless things! /

O *you hard hearts,* / you *cruel* men of Rome, /

Knew you not *Pompey*? / Many a time / and oft /

Have you climbed up to walls and battlements, /

To towers and windows, / yea, / to *chimney-tops*, /

Your infants in your arms, / and there have sat

The *livelong day*, / with patient expectation, /

To see *great Pompey* / pass the streets of Rome: /
And when you saw his chariot but appear,
Have you not made an universal shout,
That Tiber trembled underneath her banks,
To hear the replication of your sounds
Made in her concave shores?
And do you now put on your best attire?
And do you now call out a holiday?
And do you now strew flowers in his way,
That comes in triumph over Pompey's blood?
Be gone!
Run to your houses, fall upon your knees,
Pray to the gods to intermit the plague
That needs must light in this ingratitude.*

Pause. Pause is the strongest device an actor can use to create powerful emotional effects. An emotion-filled lapse of time can be highly dramatic.

A *logical pause* is a lapse in dialogue to supply necessary time for action. These pauses to *execute action* are numerous. They may be quite long if filled with business and suspense, which can be fully as interesting as lines. Pauses for action are used extensively in TV and movies, often with background music. Check TV shows for lapses in dialogue that are filled with suspense and action.

A *hold for laughs* is classified as a logical pause. An actor must pause for the audience to enjoy a laugh. When holding for a laugh, be sure to stay in character but without speaking. Pick up your lines before the laugh is finished, but only after it subsides enough so that lines can be heard. Be careful that you *do not* speak during the laugh, as it annoys the audience to feel that

* William Shakespeare, *Julius Caesar*, Act I, Scene 1.

they are missing something. They must stop laughing in order to hear. Learn to listen and to keep listening to the house.

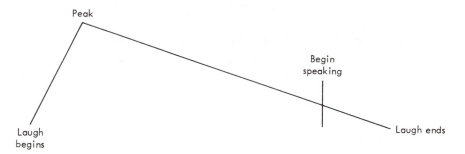

Telephone conversations must be filled with pauses. These should be long enough to be convincing, but not as long as it would take to listen in real life. Many times you start to speak in telephone conversations, then are interrupted—you stop after opening your mouth without saying a word, or stop, mouth open, in the middle of a word. What a character says might sound like this: "But this meeting isn't— Yes, I know b— of course, I know b— but— When do you?—She did!—I de— I de— I declare!"

Keep naturalness in mind when reciting lines, even with pauses. Sometimes lines are given with such speed that they seem raced. Dialogue should usually move faster than speech in real life, but it *should not seem faster.* Remember Hamlet's lines, ". . . that you o'er step not the modesty of nature." *Stage business* can be lengthened if there is emotion and suspense enough to hold audience interest.

Sometimes a character must hold for *time to think* or *to listen.* You'll find many examples of this on TV shows when a character needs time to ponder. However, this is only the *illusion* of the real amount of time needed. The real amount of time would bore the audience.

Psychological pauses are often packed with emotion. They may be used to force attention or to arouse emotions in the people watching the play. These emotions may be mild, such as enjoyment, expectancy or disappointment, or they may be strong emotions such as fear, sorrow, anger, or hatred.

The *pause to emphasize* may come just before the important idea or word, or it may follow the word. *Example:* "You can't do that (*pause*) honestly." Or, following the word: "You can't do that honestly" (*pause*). A pause can *create suspense* and emotion. An idea of sufficient importance may demand a lengthy pause.

Example: JULIET (*as she is about to drink the potion, a thought occurs to her*)
  What if this mixture do not work at all? (*Pause*)
  Shall I be married then tomorrow morning? (*Pause*)

No, no; this (*taking up dagger*) shall forbid it: lie thou there. (*Lays the dagger on the table beside the bed. Again takes up the vial, and again hesitates.*)

Suspense is often written into lines, but can be heightened by careful study and planning to create suspense that is not in the script. Here are some practice examples.

Depiction of *strong emotions* may be heightened by using pause. Every second must be filled with emotion, or it will only be a *wait*. When people are angry, their faces, body muscles, and movements tell of the emotion. Sorrow, fear, resentment, or true love can be made stronger without words.

In Susan Glaspell's TRIFLES, two women and their husbands are in a farmer's home where the farmer was hung. The men look for clues of the murder. The wives search for items that the farm wife, now in jail, might use to occupy her time. Mrs. Hale *picks up a sewing basket.*

Mrs. Hale.   Here's some red. I expect this has got sewing things in it. (*She brings out a fancy box.*) What a pretty box. Looks like something somebody would give you. Maybe her scissors are in here. (*She opens box. Suddenly her hand to her nose.*) Why— (Mrs. Peters *bends nearer, then turns her face away.*) There's something wrapped up in this piece of silk.

Mrs. Peters.   Why, this isn't her scissors.

Mrs. Hale.   (*Lifting the silk*).   Oh, Mrs. Peters—it's—

(Mrs. Peters *bends closer.*)

Mrs. Peters.   It's the bird.

Mrs. Hale (*Jumping up*).   But, Mrs. Peters—look at it! Its neck! Look at its neck. It's all—other side too.

Mrs. Peters.   Somebody—wrung—its—neck.

In the above excerpt you can find four pauses for action, five pauses for suspense, and three pauses for emphasis. Each must be filled with acting and emotion or they will become *waits*. There is never place in a theatrical performance for a wait!

In this exerpt from A DOLL'S HOUSE, by Henrik Ibsen, Nora *is filled with terror. Her husband,* Helmer, *may discover a forgery she has committed to help him. She speaks rapidly between pauses.*

Helmer.   Very well, then we'll share it, Nora, as man and wife. (*Petting her.*) Are you satisfied now? Come, come, come, don't look like a scared dove. It is all nothing—fancy. Now you must play the tarentella through, and practice with the tambourine. I shall sit in my inner room and shut both doors, please. (*Turns around in doorway.*) And when Rank comes just tell him where I'm to be found. (*He nods to her, and goes with his papers into his room, closing the door.*)

NORA (*Bewildered with terror, stands as though rooted to the ground, and whispers*). He would do it. Yes, he would do it. He would do it in spite of all the world. No, never that, never, never! Anything rather than that! Oh, for some way to escape! What to do! (*Doorbell rings.*) Doctor Rank—! Anything rather than that—anything, anything! (NORA *draws her hands over her face, pulls herself together, goes to the door and opens it.*)

Picking up cues is of greatest importance in keeping good pace; without good pickups, a play drags. However, picking up cues seems to create a difficult problem for many players. A speech should be linked to its cue. If you memorize cues as part of your own lines, the play will not drag.

First, go through your script and underscore your cues—all of them. Then memorize each cue with the speech that follows it. Make learning the cue a part of learning your own lines. When your acting partner speaks your cue, you will habitually attach your line to its cue. It works.

Sometimes your cue is for action or emotional expression without words. If that is the case, start on cue with the action. Your action may be to turn away in disgust or hide your face in your hands, but begin whatever your part calls for right on cue.

You may find yourself in a difficult situation that requires careful rehearsing. Imagine three groups on stage, acting and conversing, each with its own interest. Group C is speaking for the audience to hear, but the other conversations must continue unbroken. Group A, Nell, Francis, and Tom, discuss a new Buick; Group B, Kenneth and Helen, talk insurance; Group C, Maxine, Polly, and Betty, talk about the new Smith family in town. The audience is listening to group C, but Francis in Group A is to pick up his cue. He must seem to be conversing, but his ear is trained toward Group C to hear and pick up the cue on time.

When dialogue shifts from one group to another, or even to a character who has not been active in a scene, that character *must* perform some kind of visible action so that the audience can find the speaker. The actor may take a short step, make a hand gesture, or turn sharply toward another character.

Cutoff Speeches. When a speech is interrupted by another player's lines or action, the broken speech *must not stop.* It must continue until the speech following comes in to cut it off or some other interruption takes over, whether it is action, dialogue, or movement. There should be almost an overlapping of lines. The speaker may not be at fault for the delay, but even so it is his or her job to cover the delay by going on with the dialogue, which will be *ad lib*. Such breaks should be carefully rehearsed.

If the dialogue does not move smoothly through the break to the next speech, the fault always lies with the player who does not pick up the cue. The character with the broken line is not supposed to add words to the play; he or she does so only when a careless co-player makes it necessary.

The actor must *continue to think* of what his character was going to say. This keeps the inflection rising so that the speech *seems broken* instead of stopped. Broken speeches need to be built *up* at the break with more intensity, force, or higher pitch. Even though the speech is heightened, the player interrupting must top it. Work on these examples:

1. From THE FOOL, by Channing Pollock:

    Mrs. Gilliam (*up to tree*).   Dilly! Nobody knows better than you that I've never had a selfish thought. Mr. Gilliam—

    Dilly (*looks at Mrs. Thornbury*).   Of the Gilliam Grocery, Incorporated.

2. From THE PHILADELPHIA STORY, by Philip Barry:

    Tracy.   You mean *you* were, but now you're divorced?

    Liz.   Well, the fact is—

    Tracy.   Suds—you can't mean you're ashamed of it!

    Liz.   Of course I'm not ashamed of it.

    Mike (*staring at her*).   Wha-at?

    Liz.   It was ages ago, when I was a mere kid, in Duluth. (*Flicks ashes in tray.*)

    Mike.   Good Lord, Liz—you never told me you were—

    Liz.   You never asked.

    Mike.   I know, but—

    Liz.   Joe Smith. Hardware.

3. From THE MOLLUSC, by H. H. Davies:

    Miss Roberts.   I was telling Mr. Baxter before you came into the room—

    Mrs. Baxter (*holding out her hand*).   Give me the paper knife (Miss Roberts *gives her the knife, which she examines carefully*).

    Miss Roberts.   I told you at the beginning of the term, and several times since—

    Mrs. Baxter.   It would have been a pity if that knife had been snapped in two. (*Looks up pleasantly.*) Yes, Miss Roberts?

Miss Roberts.   I was saying that I thought—(Mrs. Baxter *drops the paper knife accidentally on the floor.*)

Mrs. Baxter.   Oh, don't trouble to pick it up. (Miss Roberts *picks it up and holds it in her hand.*) Oh, thank you, I didn't mean you to do that.

Miss Roberts.   I was saying—

Mrs. Baxter.   It isn't chipped, is it?

Ad Lib. Sometimes characters must improvise lines. Suppose a group is at a party. The play's dialogue must be heard and understood while other characters converse in lower tones—not in whispers. The same few lines are ad libbed over and over, lines with an abundance of consonants:

"The many cars at the time made driving hazardous."

"All schools close the day before Memorial Day."

"Jack and Henry are the best players on the team."

Every character should use a different sentence: one about food, another cars, another neighbors, another a public personality. Use the same line for every rehearsal, and speak as your character would, all in the mood of the play. Do not talk about your personal interests, because you will get out of character. Other reasons for ad libbing will be discussed in another chapter.

Point-Up Humor. Point-up humor is helpful for emphasis. Slapstick, a very light form of comedy, needs no pointing up, but when humor is a bit subtle a pause directly preceding the humorous word or line will help. In two of the three quotations here, you will notice that the dramatist has indicated a pause. However, in many plays, as in the third example, you must find such opportunities by studying the play.

1. North.   What would it be—the flipper? (From *Mr. and Mrs. North,* by Owen Davis.)

2. Milton.   Woman was created merely to keep man—guessing! I know—I've guessed!

3. Maggie to Mr. Whiteside.   That's my image of you—Big Lord Fauntleroy. (From *The Man Who Came to Dinner,* by George S. Kaufman and Moss Hart.)

Your voice and speech need continuous training, just as a musician keeps in training with finger exercises. A fine speaking ability with its intellectual and emotional appeal is a talent that can leave you if not exercised.

We will next consider the large part that a person's *mind* plays in high-grade acting. You may agree that it is necessary to study physical action and vocal expression for effective acting, but you may wonder what your mind has to do with playing a role other than learning lines.

You must decide mentally what each line means to the play, how it should be interpreted, what action is suitable, how you should respond to others, and many other points of acting a role. Use your imagination appropriately in planning your characterization. Decide how you can cooperate with all concerned with the production. Imagination plays a tremendous part in every production, starting with the dramatist, then the director, the scene crews and costumers, even the holder of the book who has to decide the best means to project a thought to an actor in difficulty. Your mind is a strong ally of every theatrical production.

Excerpts for Practice

SKY HIGH, by Florence Ryerson and Alice D. G. Miller, is a comedy-mystery. Five students have been enticed to Sky High Lodge during a winter vacation. They discover that all communications at Sky High have been mysteriously disconnected. TRACY *and* JILL *have just imprisoned in a hidey-hole three men whom they suspect of being Communist spies. They used a poker to bar the hidey-hole doors.*

* HANK

MRS. PETMORE,
    lodge matron
JILL, a coed
MONICA, a coed
* TOOTS, a scatter-
    brained coed

SUGGESTIONS AND
STAGE DIRECTIONS

Enunciate carefully stage whisper and back-to-audience lines. Stage whisper is almost a whisper with only a little voice. Project each word carefully to reach back rows.

[*Sounds of wood tumbling around heavily as* JILL *goes back to hidey-hole.*]

MONICA. What *is* all this mystery? 1.

MRS. PETMORE. I don't care what it is! *I'm* going to let those gentlemen out! (*Reaches toward poker.* JILL *stops her.*) Locking up my company! The idea!

JILL. Please, Mrs. Petmore!

MRS. PETMORE (*grasps poker, tries to pull it out*). What-*ever* will they think?

1. Rapid tempo of lines should prevail through the scene. However, there are many suspense-filled pauses.

JILL (*blurting*).   It doesn't matter what they think! They're *spies!*

MRS. PETMORE, MONICA, TOOTS (*together*). 2.
  Spies!
  Spies!
  Did you say *s-spies?*

2. Although these three are directed to speak at the same time, it is better not to speak simultaneously.

MONICA (*thoughtfully*).   You wouldn't say such a thing without good reason—

MRS. PETMORE (*still belligerent*).   It'd better be good!

JILL (*rapidly*).   I'll just hit the high spots. Here's how Tracy and I figure it: Oscar got rid of Simon somehow —maybe the poor old thing *was* murdered—then wormed his way in here. 3.

3. JILL, the leader in this passage, should appear confident, with an analytical mind.

MONICA.   But *why*—

JILL.   To spy on the shipping—the air field. Dr. Barto is the go-between!

MRS. PETMORE (*astringently*).   And I suppose Mr. Mundy's up here to murder all of us in our beds!

JILL.   They sent fake messages to bring Tracy and me here—blew up the tunnel—cut the wires to the phone!

MRS. PETMORE.   Great Jehosaphat! I never heard such wicked nonsense in all my life!

JILL.   You saw Dr. Barto with that gun! He was really keeping Tracy from going for help!

MONICA (*bewildered*).   But why in the world—I mean —what could they possibly want of you and Tracy?

JILL.   That's one thing I can't tell you—it's Top Secret! Please take my word it's important, so important Tracy's risking his life this very minute!

MRS. PETMORE (*breaking in, to Monica*).   Do you believe all that moonshine?

MONICA (*troubled*).   I don't know. I might not believe it if it weren't for Hank—(*with growing alarm*) Where is he? What's happened to him?

TOOTS (*going to* MRS. PETMORE).   I'm scared! 4.

4. Since TOOTS has little to say, she might listen from another stage area most of the time, before going to MRS. PETMORE.

MRS. PETMORE.   Fiddlesticks! If those three are—spies— and mind you I don't admit it, they're safely locked up.

MONICA (*stepping closer toward hidey-hole*).   I wonder!

MRS. PETMORE.   What?

MONICA (*listens at double-doors*).   Why are they so quiet? 5.

5. Beginning here, a number of speeches should be given in a stage whisper—a voiced whisper.

JILL.   That's right.

MRS. PETMORE (*knocks on door*).   Dr. Barto! Mr. Mundy! Oscar, do you hear me! 6.

6. Speaking very loud.

[*Silence in the hidey-hole continues. Worried, they look at each other, speak rapidly in low tones.*] 7.

7. Hold pauses. Lines move rapidly, but suspense-filled silences can be eloquent, and should be carefully observed.

MONICA.   I don't hear a sound.

JILL.   Not even a breath—

TOOTS.   Let's just peek in!

JILL.   No, no—it may be a trick!

MONICA.   But if it isn't—

JILL (*a new and dreadful possibility presenting itself*). *Monica, you're sure Hank*—the ghost—*went in there?*

MONICA.   Perfectly!

JILL.   And then vanished?

MONICA.   Yes!

JILL.   Then, there must be some other way out.

MRS. PETMORE.   But that's impossible! 8.

8. Speak rapidly, *clipping* the words to make them easily understood.

JILL (*turns resolutely up to hidey-hole again*).   I'm going to look!

MONICA.   But that's dangerous.

JILL.   Don't you see, we *must* know.

MONICA.   At least we ought to be prepared! (*Looks around, picks up a piece of firewood from hearth to wield as a club.*) 9.

9. Eye work is important here. Don't rush the action.

MRS. PETMORE.   This is perfectly ridiculous! (*But she picks up a pair of shears from work-box by her chair.*) I feel like a fool! 10.

10. These scissors are "planted" at this time.

JILL (*slowly, quietly pulling poker out from the handles*).   I'll use this if—(*loudly*) Don't try to come out —we're armed!

(*Brandishing their weapons,* JILL *and* MONICA *simultaneously pull the door open,* L. *and* R.) 11.

11. Action slow here, with few words now and then.

MRS. PETMORE. Why, there's nobody there!

TOOTS. *Goody!* (*A change of tone.*) But it *isn't* good, is it? If they aren't there—where are they?

MONICA (*drily, crossing R*). That's the problem.

In THE STAR WAGON, by Maxwell Anderson, the choir is gathering for its weekly rehearsal. HALLIE comes in with STEPHEN, who has had a near escape from drowning. Both are in wet clothing. Other choir members are laughing uproariously at DUFFY as he humorously imitates MRS. RUTLEDGE, the choir director, before she arrives. DUFFY lifts an imaginary baton, and the QUARTET sings.

DUFFY	HALLIE	SUGGESTIONS AND
HANUS	MRS. RUTLEDGE	STAGE DIRECTIONS
* OGLETHORPE	* DELLA	
* STEPHEN	* CHRISTABEL	

Exercise to practice laughing heartily, then trying to smother laughter.

THE QUARTET. I'm dreaming now of Hallie.
Sweet Hallie, sweet Hallie;
I'm dreaming now of Hallie,
For the thought of her is one that never dies. 1.

1. This group of friends is full of fun. They sing with exuberance, probably swaying and moving about as they sing.

HALLIE. I don't know what you think's so funny.

THE QUARTET. She's sleeping in the valley,
The Valley, the Valley
She's sleeping in the valley
And the mocking bird is singing where she lies. 2.

2. HALLIE is sedate. She might show her disgust through expression as well as words.

DUFFY (*imitating* MRS. RUTLEDGE). Now something dulcet, something really dulcet and tender! 3.

3. DUFFY steps in front of others as he directs. This gives a good opportunity for burlesque, but don't overdo it.

DUFFY (*still imitating*). And now tomorrow, nothing preventing, bring the little red hymnal after prayer-meeting, and we'll all—oh, I'm sorry, I'm late—I must rush—foreign missions—so sorry—the young ladies will remember in my absence—propriety please—in all things. 4.

4. The QUARTET must laugh *heartily* at DUFFY'S antics. Keep laughing.

(MRS. RUTLEDGE *enters. The laughter is suddenly hushed.*)

HALLIE. I'm glad if you think it's amusing, because I don't. I've heard it too often.

MRS. RUTLEDGE. I shall remember this, Mr. Duffy. 5.

(*She passes the* QUARTET *and sees* HALLIE *and* STEPHEN.)

5. QUARTET covers their snickers with hymnals or their hands.

So this is where you are. Within easy distance of my call, where you must have heard me. Hallie, have you been swimming?—You have. 6.

HALLIE.   What if I have?

(HANUS *enters with* HALLIE'S *shoes and stockings; also a chemise.*)

DUFFY.   He fell in and she pulled him out. (STEVE *sits up.*)

MRS. RUTLEDGE.   Very likely. Hanus, what are you doing with Hallie's shoes and stockings? 7.

HANUS (*dropping them*).   This always happens to me—always. (*He stuffs the chemise in his pocket.*)

MRS. RUTLEDGE.   I'm quite grateful to you. You bring in exactly the evidence I need.

6. HALLIE and STEPHEN may have dropped onto one of the front pews. Their clothing may not be evident at first.

7. MRS. RUTLEDGE is probably dressed as severely as she speaks.

In Shakespeare's MACBETH, the three WITCHES *represent the influence of supernatural evil in* MACBETH'*s rise to power and in his demise. This famous sequence shows them at work with their cauldron, throwing in bits of all sorts of creatures to make their potion. They are preparing for* MACBETH'*s visit.*

* FIRST WITCH
SECOND WITCH
THIRD WITCH

FIRST WITCH.   Thrice the brinded cat hath mewed.

SECOND WITCH.   Thrice and once the hedge-pig whined.

THIRD WITCH.   Harpier cries. 'Tis time, 'tis time.

FIRST WITCH.   Round about the caldron go: 1.
In the poisoned entrails throw.
Toad, that under cold stone
Days and nights has thirty-one
Swelt'red venom sleeping got,
Boil thou first i' th' charmed pot.

ALL.   Double, double, toil and trouble;
Fire burn and caldron bubble.

SECOND WITCH.   Fillet of a fenny snake,   2.
In the caldron boil and bake;
Eye of newt and toe of frog,
Wool of bat and tongue of dog,

SUGGESTIONS AND
STAGE DIRECTIONS

Explore the possibilities of the sounds in these words. Explore the extremes of voice and body movement. Have fun with it! For this exercise, the WITCHES may be played by any combination of men and women.

1. THE WITCHES should be engaged in a slow, erratic dance around the cauldron throughout the scene.

2. Each WITCH takes her turn throwing in various items.

Adder's fork and blindworm's sting,
Lizard's leg and howlet's wing,
For a charm of pow'rful trouble,
Like a hell-broth boil and bubble.

ALL.   Double, double, toil and trouble;
Fire burn and caldron bubble.

THIRD WITCH.   Scale of dragon, tooth of wolf,
Witch's mummy, maw and gulf
Of the ravined salt-sea shark,
Root of hemlock digged i' th' dark,
Liver of blaspheming Jew,
Gall of goat, and slips of yew
Slivered in the moon's eclipse,
Nose of Turk and Tartar's lips,
Finger of birth-strangled babe   3.
Ditch-delivered by a drab,
Make the gruel thick and slab:
Add thereto a tiger's chaudron,
For th' ingredience of our caldron.

3. You can, of course, use substitute props, or even mime them.

ALL.   Double, double, toil and trouble;
Fire burn and caldron bubble.

SECOND WITCH.   Cool it with a baboon's blood,
Then the charm is firm and good.

The scene for Victor Wolfson's EXCURSION is laid on the deck of an excursion boat. An air of confusion prevails as passengers come and go, laugh, talk, and in general amuse themselves. The play is built about New York's middle classes during depression times.

MIKE	MRS. FITCHEL	SUGGESTIONS AND
AIKENS	MRS. GEASLING	STAGE DIRECTIONS
CANDY BOY	LOLLIE	
* EXTRAS	* EXTRAS	

Picking up cues when several conversations are in progress at the same time is important to the pace of a scene, as well as the rhythm of a play.

MRS. FITCHEL.   Here, Mike. Here's a nickel. Go buy yourself a fudgicle.

MIKE.   Gee, thanks, Mrs. Fitchel! (*He runs off.*)   1.

MRS. FITCHEL.   Such a nice boy. So big already.

MRS. GEASLING.   An' eats f' three! He's an expensive proposition, Mrs. Fitchel.

MRS. FITCHEL.   I can imagine. Mr. Geasling is working?

1. MIKE need not wait until MRS. FITCHEL finishes to start his speech.

MRS. GEASLING.   Three days a week. I can't complain. An' I rented the front room out this week.   2.

MRS. FITCHELL.   So—

MRS. GEASLING.   All summer long I've been promisin' Mike a boat ride t' Coney Island. Y' can't disappoint him.

MRS. FITCHELL.   Ach! Times are still hard, I know. (*The* YOUNG MAN *walks over to* LOLLIE *who some time ago has taken out paper and pencil and has been busy writing.*)

AIKENS.   What are you doing?   3.

LOLLIE (*suddenly looking up*).   What? Oh!   4.

AIKENS.   You're writing, I see.

LOLLIE (*with a little laugh*).   Yes.

AIKENS (*looking off at the city*).   I don't blame you. It's a swell day. (*a pause*) Do you go on these things often?

LOLLIE.   Every Sunday.

AIKENS.   Really? That's a swell view, isn't it? (*A pause.*)

LOLLIE.   Yes.

AIKENS.   Gosh.   5.

MRS. FITCHEL.   You know, Mrs. Geasling, we'll have to change our name again.

MRS. GEASLING.   Again? Why?

MRS. FITCHEL.   The name of the store, I mean. The neighborhood is getting so fancy—it doesn't like to come into a store with a Jewish name.

MRS. GEASLING.   Go on! What are you talkin' about!

MRS. FITCHEL.   Yes. It's true. Business is falling off and Sarah says that's the reason. Sarah's a very smart girl.

MRS. GEASLING.   And what'll y' call the store, now, Mrs. Fitchel?

MRS. FITCHEL (*with a little shrug of the shoulders*).   The Fitch Laundry.

MRS. GEASLING (*turning it over in her mind*).   Fitch Laundry. Mmm.

MRS. FITCHEL.   Maybe with a shop at the end of it. Old Mr. Haaga's delicatessen store is now a Snack Shop.

2. This and the next speech of MRS. GEASLING are really only one. MRS. FITCHEL'S *so*, as a cue, is tossed in on top.

3. AIKENS has crossed just in time to pick up his line on cue.

4. Keep in mind the *illusion of the first time.*

5. All groups have continued their conversations and business. They converse *not in a whisper* but in full voice, although not loud. Those with lines speak above all others. Plan appropriate business, such as loading a camera and taking each other's pictures, sunning in deck chairs, eating popcorn or peanuts, playing cards, writing postcards.

Papa says— (*leans to* Mrs. Geasling *and lowers voice*) over his dead body his store will be a shop. But Papa gives in. Oh, he's asleep. He's so tired.

Mrs. Geasling.   He works hard for a little man.   6.

6. MRS. FITCHEL'S cue is *hard,* not *man.* All work to keep rising inflections, sentence ends lifted.

Mrs. Fitchel.   Hard. You have no idea how hard, Mrs. Geasling. The neighborhood gets richer, but the shirts and pillow cases and towels are *still* dirty. It breaks my heart to see him standing all day long over the hot irons. You see? He's so tired he don't even enjoy the excursion.

Mrs. Geasling (*gently*).   Poor man. The ocean air'll do him good.

Mrs. Fitchel.   I hope so.

Aikens.   I get mad as all get-out every time I think of it!   7.

7. MRS. GEASLING and MRS. FITCHEL gradually retard the volume of their talk.

Lollie.   What?

Aikens.   Oh, the millions of people out there who can't even get away for a single day. The millions of people who sweat out their lives day in an' day out—without a chance of asking why. Makes me sore! Some day I'll write something for those people like what *Uncle Tom's Cabin* was for the slaves. You watch. (*He indicates the paper in her lap.*) You write—poetry?   8.

8. CANDY BOY'S chant should be heard much before he comes in sight. All groups keep up the clatter of voices, not just a mumble.

Lollie.   Letters. Letters to my Aunt Sophie in St. Louis.

Aikens.   Oh. (*He stands quietly, disappointed a moment—then walks off, whistling the "Internationale."* Candy Boy *enters with a basket.*)

Candy Boy (*calling*).   Here y' are—get y' souvenirs of the *S. S. Happiness.* Y' last chance of the season t' get y' Happiness Souvenirs. Here y' are— (*His way is blocked by* Mr. Fitchel, *asleep in his chair.*) Get your souvenirs—(*He almost dumps him out of his chair.*) 9.

9. Grouping, stage pictures, movement, regrouping, all stage business—all call for careful rehearsal in this. Keep working for an over-all mood and atmosphere.

Fitchel (*wakes up—startled*).   What's a matter, Mama!

Boy.   Have a souvenir, mister, sellin' out cheap!

Fitchel.   Mama! I thought the boat was sinking already!

Mrs. Fitchel.   No souvenirs, t'ank you.

BOY. Let y' have it for half a dollar. How about it? Let y' have it for a quarter——

FITCHEL. Go 'way, please. I'm tired out!

BOY (*thrusts the pennant into his hands*). Go on— take it for fifteen cents——

FITCHEL (*shouts*). No!!

BOY (*backs away*). All right, mister, all right. Don't get excited.

CYRANO is a musical version of CYRANO DE BERGERAC by Edmond Rostand, a play set in 1640 France. The libretto for CYRANO is by Jacquez Deauville, the lyrics and music by Charles George. CYRANO, a poet, is terribly disfigured by his extremely long nose, and is constantly in fear of ridicule. He is romantically in love with his cousin ROXANNE, but will not express his feelings to her for fear she may jest to others about marriage to one so disfigured. In this scene DUENNA, ROXANNE'S chaperone, arrives to announce that ROXANNE is coming to congratulate CYRANO on having defeated COMTE DE GUICHE in a duel.

| CYRANO | ROXANNE | SUGGESTIONS AND |
| * CAPTAIN | DUENNA | STAGE DIRECTIONS |

CYRANO. Strange matters, these affairs of the heart. (*Sighs*) Poor Ragueneau! How quickly one can throw one's heart away.

CAPTAIN. Aye! (*Goes to L. U.*) I shall return later. (*Exits. Duenna enters door at R.*)

DUENNA. Monsieur, my lady approaches! (*With bated breath Cyrano watches Roxanne enter from R. She carries a lorgnette mask over her face*)

CYRANO. (*doffing his hat and bowing to Roxanne*). May this moment above all other moments be blessed, when, ceasing to forget that I humbly exist, you came here to grant me this precious moment. 1.

1. CYRANO is extremely happy. He beams until she says that the man she loves is handsome. CYRANO'S elation then suddenly fades.

ROXANNE. (*unmasking*). You are very kind, Cousin.

CYRANO. Do, pray, be seated! (*Brings down a chair at R.*)

ROXANNE. Thank you, Cousin.

CYRANO. (*to DUENNA who has gone to L. C.*). Are you fond of cakes?

DUENNA.   Fond enough to make myself sick with them.

CYRANO.   Splendid! (*Gives her a coin*) Go inside and make yourself ill.

DUENNA.   Thank you, Monsieur.

CYRANO. (*giving her several more coins*).   On second thought, buy yourself several bags full of sponge cake, jelly tarts and whatever you see that may strike your fancy. (*Urges her gently to door at L.*) Stuff yourself into delicious agony.

DUENNA. (*elatedly*).   I shall expire from joy!

CYRANO.   Pray do! (DUENNA *is gone. Quickly he comes back to* ROXANNE) May I sit beside you?

ROXANNE.   Please do!

CYRANO. (*sitting*).   Thank you!

ROXANNE.   First of all, let me thank you because that knave, that fop you checkmated in brave sword play, is the one. . a great lord in love with me. . .

CYRANO.   The Comte De Guiche?

ROXANNE.   Tried to impose upon me as a husband. . as a substitute for himself. . (*Shudders*) But for the confession I am going to make, I must think of you once more as the. . almost brother. . I used to play with in the park. . near the lake. It was a time for merry games. The time when you did everything I wished.

CYRANO.   Roxanne, in short dresses, called Madeleine.

ROXANNE. (*coquetishly*).   Was I pretty then?

CYRANO.   You were not ugly. (*They laugh*) Ah, those were happy times.

Cyrano and Roxanne

Lyrics and Music by
CHARLES GEORGE

Moderato

(CYRANO)

I pray you, tell me quick-ly,___ What you
(ROXANNE) He's young and proud and hand-some,___ A ca-

(ROXANNE)

came ___ here to say. Yes, now I dare to tell you, ___ I'm in
det ___ in your corps. In face and form the grand sum ___ Adds to

love, ah! bless the day. As yet he does not ___ know it, But
all I do a - dore. As yet we have not ___ spo-ken, Ex-

soon he'll be ___ a - ware. ___ He has loved me but can't
cept with eyes ___ a - lone. ___ But a glance a si - lent

(CYRANO)

show it, He's so tim - id, he does not dare. Ah! who ___ can he
to - ken, Binds me to him, he's mine, mine own. His name, ___ tell me

be? Ah! please ___ tell ___ me! Who is this for - tu - nate
pray? With - out ___ de - lay! (ROXANNE) Chris-tian de Neu - vill - ette,

man? The one who fills your heart with plea - sure,
Joined your guard to - day, 'Tis true with Ja - loux,

Who is this trea - sure? Do tell who doth in great
What is the mat - ter? You start. How quick - ly can

mea - sure So cast ___ his ___ spell?
one throw a - way ___ one's ___ heart?

CHAPTER 6

Your Mind

Your interest in acting grows with an active mind. Perhaps you are one who enjoys plays only through watching or reading. You get insight into people's lives, motives, tastes, and associations and see the twists of circumstances, entanglements, and other elements that cause people to act and react as they do—a good reason for interest in the theater, and in this book.

But now let us consider those of you who want to act in plays, who wish to know how your mind can help you and what steps you should take. Let's suppose that you hope to be cast in a role in a community play. You have read about the play, and now you want to read and study it. You hope to know the characters intimately and get acquainted with relationships, so that their actions and reactions seem plausible.

YOUR MIND SEARCHES

Great actors know the value of delving deeply into a play. They study the background, locale, environment, habits, associates, and moods of the characters they are to portray. The novice actor must also learn all he or she can about the play and its characters.

Real mental work starts when you explore the play: the environment, the characters, their attitudes toward each other. You explore what you would do or say if you found yourself in the same circumstances as any one of the characters, without, of course, the author's directions.

When you are cast in a play, you *research* the playwright's background, the kind of people that the author knew, the locale of the play, and any other element that may have influenced the play's inception.

After you begin rehearsals, you still search for *implications* about your character in the way other characters act toward you and speak about you. You creatively construct your character's feelings, devising a voice, kinds of movements, and emotional reactions appropriate to your character.

It is your mind that *ties together* and controls your body, your voice, and your emotions, unifying them into a whole. Without it you are a mechanical actor, speaking playwrights' lines and performing suggested gestures and stage movements with little or no inner feelings.

YOUR MIND RELAXES

Relaxation of the mind and of the body are closely related. In the chapter entitled "Your Body," you practiced relaxing your physical muscles and also relaxed your mind to some extent.

When you are nervous or overly concerned about something your mind doesn't "behave." *Your mind wanders* aimlessly so that you can't concentrate, can't think; you become frustrated; you suffer from stage fright. Try to relax your brain and think, to feel comfortable but alert to the situation. Sometimes if you work at frustration, it grows. Yet being relaxed does not mean that you should be in a state of mental inactivity. You must stay alert, interested, eager, and ready to participate actively.

Exercises to Relax Your Mind

1. When you begin to tense up, recall the appearance of a chair, vase, or book you have in your home. Recall the color, when it was last used, exact shape, and exact size the last time you saw it, whether it has scars or shows wear, how and where you procured it. Your tensions will clear.

2. Recall a childhood friend: his or her eyes, length and care of hair, how and where you first met. How often did you meet and under what circumstances?

3. Close your eyes, breathe deeply, and recall a trip you took or some other experience that greatly interested you several years ago. Why did you like this experience? Have you recalled the situation many times since you experienced it? Who else knows how you feel about the experience?

4. Relax your mind by thinking of physical exertion. Your car is stalled. Imagine pushing it, shaking it; get mad, kick a tire. Examine everything under the hood. Try as many ways to start it as you can think of.

5. Learn to physically relax when you will it. Sit in a chair. Go limp. Think of each part of your body as you allow it to relax: your eyelids and jaw droop; your head swings downward on to your chest; your arms and hands are relaxed. Suddenly tighten all your muscles: toes, shoulders, neck, abdomen —all. Then begin slow, regular breathing as you slowly relax.

YOUR MIND CONCENTRATES

Concentration is related to and largely dependent on relaxation that helps consciousness flow freely into new and vivid patterns of experience. Relaxation and concentration are two aspects of one state of mind and body. Concentration is the quality which permits us to turn all our heart and mind toward the accomplishment or conclusion of a purpose.

Exercises in Concentration

1. While a few members of class rehearse a short scene, others keep a record on paper of number of times each of the five vowels are used in words of scene.

2. Work in pairs in class, each member preparing for another a column of figures, twelve or more in column, to be added by partner. While one adds, the other must keep up a line of chatter.

3. Class is given a short glance at a familiar object, then each is required to sketch or describe it.

4. Listen to sounds outside the room and tell what you hear. Some may need to concentrate intently to hear sounds others are hearing.

5. (This exercise is similar to one of Stanislavski's.) Group counts together to thirty, clapping hands once when number can be divided by three, clapping twice when it can be divided by five, and clapping three times when it can be divided by both three and five.

6. Half the class closes eyes while the others make familiar noises—tearing paper, patting shoes, etc.; the sightless people must guess the noises.

7. While others near you converse, pay attention while at the same time recalling things that occurred years ago, such as your first try at playing ball with a team, or your first day at high school.

8. Sit in a circle of ten or twelve people. Choose a partner across the circle. Hold a conversation with that person while others in the circle do the same with their partners. Avoid shouting. Use crisp, exaggerated diction, and concentrate! Focus not only on the sounds but on the lips of the speaker.

Control Your Thinking. School yourself to *control your thoughts*, to be aware of many things simultaneously but ready to attack any one of them. If you pay close attention to dialogue on stage, it will help your nervous mind unwind, forgetting all but the play. Keep listening; even if your mind wanders, bring it back. Stay with the play just as the character you are enacting would.

Sometimes when you have your own lines and cues down pat, you find that your mind wanders. You have heard those speeches in rehearsal after rehearsal after rehearsal, and your mind has become dulled to the sound. But snap back! *Keep hearing the lines with your mind.* Become like a child again. Pretend fully that it is the thing it is intended to be. Feel that the characters are those real people living, acting, speaking, in the time and place in which the author placed them.

School your mind to be ready for the *unexpected*. Mistakes do happen, even among the best: an electrician forgets to switch on an electric lamp, a chair is missing, or there's a disturbance in the audience. In the experience of one of the authors, a toddler came smilingly on stage through a rear entrance. We actors tried to ignore her and to stifle our nervous laughter. One of us could have covered with, "Oh, Jennie has climbed out of her crib," picked up the child and taken her off-stage. Actually, we handled the situation badly—we laughed, so the audience also laughed heartily.

During a performance of a professional group, an actor fell asleep backstage and missed his entrance. An off-stage player roused him and pushed him on-stage. He, half asleep, didn't know what scene was being played or what he was to do. However, the actors on stage handled the situation splendidly, and carried on impromptu dialogue until the sleepy actor got into his part.

We never expect emergencies during a performance, and they seldom occur. However, it is wise to train for them as much as you can so that, *if* and *when* the unexpected happens, you won't panic. Your director may plan some surprise disturbance which will force you to think and react appropriately, so that an audience might not realize there had been a *faux pas*.

Man of La Mancha by Dale Wasserman, Mitch Leigh, Joe Darion. Presented in Grove City College, with William Kennedy and James Dixon as directors. Eyes suggest imagination or fear or mental wonder.

The Increased Difficulty of Concentration by Vaclav Havel. Presented by New York University. Directed by Lois F. Alexander. The two seem to be concentrating on something.

YOUR MIND IMAGINES

Theater, from beginning to end, is built on *imagination*. A dramatist starts with a germ of an idea; then, by using full-scale imagination, develops it into a play. A director takes a dramatist's play and visualizes a production, including images of the stage, movement, characters, props, lighting effects, and costumes. The head of each department develops, through imagination, that part of the play for which he or she is responsible.

Your imagination is essential for successful acting. Many great actors have declared that imagination is the most important quality for good acting. An example: Helen, a frail elderly lady, is helping her grandson by mending his coat. He accidently steps on her foot with his full weight. Both you and the audience know that she has not been injured, but in playing the scene your character must believe he has seriously injured the lady, and must react accordingly. Although the audience knows the truth, they also react to the situation. Imagination helps you sense images for the characters the author has invented.

Creating *improvisations* is good practice in developing imagination. The following example shows how one person used the given props to create a plausible situation. Other situations for improvisations follow.

Students had been asked to create improvisations using a table with two pencils on it to represent different instruments. During the improvisations they were to purse their lips and blow, stoop to the floor, and talk to one or more persons present. One student improvised by picking up one pencil and using it as a chalk eraser; he then cleaned the chalkboard with it. While talking to a class he dropped the eraser, picked it up off the floor, blew dust off his hands, and used the other pencil as a piece of chalk with which to write on the board.

1. A chair is up-ended, and a kerchief hangs on one chair leg. A small pan of water is on the floor nearby. You are to talk to one person in the room using these items.

2. On coming home you find two books, a pad of paper, a stick of chewing gum, and a leaky pen. They are neatly hidden beneath a pillow. You are to laugh heartily as you call to some friends through a window, explaining the things you found and what they mean.

3. You are furnished two pencils, a sealed empty envelope, a man's top-coat with a business paper in the pocket. You hear somebody coming. You hide, but soon come out of hiding to accuse that person of a crime while using all those items.

4. You are given a yard-long ruler or pointer, a small container of pills, a drinking cup, and a table with papers on it, but no chair. You speak breathlessly to a group of people.

No other art can depict human emotions as clearly and as appealingly as can the field of theater. The more proficient you become with your imagination, the greater will be your success in the art.

Exercises in Imagination

Imagination will help you enact the following situations. Make clear, through action, what you are doing and why. Plan some logical motivation for each exercise.

1. Tiptoe into a room carrying a small object in your cupped hands. Suddenly hurry to hide it.
2. In bare or stocking feet walk on sand, a messy street, pebbles, hot sun-baked stones, soft green spring grass, ankle-deep snow.
3. Overhear a one-sided telephone conversation. Write some notes on a slip of paper, hand it to the person on the phone. Hurry out.
4. Wheel a cart into a food store. Look over items on counters, move away rapidly, whisper to a customer, leave the cart behind.
5. Bring a chair into the room, set it upside down, place the coat that you are carrying on it. Sit in another chair and look intently at the coat.
6. Approach an injured child, a fierce dog, a poisonous snake, your long-lost love.
7. Lift imaginary objects: a cup of coffee, a two-gallon pail of water, a fluffy kitten, a small bird with a broken wing, an automobile tire, a rose with a prickly stem.

GOING INTO YOUR ROLE

It is customary to have a reading rehearsal first. At this time each player is given his or her part (or sides) and is asked to study it soon. Memorization *is not* the first part of study. Do not attempt to memorize lines apart from the action they accompany. Do not memorize lines without first moving through the action of the play. However, following your first rehearsal you may wish to underscore your speeches and your cues. Memorize each cue with its speech, as a unit.

Study the Play Thoroughly. Study the whole play to locate every line or implication that tells you something about the plot, the mood, and your role.

Decide why your character has been included in the play. How does he or she relate to others in the play as a whole?

Lady Windermere's Fan by Oscar Wilde, as presented in Washburn University by Miriam A. Franklin, director. Lady Windermere seems to be undecided and pondering; Mrs. Erlynne is pleading.

Bell, Book and Candle by John Van Druten was presented by Washburn University Players, with Hugh G. McCausland directing. The two reveal very different thoughts in their eyes and faces. Both are very good dramatically.

The Natural by Regge Life. Presented by New York University. Regge Life, director; Steve Friedman, photographer. Both actors show minds alert—suspicion, wonder, waiting.

How does each main character contribute to the play? (Keep talking to your character and listening to the answers.)

If you are not fully acquainted with the locale of the story, read other material that will help you learn about it.

Do similar research about the people of the play, unless you have lived with people like them.

Learn from remarks and actions other characters make in relation to your character. Why is *your character* in the play?

Close your eyes to visualize your character's stance, walk, mannerisms, actions, and reactions. See yourself as that person.

Analyze each scene in which you appear. Decide how you can develop mood and plot.

Try to become so well acquainted with your character that you know what the person thinks about when alone and how he or she feels toward other characters in the play.

Aides to Memorization. When the first rehearsal is over and a thorough study of your character has at least been started, it is time to memorize lines. There are different useful tools for this. Some people are "quick studies" and are able to memorize quickly. For the average player, however, here are some helpful ideas.

1. Go through the whole script and mark all your cues. They are the three, four, or five words of the speech just preceding yours. Cues must catch your eye and your mind, and are very important to you. Action may be your cue.

2. Take each of your speeches alone to locate the key words. Underscore these to be sure you memorize and will project the meaning.

3. If you are to play a dialect character, you may wish to write your lines in phonetic spelling and transpose words to arrange them in the language of that dialect. Work especially to cultivate appropriate intonations (tune) of the dialect. Try to listen to records of that dialect.

4. It may help to place vertical lines between phrases before you begin memorizing. These help to bring out the full meaning of a speech and to keep phrases from running on and on without breaks.

5. Locate lines related to the plot and their implications.

6. Following rehearsals, after you receive your director's suggestions, read each of your scenes aloud several times to help you understand how others' lines relate to you.

7. Move through each scene, pantomiming business as it is planned by your director. This helps you memorize in several ways: through *sight* (the page), through *hearing* (the sound), and through *movement.*

8. Work on your speeches and their cues. Then, for practice, ask a friend to mix up cues and toss them to you. This helps you avoid slow pickup on cues.

9. In bed at night, cultivate your memory by recalling each activity of your whole day. Recall each concrete detail: the clothes you selected to wear and why, each diversion or interruption of the early morning, noon, and night, what food you ate, how it was prepared, who you saw,—everything.

A Cue Exercise

Memorize the following speeches *with their cues*. Then for practice, ask a friend to mix cues and give you cues alone. You are to follow each with the appropriate speech. In this connection, it is essential that every actor *give the right cues;* otherwise the acting partners will become very confused.

1. FRAN.   . . . I feel so gloriously happy. I want to dance and whirl and whirl and whirl.
   ARTHUR.   Fran, dear, you look exhausted. Stop this right now! (*He catches her by the arm.*) Stop now! Stop! You will . . .
   FRAN.   No, no! Not now. This is life!

2. ETHEL.   . . . I don't know why I said that to her. You see, she was . . .
   RALPH.   You lost control. She's much too dainty for you, has been . . .
   ETHEL.   Possibly you're right. But when I started reminding her . . .
   RALPH.   No, no. Don't repeat that. Wipe it out of your mind.

3. CLEMENT.   . . . that you have this one evening. Now is your . . .
   ELIZABETH.   Whether it's this time or some other time, I'm not interested in romance for me. That's for younger . . .
   CLEMENT.   You're young for your age forget about years until . . .

4. JANICE.   I wish Royce wasn't so bashful or something. He just said . . .
   POLLY.   He'll bring up the subject when he drops by with the book.
   JANICE.   Oh, that book!

5. GEORGE.   How could I have been such a fool? But I didn't mean anything.
   SAM.   Oh, no! You couldn't mean anything. The chump who rocked the boat didn't mean anything. But what he did . . .
   GEORGE.   I didn't suppose . . .
   SAM (*moving closer*).   Now see here . . . you've been in college for four years, you think you've learned. But there's one subject about which you'll never know much, if you study for fifty years, and that is woman!

In the next chapter you will study acting's most important requisite— the depiction of human emotions. Unless a player shows emotion, he or she is only reading lines. Do you know the degrees of love, fear, sorrow, anger, dislike? Each has directions and intensities.

Excerpts for Practice

This scene is from THE PLAYBOY OF THE WESTERN WORLD, by John M. Synge. Christy Mahon *has travelled a long distance, running from his home where he killed his father (or so he thinks). The people of the county Mayo, where he has arrived, begin to think him a brave soul as he tells his story. He is actually a meek fellow who begins to puff up with pride as he finds people that make him a hero. One of the persons he has impressed is* Pegeen Mike, *the daughter of the owner of the local pub.*

CHRISTY MAHON　　　　　PEGEEN MIKE

This scene requires attention to several items: the Irish dialect; the vivid imagination of CHRISTY; the emotions of wonder, jealousy, affection, and fear. Concentration is essential to keep all of these *in balance.*

PEGEEN.　Let you stretch out now by the fire, young fellow. You should be destroyed travelling.

CHRISTY (*shyly again, drawing off his boots*).　I'm tired, surely, walking wild eleven days, and waking fearful in the night.

(*He holds up one of his feet, feeling his blisters, and looking at them with compassion.*)

PEGEEN. (*standing beside him, watching him with delight*). You should have had great people in your family, I'm thinking, with the little, small feet you have, and you with a kind of a quality name, the like of what you'd find on the great powers and potentates of France and Spain.　1.

1. Note how she plays up to him throughout the scene, using her own imagination to make him more than he really is. CHRISTY willingly goes along with it, and begins to believe it himself.

CHRISTY (*with pride*).　We were great surely, with wide and windy acres of rich Munster land.

PEGEEN.　Wasn't I telling you, and you a fine, handsome young fellow with a noble brow?

CHRISTY (*with a flash of delighted surprise*).　Is it me?

PEGEEN.　Aye. Did you never hear that from the young girls where you come from in the west or south?

CHRISTY (*with venom*).　I did not then. Oh, they're bloody liars in the naked parish where I grew a man.

PEGEEN.　If they are itself, you've heard it these days, I'm thinking, and you walking the world telling out your story to young girls or old.

CHRISTY. I've told my story no place till this night, Pegeen Mike, and it's foolish I was here, maybe, to be talking free, but you're decent people, I'm thinking, and yourself a kindly woman, the way I wasn't fearing you at all.

PEGEEN (*filling a sack with straw*). You've said the like of that, maybe in every cot and cabin where you've met a young girl on your way. 2.

2. She is preparing a bed for him throughout the following sequence.

CHRISTY (*going over to her, gradually raising his voice*). I've said it nowhere till this night, I'm telling you, for I've seen none the like of you the eleven long days I am walking the world, looking over a low ditch or a high ditch on my north or my south, into stony scattered fields, or scribes of bog, where you'd see young, limber girls, and fine prancing women making laughter with the men.

PEGEEN. If you weren't destroyed travelling, you'd have as much talk and streeleen, I'm thinking, as Owen Roe O'Sullivan or the poets of the Dingle Bay, and I've heard all times it's the poets are your like, fine fiery fellows with great rages when their temper's roused.

CHRISTY (*drawing a little nearer to her*). You've a power of rings, God bless you, and would there be any offence if I was asking are you single now?

PEGEEN. What would I want wedding so young?

CHRISTY (*with relief*). We're alike, so.

PEGEEN (*she puts sack on settle and beats it up*). I never killed my father. I'd be afeard to do that, except I was the like of yourself with blind rages tearing me within, for I'm thinking you should have had great tussling when the end was come.

CHRISTY (*expanding with delight at the first confidential talk he has ever had with a woman*). We had not then. It was a hard woman was come over the hill, and if he was always a crusty kind when he'd a hard woman setting him on, not the divil himself or his four fathers could put up with him at all.

PEGEEN (*with curiosity*). And isn't it a great wonder that one wasn't fearing you?

CHRISTY (*very confidentially*).   Up to the day I killed my father, there wasn't a person in Ireland knew the kind I was, and I there drinking, waking, eating, sleeping, a quiet, simple poor fellow with no man giving me heed.

PEGEEN (*getting a quilt out of the cupboard and putting it on the sack*).   It was the girls were giving you heed maybe, and I'm thinking it's most conceit you'd have to be gaming with their like.

CHRISTY (*shaking his head, with simplicity*).   Not the girls itself, and I won't tell you a lie. (3) There wasn't anyone heeding me in that place saving only the dumb beasts of the field.

(*He sits down at fire.*)

3. CHRISTY comes down to earth for a while and is his plain, simple self again.

PEGEEN (*with disappointment*).   And I thinking you should have been living the like of a king of Norway or the Eastern world.

(*She comes and sits beside him after placing bread and mug of milk on the table.*)

ANTIGONE, adapted by Lewis Galantiere from the play by Jean Anouilh, is a modern version of the ancient Greek story of ANTIGONE, *the daughter of* OEDIPUS. ANTIGONE'*s two brothers have killed each other in a civil war. Her uncle* CREON, *now the ruler, has given proper burial to one of the brothers,* ETEOCLES, *but has left the body of the other,* POLYNICES, *to rot in the sun as a warning against future rebellion.* ANTIGONE *has spoken to her sister,* ISMENE, *about defying* CREON'*s order.* ISMENE *here discovers* ANTIGONE *up before dawn.*

ANTIGONE
ISMENE

SUGGESTIONS AND
STAGE DIRECTIONS

Note the emotional propensity of each of these two characters: ISMENE toward fear and ANTIGONE toward anger. Use the mind to concentrate on and to fully imagine the vivid images in this scene.

ISMENE (*moves to above Center of table*).   Aren't you well?

ANTIGONE.   Yes, of course. Just a little tired. Because I got up too early.

(ANTIGONE *goes to chair Right and sits, suddenly tired.*)

ISMENE (*moves to upper Right end of table*).   I couldn't sleep, either.

ANTIGONE.   Ismene, you ought not to go without your beauty sleep.

ISMENE. Don't make fun of me.

ANTIGONE. I'm not, truly. This particular morning, seeing how beautiful you are makes everything easier for me. Oh, wasn't I a nasty little beast when we were small? (*She takes* ISMENE'*s hand in hers.*) I used to fling mud at you, and put worms down your neck. I can remember tying you to a tree and cutting off your hair. Your beautiful hair! (*She rises and strokes* ISMENE'*s hair.*) How easy it must be never to be unreasonable with all that smooth silken hair so beautifully set around your head.   1.

ISMENE (*takes* ANTIGONE'*s hand in hers*).   Why do you insist upon talking about other things?

ANTIGONE. I am not talking about other things.

ISMENE. Antigone, I've thought about it a lot.

ANTIGONE. Did you?

ISMENE. I thought about it all night long. Antigone, you're mad.

ANTIGONE. Am I?

ISMENE. We cannot do it.

ANTIGONE. Why not?

ISMENE. Creon will have us put to death.

ANTIGONE. Of course he will. But we are *bound* to go out and bury our brother. That's the way it is. What do you think *we* can do to change it?

ISMENE (*releases* ANTIGONE'*s hand; draws back a step*). I don't want to die.

ANTIGONE. I'd prefer not to die, myself. (ANTIGONE *crosses below the table over to front of upstage part of arch Left; faces toward the arch.*)

ISMENE (*backs away a few steps Right as she turns to* ANTIGONE).   Listen to me, Antigone. I thought about it all night. I may be younger than you are, but I always think things over, and you don't.

ANTIGONE. Sometimes it is better *not* to think too much.

ISMENE. I don't agree with you! (ISMENE *moves to upper Right end of table and leans on end of table top, toward* ANTIGONE.) Oh, I know it's horrible. I *know* Polynices was cheated out of his rights. That he made

1. Obviously, it helps if ISMENE has long hair. ANTIGONE's can be short as she has always been boyish, as this speech reveals.

war—that Creon took sides against him, and he was killed. And I pity Polynices just as much as you do. But all the same, I sort of see what Uncle Creon means. Uncle Creon is the *king* now. He *has* to set an example!

ANTIGONE (*turns to* ISMENE). Example! Creon orders that our brother rot and putrefy, and be mangled by dogs and birds of prey. (2) That's an offense against every decent human instinct; against the laws of God and Man. And you talk about examples!

2. ANTIGONE must visualize and fully imagine this scene to be revolted by it.

ISMENE.   There you go, off on your own again—refusing to pay the slightest heed to anybody. At least you might try to understand!

ANTIGONE.   I only understand that a man lies rotting, unburied. And that he is my brother, (*She moves to chair* L. *of the table.*) and that he must be buried.

ISMENE.   But Creon won't let us bury him. And he is stronger than we are. He is the king. He has made himself King.

ANTIGONE (*sits*).   I am not listening to you.

ISMENE (*kneels on stool, facing toward* ANTIGONE).   You *must!* You know how Creon works. His mob will come running, howling as it runs. (3) A thousand arms will seize our arms. A thousand breaths will breathe into our faces. Like one single pair of eyes, a thousand eyes will stare at us. We'll be driven in a tumbril through their hatred, through the smell of them and their cruel roaring laughter. We'll be dragged to the scaffold for torture, surrounded by guards with their idiot faces all bloated, their animal hands clean-washed for the sacrifice, their beefy eyes squinting as they stare at us. And we'll know that no shrieking and no begging will make them understand that we want to live, for they are like trained beasts who go through the motions they've been taught, without caring about right or wrong. And we shall suffer, we shall feel pain rising in us until it becomes so unbearable that we *know* it must stop: but it won't stop: it will go on rising and rising, like a screaming voice— (ANTIGONE *suddenly sits erect.* ISMENE *sinks*

3. ISMENE's imagination serves to fuel her fears and make them even worse. She sees, hears, smells, and feels intensely the imaginary scene she describes.

down onto the stool, buries her face in her hands and sobs.) Oh, I can't, I can't, Antigone!

(*A pause.*)

ANTIGONE.   How well you have thought it all out.

ISMENE.   I thought of it all night long. Didn't you?

ANTIGONE.   Oh, yes.

ISMENE.   I'm an awful coward, Antigone.

ANTIGONE.   So am I. But what has that to do with it?

ISMENE (*raises her head; stares at* ANTIGONE).   But Antigone! Don't you *want* to go on living?

ANTIGONE.   Go on living! Who was always the first out out of bed every morning because she loved the touch of the cold morning air on her bare skin? (*She rises; goes to Left of* ISMENE.) Or the last to bed because nothing less than infinite weariness could wean her from the lingering night?

ISMENE (*clasps* ANTIGONE'*s hands, in a sudden rush of tenderness*).   Antigone! My darling sister!

ANTIGONE (*repulsing her*).   No! For pity's sakes! Don't! (*A pause as she crosses behind* ISMENE *to upstage Right Center, just below bottom step.*) You say you've thought it all out. The howling mob: the torture: the fear of death: (*She turns to* ISMENE.) *They've* made up your mind for you. Is that it?

ISMENE.   Yes.

ANTIGONE.   *All right.* They're as good excuses as any. (ANTIGONE *moves down to Right of* ISMENE *and stands facing Right.*)

ISMENE (*turns to* ANTIGONE).   Antigone, be reasonable. It's all very well for *men* to believe in ideas, and die for them. But you are a *girl!* Antigone, you have everything in the world to make you happy. All you have to do is—reach out for it. (*She clasps* ANTIGONE'*s left hand in hers.*)

THE RUNNER STUMBLES, by Milan Stitt, is a sensitive play about a youthful, loving nun who challenges the basic beliefs of a priest who is locked in the old traditions. In this scene MRS. SHANDIG, *the cleaning*

woman, finds herself in the middle of a theological disagreement be-
tween the priest, FATHER RIVARD, *and the nun,* SISTER RITA. *The disagree-*
ment grows into a very personal argument.

PRIEST (FATHER RIVARD)   NUN (SISTER RITA)
MRS. SHANDIG

Acting involves use of
the mind, even when the
actor is silent. This is
evident in the first
portion of the scene.
Throughout the rest of
the scene, the mind must
be operative in control-
ling emotions and in
holding back outbursts.

NUN. (PRIEST *takes harness and a chair and sits* R. NUN
crosses D. R. *and moves cell stools slightly* U. *to form a*
"window seat." She gets her scissors and brown
paper. She waits in hopes PRIEST *will speak. The wind*
outside and a ticking clock in the hall can be heard
under scene. NUN *crossing toward* PRIEST.) Father? A
month. It's been a month since Monsignor visited.
Four weeks, Father, and— (*Silence as* PRIEST *con-*
tinues polishing harness with vigor. NUN *sits on* L. *stool*
and watches MRS. SHANDIG *enters with bowl of apples.*
MRS. SHANDIG *pulls a chair* D. C., *slightly above* PRIEST'S.
She offers him apple, which PRIEST *refuses.* MRS. SHAN-
DIG *sits and begins paring apples.* NUN *is frustrated by*
silence, looks out window to valley, fights back tears
of frustration. She takes a chair from the study and
brings it down and sits in front of "window seat." She
begins to noisily cut a design in the brown wrapping
paper. Eventually, the PRIEST *throws down harness*
with annoyance. He takes missal from pocket and
begins to read. NUN, *catching a look from the* PRIEST,
tries to cut more quietly. Thereby making even more
noise.)

MRS. SHANDIG (*Unable to bear tension in the room*).
What are you making?   1.

1. The tension must be
palpable, created by
the silent concentration
in the preceding mime.

NUN.   Oh, for the school. Flowers. (*She holds up de-*
sign.) I thought the younger children could paint
them bright colors, and Louise could put them up
with the compositions.

MRS. SHANDIG (*Worried about* PRIEST, *trying to stop con-*
versation).   I see.

NUN.   There are so few flowers in the drought. The few
in my garden will be gone by the weekend. Fridays I
let them take little bouquets home. Everything so
brown, these will be . . . (*Realizing no one is listen-*

ing.) . . . nice. Nice. (NUN *tries to continue her work quietly, but aware* PRIEST *is more annoyed, she takes paper and scissors and puts them on* U. *table.* NUN, *unable to find anything to take her attention.*) Would you like to resume the reading lessons after All Saints? (NUN *returns to sit on* L. *stool.*)

PRIEST.   I didn't know you had stopped, Mrs. Shandig.

MRS. SHANDIG.   What's the use? There's no time. No time, Father.

NUN.   We'll be all cooped up in here when it snows. Some days the children can't even get up the hill they told me. By spring you could be a wonderful reader. (*Silence.*) Why do you burn your lamp so late at night, Mrs. Shandig? It makes a square of light on the ground. (NUN *sits.*)

MRS. SHANDIG.   I hear you walking, Sister, so I work on the mending.

NUN (*Standing*).   I didn't know you could hear me. I pray. Do you ever pray standing up?

MRS. SHANDIG.   You must walk when you pray too, Sister.

NUN.   I'm sorry. I didn't know you could hear me. (*She waits for someone to speak,* (2) *then, looking out window.*) I like to look at the few lights down in the valley, try to imagine (3) why those three or four windows have a warm glow so late at night. Someone sick, a party, a student preparing for an exam, a baby being born. Do you ever do that? (*Silence.*) Then I look up at those trees behind the convent. Trees. They catch the stars, darken the ground. It's like you said, Father. I pray against the dark. (*Silence.*) Do you know what I mean, Mrs. Shandig? About praying.

2. These silences are awkward for all the characters and must be observed.

3. She uses her imagination, even as she talks. She really does see the lights, the trees, the stars. Take time with this; the character should almost lose herself in her thoughts.

MRS. SHANDIG.   I don't know, Sister. You are a nun. I never know what to say about such things. I don't stand when I pray. I didn't think you are supposed to. Are you, Father? I'm sorry. You want to read, don't you?

NUN.   It is not disrespectful if you want to pray, Mrs. Shandig. God gave us a brain after all, and I think He expects us to use it.

MRS. SHANDIG (*Rising, crossing behind Priest*).   Father, I wish Sister wouldn't talk personal like this. I don't understand things the way you do, Sister. (*Silence.*)

NUN.   Well you talk personal with the other sisters. I hear you, Mrs. Shandig.

MRS. SHANDIG.   Not blasphemy, Sister.

PRIEST (*Standing*).   Mrs. Shandig. Let me talk to Sister. We'll say the rosary later.

MRS. SHANDIG (*As she exits*).   Yes, Father. (*Silence.*)

NUN.   Can we, can't we just discuss it?

PRIEST.   Don't you know we are very close to serious difficulty?

NUN.   No. Why?

PRIEST.   We cannot talk like this, Sister.   4.

NUN.   We cannot talk. We have not spoken a single word for a month.

PRIEST.   Exactly as it should be, Sister.

NUN.   No. I'm here, and you've got to let me help you. It's useless to stay locked in your study, striking out at poor Mrs. Shandig when all you need to— I don't live in the convent. I won't be ignored.

PRIEST.   I want you to think what you've said. (*Silence.*) Then you tell me. In the Confessional. That is the appropriate place for you to speak to me.

NUN.   Well, I suppose it all sounds especially Protestant to your particularly Catholic ears. (NUN *turns to exit.* PRIEST *grabs her.*)

PRIEST.   Yes, it does. It sounds like, like . . . (*Silence. They face each other for a long moment.*)

NUN (*Defeated, crossing to window seat*).   I am trying to be a good nun, Father.

PRIEST.   I know.

4. The PRIEST insists on maintaining a strict decorum in his relationship with the NUN. She is starving for joy and companionship.

THE CRUCIBLE, a powerful play by Arthur Miller, is based on the Salem witch trials in Massachusetts in 1692. ABIGAIL WILLIAMS, *once a serving girl to* JOHN *and* ELIZABETH PROCTOR, *was dismissed by the* PROCTORS *after* JOHN *committed adultery with her on a single occasion.*

ABIGAIL *has since led a group of girls as lead witnesses in an hysterical witch hunt.* JOHN *has gone to court to denounce* ABIGAIL *as witness.* MARY WARREN *is another serving girl, whom* JOHN *has coached to tell the truth against* ABIGAIL. REV. HALE *is an expert in witchcraft but is growing sympathetic to the* PROCTORS.

JUDGE DANFORTH
JOHN PROCTOR
* REV. HALE
* EXTRA MEN (may be cut for this scene)

ABIGAIL WILLIAMS
MARY WARREN
* MERCY LEWIS
* SUSANNA WALCOTT

SUGGESTIONS AND STAGE DIRECTIONS

PROCTOR.   She only thought to save my name!   1.

HALE.   Excellency, it is a natural lie to tell; I beg you, stop now; before another is condemned! I may shut my conscience to it no more . . . private vengeance is working through this testimony! From the beginning this man has struck me true. I believe him now! By my oath to heaven, I believe him, and I pray you call back his wife before we . . .

DANFORTH.   She spoke nothing of lechery, and this man lies!

HALE (*He cries out in anguish*).   I believe him! I cannot turn my face from it no more. (*Pointing at* ABIGAIL.) This girl has always struck me false! She . . . (ABIGAIL *with a weird cry screams up to ceiling.*)   2.

ABIGAIL.   You will not! Begone! Begone, I say! (MERCY *and* SUSANNA *rise, looking up.*)

DANFORTH.   What is it, child? (*But* ABIGAIL, *pointing with fear, is now raising up her frightened eyes, her awed face, toward ceiling—the girls doing the same —and now* HATHORNE, HALE, PUTNAM, CHEEVER *and* DANFORTH *do the same.*) What's there? (*He lowers his eyes from the ceiling and now he is frightened there is real tension in his voice.*) Child! (*She is transfixed—with all the girls, in complete silence, she is open-mouthed, agape at ceiling, and in great fear.*) Girls! Why do you . . . ?

MERCY.   It's on the beam!—behind the rafter!

DANFORTH (*Looking up*).   Where!

ABIGAIL.   Why . . . ? Why do you come, yellow bird?

This scene requires the utmost in concentration as it builds to the climax. The girls must use a great deal of imagination in "seeing" the great winged bird in the rafters. Careful blocking is essential for the entire scene.

1. ELIZABETH PROCTOR, who has been imprisoned for suspected witchcraft, was brought in to verify what JOHN has said against ABIGAIL. Against her nature, ELIZABETH lied to the court, thinking she was saving JOHN.

2. Here begins the "vision" of the great bird. The actresses playing ABIGAIL and MERCY must have vivid imaginations. Place the bird consistently in one location in the rafters (above the heads of the audience).

PROCTOR (*A tone of reason, firmly*).   Where's a bird? I see no bird!

ABIGAIL.   My face? My face!?

PROCTOR.   Mister Hale . . .

DANFORTH.   Be quiet!

PROCTOR (*To* HALE).   . . . Do you see a bird?

DANFORTH.   Be quiet!!

ABIGAIL (*To ceiling, in a genuine conversation with the "bird," as though trying to talk it out of attacking her*).   But God made my face; you cannot want to tear my face. Envy is a deadly sin, Mary.

MARY.   Abby!

ABIGAIL (*Unperturbed, continued to "bird"*).   Oh, Mary, this is a black art to change your shape. No, I cannot, I cannot stop my mouth; it's God's work I do. . . .

MARY.   Abby, I'm *here!*

PROCTOR.   They're pretending, Mister Danforth!

ABIGAIL (*Now she takes a backward step, as though the bird would swoop down momentarily*).   Oh, please, Mary!—Don't come down. . . .

SUSANNA.   Her claws, she's stretching her claws!

PROCTOR.   Lies—lies——

ABIGAIL. (*Backing further, still fixed above*).   Mary, please don't hurt me!

MARY (*To* DANFORTH).   I'm not hurting her!

DANFORTH (*To* MARY).   Why does she see this vision?

HALE.   You cannot believe them.

MARY (*Rises*).   She sees nothin'!

ABIGAIL (*As though hypnotized, mimicking the exact tone of* MARY's *cry*). She sees nothin'!   3

MARY.   Abby, you mustn't!

ABIGAIL (*Now all girls join, transfixed*).   Abby, you mustn't!

MARY (*To all girls, frantically*).   I'm here, I'm here!

ABIGAIL (*With all girls*).   I'm here, I'm here!

3. These repetitions become more and more maddening as MARY becomes more and more frantic. Volume and tempo increase throughout.

DANFORTH.   Mary Warren!—Draw back your spirit out of them!

MARY.   Mister Danforth . . . !

ABIGAIL (*And all girls*).   Mister Danforth!

DANFORTH.   Have you compacted with the Devil? Have you?

MARY.   Never, never!

GIRLS.   Never, never!

DANFORTH (*Growing hysterical*).   Why can they only repeat you?!

PROCTOR.   Give me a whip—I'll stop it!

MARY.   They're sporting . . . !

ABIGAIL (*And all girls, cutting her off*).   They're sporting!

MARY (*Turning on them all, hysterically and stamping her feet*).   Abby, stop it!

ABIGAIL (*And all girls, stamping their feet*).   Abby, stop it!

MARY (*Screaming it out at top of her lungs, and raising her fists*).   Stop it!!

ABIGAIL (*And all, raising their fists*).   Stop it!!

MARY.   Stop it.

GIRLS.   Stop it.

(MARY *utterly confounded, and becoming overwhelmed by* ABIGAIL's,—*and the girls'—utter conviction, starts to whimper, hands half raised, powerless—and all girls begin whimpering exactly as she does.*)

DANFORTH.   A little while ago you were afflicted. Now it seems you afflict others; where did you find this power?

MARY (*Staring at* ABIGAIL).   I . . . have no power.

ABIGAIL and ALL GIRLS.   I have no power.

PROCTOR.   They're gulling you, Mister!

DANFORTH.   Why did you turn about this past two weeks? You have seen the Devil, have you not?

MARY.   I . . .

GIRLS. I . . .

PROCTOR (*Sensing her weakening*). Mary, Mary, God damns all liars!

DANFORTH (*Pounding it into her*). You have seen the Devil, you have made compact with Lucifer, have you not?

PROCTOR (*Quietly*). God damns liars, Mary! (MARY *utters something unintelligible, staring at* ABIGAIL *who keeps watching the "bird" above.*)

DANFORTH. I cannot hear you. What do you say? (MARY *utters again unintelligibly.*) You will confess yourself or you will hang! (*He turns her roughly to face him.*) Do you know who I am? I say you will hang if you do not open with me!

PROCTOR. Mary, remember the angel Raphael . . . do that which is good and . . .

ABIGAIL (*Pointing upward*). The wings! Her wings are spreading! Mary, please, don't, don't . . . ! She's going to come down! She's walking the beam! Look out! *She's coming down!* (*All scream.* ABIGAIL *dashes across stage as though pursued, the other girls streak hysterically in and out between the men, all converging* D. S. R.—*and as their screaming subsides only* MARY WARREN'*s is left. All watch her, struck, even horrified by this evident fit.*) 4.

4. The movements of the girls here must be planned to insure that they go off in all directions and criss-cross the entire stage before they converge downstage right, kneeling and huddling together.

PROCTOR (*Leaning across the table, turning her gently by the arm*). Mary, tell the Governor what they . . .

MARY (*Backing away*). Don't touch me . . . don't touch me!

PROCTOR. Mary!

MARY (*Pointing at* PROCTOR). You are the Devil's man!

CAMELOT, by Alan Jay Lerner and Frederick Loewe, is a musical play based on the famous King Arthur story. ARTHUR *became king by using his strength to pull out a sword which was imbedded in a stone. He disliked and feared his kingship until beautiful* GUENEVERE *became his bride. Her principal delight was in causing others embarrassment, even dismay, as she sought excitement and prettily forced people to pay her homage.*

ARTHUR (*Exasperated*).   Jenny, at the risk of disap-
  pointing the other knights, I ask you to withdraw your
  permission from all.

GUENEVERE.   Arthur, I believe you're jealous of the
  Knights and their attentions to me. Are you, my
  love?   1.

1. GUENEVERE uses
cunning and finesse to
get what she wants. She
leads her victims into
a mental trap.

ARTHUR (*Fuming*).   Jealous?! Jealous?! What absolute
  rubbish! You know perfectly well I'm delighted the
  Court adores you. I'd be astonished if they didn't.
  And I trust you as I do God above. They've carried
  your kerchief in tournament a hundred times, and . . .
  and . . . and . . . Jenny, you've dragged me off the subject and I want to get back on it. Will you withdraw
  your permission?

GUENEVERE (*Quietly and firmly*).   Only if you command
  me—as King.

ARTHUR (*Gently*).   And if I do, you will forgive me?

GUENEVERE.   Never.

ARTHUR.   If I ask as your husband, will you, as a favor? 2.

2. Work for character-
istic actions to
indicate their moods.

GUENEVERE.   No. The knights are against him, and I
  quite agree with them. I find him just as overbearing
  and pretentious as they do.

ARTHUR (*At the peak of exasperation*).   That is not the
  issue. The issue is your kerchief. Can we not stay on
  the subject?

GUENEVERE (*Calmly*).   There is nothing more to be said.
  If the King wishes me to withdraw permission, let
  him command me! And Yours Humbly will gra-
  ciously obey. What? What?

(*She turns and exits*)

ARTHUR.   What!! (*Raging*) Blast! (*He paces up and
  down*) Blast you, Merlyn! This is all your fault! (*He
  sings*)

You swore that you had taught me ev'rything from
    A to Zed,
With nary an omission in between.   3.
Well, I shall tell you what
You obviously forgot:

3. Use the opportunity
here to recite the first
three verses with varied
action that shows
ARTHUR's agitation.

That's how a ruler rules a Queen!

(*He continues pacing*)

And what of teaching me by turning me to animal
  and bird,
From beaver to the smallest bobolink!
I should have had a whirl
At changing to a girl,
To learn the way the creatures think!

(*He paces again. Then a thought occurs to him*)

But wasn't there a night, on a summer long gone by,
We pass'd a couple wrangling away;
And did I not say, Merlyn: What if that chap were I?
And did he not give counsel and say . . .

(*He tries to remember*)

What was it now? . . . My mind's a wall.
Oh, yes! . . . By jove, now I recall.

How to handle a woman?   4.
There's a way, said the wise old man;
A way known by ev'ry woman
Since the whole rigmarole began.

Do I flatter her? I begged him answer . . .
Do I threaten or cajole or plead?
Do I brood or play the gay romancer?
Said he, smiling: No indeed.
How to handle a woman?
Mark me well, I will tell you, Sir:
The way to handle a woman
Is to love her . . . simply love her . . .
Merely love her . . . love her . . . love her.

(*The music continues.* ARTHUR *doesn't move from his
position. He ponders a moment, then turns his head
and looks in the direction of* GUENEVERE)

What's wrong, Jenny? (*He walks a few steps, then
stops and looks off again*) Where are you these days?
What are you thinking? (*He walks again and stops
again*) I don't understand you. (*After a moment*) But
no matter. Merlyn told me once: Never be too dis-
turbed if you don't understand what a woman is
thinking. They don't do it often. (*He walks again*) But

4. Begin singing. Move,
pause, act as you sing.

what do you do while they're doing it? (*He smiles as he remembers*)

How to handle a woman?
Mark me well, I will tell you, Sir:
The way to handle a woman . . .
Is to love her . . . simply love her . . .
Merely love her . . . love her . . . love her.

(*He stands quietly, as the lights dim out*)

How to Handle a Woman

Words by
ALAN JAY LERNER

Music by
FREDERICK LOEWE

How to han-dle a wom-an, There's a way, said a wise old man. A way known by ev-'ry wom-an since the whole rig-ma-role be-gan. "Do I flat-ter her?" I begged him an-swer. "Do I threat-en or ca-jole or plead? Do I brood or play the gay ro-man-cer?" Said he, smil-ing, "No, in-deed." How to han-dle a wom-an, Mark me well, I will tell you, sir. "The way to han-dle a wom-an is to love her,_____ Sim-ply love her,_____ Mere-ly love her, love her, love her!"_____

CHAPTER 7

Build Your Emotions

One of the essentials for the successful actor is the ability to depict human feelings and to project them to the audience. You, as an actor, are not actually living the events of a play, but your emotions are deep enough to project ideas and feelings to the audience. You have many aids to help you: a compelling story, fascinating dialogue, music, artistic settings, and the contributions of other arts that the theater has assimilated. Yet fundamentally theater is based on the most intangible art of all, that of expressing human emotions to create aesthetic beauty. A good actor is able to show emotional tension without unduly taxing his or her own feelings by using a minimum of exertion. After the last curtain, the actor leaves the role behind, hoping he or she has succeeded—and success is measured by whether the appropriate emotion has been carried to the hearts and minds of the spectators.

RECALLING EMOTIONS

In the course of your acting training, make an effort to recall, step by step, emotions you have felt. By going systematically over an incident which aroused emotions of fear, anger, delight, sorrow, frustration, or humiliation, you will again experience some of that feeling. In anger you may feel the blood rush to your face, your muscles tighten, your eyes narrow, and your jaw set. These reactions will come from inside you, and will reveal themselves on the outside. Try to recall some sorrow or disappointment. Perhaps you received shocking news in the mail. As you thought about it perhaps your muscles seemed to become limp. In recalling this, tears may flow as the memory returns. As you cry, you may feel the hurt much more keenly than you did when first recalling it. Experiencing an emotion again often helps in enacting it in a play.

Recall incidents, minute by minute, that brought on the following emotions:

Affection	Happiness
Anger	Humility
Delight	Sorrow
Disappointment	Submission
Disgust	Surprise
Dread	Terror
Embarrassment	Worry
Expectancy	

EMPATHY

Empathy, a word of Greek derivation that means "in-feeling," refers to experiencing something of the same emotion as that of another. Your purpose as an actor is to communicate emotional experiences to the audience, to project ideas so effectively that your audience actually identifies with your character and feels empathetic responses. Your smile begets their smile, your frown makes them frown. They too, cringe before the blow of the villain. As your muscles tighten and relax, theirs also respond.

In real life, moods and emotions are often contagious. Others' happiness affects us, their worry makes us worry, their sorrow affects us deeply. Consider these examples:

1. Ken aims a blow at Ralph's chin. Spectators inwardly cringe away from the punch.
2. Molly relates the injury of her boss's remarks. She clenches her teeth and tightens her lips. Spectators, do the same.
3. Bob's mother weeps over her son's automobile accident and death. Spectators' throats also tighten as they squeeze back their tears.

Death Takes a Holiday by Walter Ferris. Presented at Grove City College. Miriam A. Franklin, director. The two characters are nicely arranged as they express love for one another with their eyes.

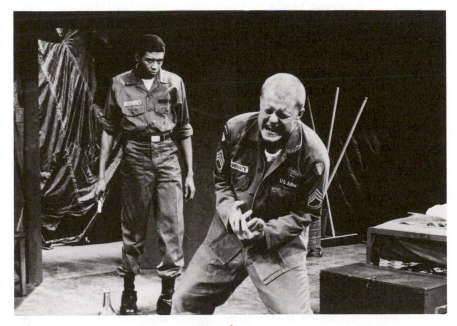

Streamers by D. Rabe was presented by University of Kansas Theatre. Jem Graves directed. Deep emotion and pain show in faces and body positions.

Stage settings, lights, costumes, and general mood heighten the "in-feeling" process. However, it is the actor's mind that, through speech and sensitive muscular responses and movements, elicits empathy from your audience.

ENACTING EMOTIONS

The enactment of emotions cannot be learned by obeying rules. Words, pantomime, and characterization are roads leading to the expression of fear, resentment, hatred, and love, but the players add their talent while obeying certain principles for the expression of emotions. Expression must be adjusted to the play's needs.

Comedy incites emotions of mirth, hilarity, joy, and fun. Subtle comedy is difficult to play effectively. To become a comedian, you need a comic sense, which few people have.

If people could learn from a book how to become comedians, there would be more fun-makers than plays for them. Many people can recite gags, use horseplay, and go through antics that bring laughs. Laughs are usually an indication that the humor of the play is being projected to the audience. This is not always true, however. Horseplay can be inappropriately inserted where it doesn't belong, bringing undesirable laughs from certain sections of the audience. Never insert anything for a laugh unless it is in good taste. Laughter is no criterion by which to judge a play's success.

A *comedy sense* is a rare gift that only a few people have. Comedy sense doesn't mean a sense of humor, it means successfully *conveying* humor. Sometimes a player works too hard trying to be funny and then the humor appears labored. Pointing up humor should always appear easy.

Several types of humor find their way into the theater. *Farce* is light dramatic composition intended to make the audience laugh. It may conceal a serious central idea by using mockery. Farce can be funny, droll, even ludicrous, but it is usually good healthy humor. *Slapstick* is very broad comedy, such as when we laugh at somebody's humorous misfortune. *Burlesque* may be very rowdy, with exaggerated business and lines. *Farce* makes little attempt to depict characters realistically, the story and the character's actions being highly overdrawn, but near enough to life to be accepted.

Both *light* and *high comedy* are on a higher level. They require careful timing, action, and reaction to show skill. High comedy is usually subtle enough to demand careful study to locate and execute the humor. Such comedy may embody satire and keenly witty lines.

Any of the varieties of comedy can be artistic and good theater; all demand careful timing. Light comedy and farce are usually played in fast tempo, with staccato, clipped words; conversely, sometimes a very slow-moving, slow-speaking character provides the comedy.

Pointing up lines most effectively often requires contrast. If comedy is produced by slow moving and acting, it will be heightened if other characters use rapid repartee. They may move fast, speak rapidly, and step on cues. A *pause* before the comic words will also point up and add value. Because comedy lines often come in rapid succession, actors must give the audience an opportunity to appreciate them. Lines should be separated and pauses provided for laughs.

There are a number of ideas you may keep in mind to help you heighten comedy effects. Try to use *variety of rendition*. Sometimes a character, very funny early in the play, grows stale later. He needs to use changes that will give variety in order to keep people enjoying him. He may insert a piece of different business that will make the audience roar with laughter.

Reaction to other characters may be a means of producing humor, but it needs to be pointed up. Often two characters working together can bring out humor effects—one giving the line, the other producing the laugh by his reaction to it. This is an old vaudeville method.

Some characters can use a trifling piece of business; such as puffing a cigar, toying nervously with a hat, or tapping a foot. That character may *feed* a laugh for some time after its inception with his particular amusing piece of business.

Comedy lines in some plays are pointed *straight front*. This technique was used a great deal in period plays, but is less popular today. It is employed in reciting gags and in funny facial business and stunt reactions. Because the comedian produces the laughs, he should be in a prominent stage position, his face in view of the audience, and usually he is located well downstage.

There are several principles which often help in playing light comedy: rapid pace, clipped words, speaking down stage, tossing lines toward the audience. A very slow-speaking character may provide humor, even a "dumbbell" type.

Here are some *do's* and *don'ts* to keep in mind for playing comedy.

DON'T:

Drop humor-provoking words	Emphasize wrong words
Kill a laugh at its inception	Face away from audience
Move on a punch line	Speak while audience laughs
Stop acting	Wait for laugh to die completely before speaking
Get out of character	

DO:

Use face to point comedy	Have all characters hold during laugh
Hold lines till audience has enjoyed laugh	Keep laugh line lifted to the end
	Choose laugh lines carefully
Keep in character	Study comedian's style

Personality is the most important factor in playing humor.

Varying your depiction. Don't try to show feelings in voice and face only. Your fingers, head, leg muscles, stance, all parts of your body are acting the emotions. Work on the suggested various emotions, using your whole body.

It is often necessary to *dress the emotions* you are playing, to adjust or make rapid changes. An emotion must fit every aspect of the play: plot, locality, year or period, and the sex, personality, and social status of characters.

Sometimes there must be fast *change* from one emotion to another. For instance, perhaps a character enters and tells you of a bad bus accident. You know your brother was on that bus. You are filled with fear and anxiety. Then a phone call comes from the brother telling you that he was not injured. Your anxiety changes to relief and joy. The more you work at showing a character's feelings, the easier it will be to change to a different one. Even though there are many you may never need to show, it is well to practice them.

There are times when you show *two emotions simultaneously*. Suppose that your wedding has just taken place. You are dressed for traveling, ready to go with your spouse to make your home far away. You are full of joy and happiness for your marriage but also are sorry to leave your lifelong home, loving family, and friends. There will be smiles but sad eyes.

There are different *intensities of emotion*. You are happy that your friend has been hired for the job he sought, but greater joy is experienced when you are told that your father's operation showed no signs of a malignancy.

Here are some warnings: *Do not overact.* Deep sorrow is made more effective with only a suggestion of grief than with heart-rending sobs. Be careful that you *do not accept compliments* too seriously. Steel yourself against believing praise. Accept it gracefully and gratefully, but keep in mind that you have a long way to go to deserve praise such as good friends lavish. Work to improve.

Laughter. To *laugh* audibly and heartily is hard for many players. A stage laugh is not a natural reaction. A hearty laugh demands action of the diaphragm. Air is expelled from the lungs in bursts, repeated in rapid succes-

Romeo and Juliet by William Shakespeare, presented by University of Arizona. Dale Luciano was director, Jeff Warburton photographer. Great anxiety and sorrow show in posture and faces.

Bosoms and Neglect by John Guare was a Yale Repertory presentation. Steven Robman directed it and Gerry Goodstein was the photographer. This is an excellent expression of intense emotion.

Build Your Emotions   **113**

sion. Begin by coughing *ha-ha-ha*, slowly at first, then faster and faster, until you are out of breath.

Draw a fast deep breath and continue coughing.
Inhale sharply, audibly, and cough some more.
Fill your lungs again and expel most of the air without coughing.
Finish the last of the breath with coughs.

Practice with others. As you laugh, try to notice *exactly* what you are doing and how. Feel the cool stream of air as it rushes down your throat, followed by a push of the diaphragm and hardening of the abdominal muscles, as the air is "coughed" out.

A *sensitive ear* is a great asset in playing emotions. If you can hear shades of thought and feeling, if you have an acute ear for the slightest variation of tone, you are fortunate. More important, however, is your ability to speak with nuances of feeling, to *speak with implications.*

Exercises in Emotions

1. *Animation:* You feel good, full of life. You have been working on assignments for hours, now completed them. It is spring and the out-of-doors beckons. You express pent-up feelings with some leaps and yells.
2. *Happiness:* The moon is full, the lake is smooth, and you are canoeing with your sweetheart.
3. *Exhilaration:* It is very near the end of the homecoming football game. The score is 12 to 11 in the opponent's favor. In the last minute of the game your buddy breaks through the line with the ball and scores a touchdown.
4. *Joy:* A letter arrives. As you read it you learn that you have won first prize in the short story contest and its award of a new car.
5. *Anger:* The driver behind your car insistently blows his horn at you in a long line of slow traffic.
6. *Exasperation:* Every month you attempt to straighten out your (wife's/husband's) jumbled checking account.
7. *Fear:* You are alone at night in a cabin in the woods. You hear footsteps outside, and you sense that eyes are peering through a window.
8. *Despair:* After the third try to pass your driver's test, you are told that you have again failed.
9. *Sorrow:* A ten-year-old boy chokes back tears as he tells you that he received no Christmas gifts.

IMAGERY

Imagery is a general term for all sensory feelings. When a playwright gives you an opportunity, through your lines, to use imagery, try to make your hearers "taste" the words. The following is a list of sense images. Speak and act each to create a vivid sensation.

Visual (*sight*): We saw the great elm tree fall.

Auditory (*hearing*): We heard the crack and crunch when it fell.

Olfactory (*smell*): We got a whiff of brewing coffee.

Gustatory (*taste*): Honey on hot bisquits was our treat.

Tactile (*touch*): Soft white sand sifted through our fingers.

Motor (*movement*): They shoved us aside.

Thermic (*heat and cold*): The open fire burned our faces.

Kinesthetic (*muscular*): We heaved the stone into place.

Organic (*inner organs*): I felt nauseated on the boat.

Sensory (*nerves*): I began to feel frustrated with the confusion.

Richard Boleslavski said "The man who can stand in an imaginary snowdrift and actually make an audience shiver, has mastered the reality of his art." Stanislavski said, "Art cannot be taught, art is talent."

Sensing Imagery. Several of us were waiting at an air station in a desert town (*sensory*). The plane was late. Someone thought he heard the plane's whir (*auditory*). All of us listened, ears cocked, in the direction of the sound (*visual*). As passengers went outside (*visual*) to board, the wintry blast (*thermic*) struck and chilled us. A ruffian shoved us aside (*motor*) to get ahead of us. As we got on the plane, we could smell coffee brewing (*olfactory*). We fastened our seat belts (*motor*), then started the dizzying climb (*sensory*), but we knew that roast beef dinners (*gustatory*) would soon be passed to us. We all sincerely hoped that none of us would get squeamish (*sensory*) while flying and eating our dinner.

Exercise in Sensing Imagery

Practice reading aloud the following imagery-filled lines so that those listening will sense the appropriate images. "Taste the words, feel them," as somebody has suggested. Every image can be made vivid with vocalized feeling. Classify on paper all images you find, just to check yourself.

As I pulled into our driveway, my parents came to meet me at the gate. It was merely noon, but already the day was so humid and sticky that the back of my shirt was wet with perspiration and my drippy hands almost stuck to the steering wheel.

Mother knows what summer foods I like best so she had prepared my favorites: firm sliced tomatoes with blue cheese dressing, fresh cold buttermilk with its sweet-sour flavor, biscuits so piping hot that they burned my fingers when I buttered them, and for dessert an icy wedge of sweet, red, juicy watermelon. After lunch I lay in the hammock on the porch where the breeze swung me back and forth, back and forth, back and forth.

The last time I had been at home was in the dead of winter. My car stuck in a snow-drift just a short way from home. I tried to move forward slowly, then I tried giving it the gas. The car couldn't budge.

I turned up my collar, ducked my head against the biting wind, and put my shoulder against the rear end of the car. I heaved and heaved, and pushed and pushed, then rested and pushed some more. I couldn't move it an inch. My feet, ears, and fingers tingled and ached, while the swirling bits of ice in my eyes blinded me. I became exhausted and the frigid air that I was inhaling through my mouth nearly strangled me. Finally I gave up. I dropped in behind the steering wheel, lay my head on my folded arms over the wheel and closed my eyes.

I was numb with exhaustion until I heard the distant chug of a tractor. It slowly grew nearer. Then I could begin to see the dim outline. Could it be? Yes, it was our good neighbor Tom Evans, bundled in his sheepskin-lined coat, cap tabs pulled over his ears, and his hands in clumsy mittens. Tom knew somebody needed help, so even in the worst of weather, he came.

The smell of his tractor fumes was sweet fragrance to me that day. I forgot about my aching ears and fingers. The tractor had the power, my car lunged forward and I guided it through Tom's tracks up to my old home and under the lean-to shed.

Pantomimes for Sensing

1. The temperature is ten below zero. You dash out, hunt for, and find the morning paper, and then run back to the house.
2. Trim dead branches from a rosebush.
3. Walk barefoot on velvety blue-grass in summer.
4. A neighbor's house is on fire. Fight your way through blinding smoke to help carry out the young children.
5. Swallow a dose of the worst-tasting medicine you ever had.
6. It is a very hot summer day. You have just finished a tennis game and you sit down to rest.
7. Take a cake from the oven. You use a holder, but it slips and you burn your fingers. Try again. Drop the pan. Pick it up.
8. Pick up these items from the floor: needle and thread, broken glass, a pile

of laundry, a fluffy kitten, a toddler who fell, a piece of bread drippy with syrup, an overstuffed chair.

9. You are on a country road, a mile from home. You walk through 18-inch-deep snow while facing a blinding snowstorm.
10. In a similar way, face a drenching rain.
11. Feel your way through a very dense fog at night.
12. A piece of iron falls from a scaffold onto your left hand.
13. Start to wash dishes in a sink. The dishwater is terribly hot; it burns your hands.
14. Cuddle a three-month-old baby.
15. While reading the morning newspaper, fold it to inner pages as you glance at the headlines.

Pantomimes for Expressing Emotion

Here are a number of ideas for pantomimes. Let each student plan his or her own pantomimes built around these ideas or emotions. Make up lines if you prefer.

1. *Happy surprise:* Your mother arrives at college to see you in the college play.
2. *Delight:* Your fraternity president meets you on the street and tells you that your group has received highest scholastic honors.
3. *Horror:* Ahead of your car you see two other cars collide.
4. *Fear:* While you are visiting the zoo, a tiger escapes from his pen.
5. *Expectation:* You are at the Field House with a friend, waiting for your winning basketball team to return from a game.
6. *Animation:* You are returning from an evening with a new date, the nicest one ever!
7. *Disgust:* A drunk leers at you and makes a repulsive remark.
8. *Despair:* You have just returned home after days of unsuccessfully looking for work.
9. *Anger:* You see a man whipping a skinny stray dog.
10. *Grief:* You have just returned home from the funeral of a loved one.

Depicting emotions is a large part of acting. The next phase of your study will give you practice in representing unusual characters. However, showing emotion is part of every character in every play. Learning to express the feelings of your character may be challenging, but it is gratifying when you accomplish your end.

Excerpts for Practice

In Shakespeare's MUCH ADO ABOUT NOTHING, BEATRICE *and* BENEDICK *have long engaged in a battle of wits that has covered the growing love between them. In this scene,* BENEDICK *finally tells* BEATRICE *of his love for her, while* BEATRICE *asks him to execute revenge against his close friend* CLAUDIO *for unfair accusations made against her cousin* HERO.

BENEDICK   BEATRICE

SUGGESTIONS AND
STAGE DIRECTIONS

BENE.   Lady Beatrice, have you wept all this while? 1.

BEAT.   Yea, and I will weep a while longer.

BENE.   I will not desire that.

BEAT.   You have no reason, I do it freely.

BENE.   Surely I do believe your fair cousin is wrong'd.

BEAT.   Ah, how much might the man deserve of me that would right her!

BENE.   Is there any way to show such friendship?

BEAT.   A very even way, but no such friend.

BENE.   May a man do it?

BEAT.   It is a man's office, but not yours.

BENE.   I do love nothing in the world so well as you— is not that strange?

BEAT.   As strange as the thing I know not. It were as possible for me to say I lov'd nothing so well as you, but believe me not; and yet I lie not: I confess nothing nor, I deny nothing. I am sorry for my cousin.   2.

BENE.   By my sword, Beatrice, thou lovest me.

BEAT.   Do not swear and eat it.

BENE.   I will swear by it that you love me, and I will make him eat it that says I love not you.

BEAT.   Will you not eat your word?

BENE.   With no sauce that can be devis'd to it. I protest I love thee.

BEAT.   Why then God forgive me!

BENE.   What offense, sweet Beatrice?

Be careful to play the various emotional levels at work in the scene: tenderness, weeping, anger, humor (it is a comedy, after all), and through it all, of course, love.

1. Have BEATRICE sitting on a bench as the scene begins.

2. She starts to leave and stops short on his next line.

BEAT. You have stay'd me in a happy hour, I was about to protest I lov'd you.

BENE. And do it with all thy heart.

BEAT. I love you with so much of my heart that none is left to protest.

BENE. Come, bid me do any thing for thee.

BEAT. Kill Claudio. 3.

BENE. Ha, not for the wide world.

BEAT. You kill me to deny it. Farewell. 4.

BENE. Tarry, sweet Beatrice.

BEAT. I am gone, though I am here; there is no love in you. Nay, I pray you let me go.

BENE. Beatrice—

BEAT. In faith, I will go.

BENE. We'll be friends first.

BEAT. You dare easier be friends with me than fight with mine enemy.

BENE. Is Claudio thine enemy?

BEAT. Is 'a not approv'd in the height a villain, that hath slander'd, scorn'd, dishonor'd my kinswoman? O that I were a man! What, bear her in hand until they come to take hands, and then with public accusation, uncover'd slander, unmitigated rancor—O God, that I were a man! I would eat his heart in the market-place. 5.

BENE. Hear me, Beatrice—

BEAT. Talk with a man out at a window! (6) a proper saying!

BENE. Nay, but, Beatrice—

BEAT. Sweet Hero, she is wrong'd, she is sland'red, she is undone.

BENE. Beat—

BEAT. Princes and counties! Surely a princely testimony, a goodly count, Count Comfect, a sweet gallant surely! O that I were a man for his sake! or that I had any friend would be a man for my sake! But manhood is melted into cur'sies, valor into compli-

3. Make the transition from love to revenge a jarring one, vocally and physically; he must be shocked by her sudden change.

4. She attempts to leave again, but is physically detained.

5. She gives her anger full vent. Use voice, body, and strong movement.

6. This is what CLAUDIO accused her of doing.

ment, (7) and men are only turn'd into tongue, and trim ones too. He is now as valiant as Hercules that only tells a lie, and swears it. I cannot be a man with wishing, therefore I will die a woman with grieving.

BENE. Tarry, good Beatrice. By this hand, I love thee.

BEAT. Use it for my love some other way than swearing by it.

BENE. Think you in your soul the Count Claudio hath wrong'd Hero?

BEAT. Yea, as sure as I have a thought or a soul.

BENE. Enough, I am engag'd, I will challenge him. I will kiss your hand, and so I leave you. By this hand, Claudio shall render me a dear account. As you hear of me, so think of me. Go comfort your cousin. I must say she is dead; and so farewell. [*Exeunt.*]

7. Her anger is slowing, settling into grief.

In THE GLASS MENAGERIE, by Tennessee Williams, AMANDA WING-FIELD *and her two grown children,* TOM *and* LAURA, *live in a small tenement apartment in St. Louis.* LAURA *is an extremely shy girl, deeply inhibited by a very slight crippled condition.* AMANDA, *in an effort to bring* LAURA *out of herself, has asked* TOM *to bring home a friend from work so that* LAURA *can have a "gentleman caller."*

AMANDA
LAURA

SUGGESTIONS AND STAGE DIRECTIONS

Note the rising emotional contrast as the scene progresses: LAURA'S fear and AMANDA'S insistence, frustration, and then anger. AMANDA speaks with a Southern accent.

AMANDA. I hope they get here before it starts to rain. I gave your brother a little extra change so he and Mr. O'Connor could take the service car home. (LAURA *puts flowers on armchair* R., *and crosses to door* R.)

LAURA. Mother!

AMANDA. What's the matter now? (*Re-entering room.*)

LAURA. What did you say his name was?

AMANDA. O'Connor. Why?

LAURA. What is his first name?

AMANDA (*Crosses to armchair* R). I don't remember —— Oh, yes, I do too—it was—Jim! (*Picks up flowers.*)

LAURA. Oh, Mother, not Jim O'Connor!

AMANDA. Yes, that was it, it was Jim! I've never known a Jim that wasn't nice. (*Crosses* L., *behind day-bed, puts flowers in vase.*) 1.

LAURA. Are you sure his name was Jim O'Connor?

AMANDA. Why, sure I'm sure. Why?

LAURA. Is he the one that Tom used to know in high school?

AMANDA. He didn't say so. I think he just got to know him— (*Sits on day-bed.*) at the warehouse.

LAURA. There was a Jim O'Connor we both knew in high school. If that is the one that Tom is bringing home to dinner—— Oh, Mother, you'd have to excuse me, I wouldn't come to the table!

AMANDA. What's this now? What sort of silly talk is this?

LAURA. You asked me once if I'd ever liked a boy. Don't you remember I showed you this boy's picture?

AMANDA. You mean the boy in the year-book?

LAURA. Yes, that boy.

AMANDA. Laura, Laura, were you in love with that boy?

LAURA. (*Crosses to* R. *of armchair*). I don't know, Mother. All I know is that I couldn't sit at the table if it was him.

AMANDA (*Rises, crosses* L. *and works up* L. *of day-bed*). It won't be him! It isn't the least bit likely. But whether it is or not, you will come to the table— you will not be excused.

LAURA. I'll have to be, Mother.

AMANDA (*Behind day-bed*). I don't intend to humor your silliness, Laura. I've had too much from you and your brother, both. So just sit down and compose yourself till they come. Tom has forgotten his key, so you'll *have* to let them in when they arrive.

LAURA. Oh, Mother—*you* answer the door! (*Sits chair* R.). 2.

AMANDA. How can I when I haven't even finished making the mayonnaise dressing for the salmon?

1. AMANDA'S handling of her lines and of the flowers indicates nonchalance, while LAURA reflects tension and rising fear.

2. LAURA'S fear makes her incapable of responding with anything more than variations on this line until the end of the next scene.

LAURA.   Oh, Mother, please answer the door, don't make me do it! (*Thunder heard offstage.*)

AMANDA.   Honey, do be reasonable! What's all this fuss about—just one gentleman caller—that's all—just one! (*Exits through living-room curtains. TOM and JIM enter alley R., climb fire-escape steps to landing and wait outside of closed door. Hearing them approach, LAURA rises with a panicky gesture. She retreats to living-room curtains. The doorbell rings. (3) LAURA catches her breath and touches her throat. More thunder heard offstage.*)

3. These sounds are triggers that heighten LAURA'S fears even more.

AMANDA (*Offstage*).   Laura, sweetheart, the door!

LAURA.   Mother, please, you go to the door! (*Starts for door R., then back.*)

AMANDA (*Offstage, in a fierce whisper*).   What is the matter with you, you silly thing? (*Enters through living-room curtains, and stands by day-bed.*)

LAURA.   Please you answer it, please.

AMANDA.   Why have you chosen this moment to lose your mind? You go to that door.

LAURA.   I can't.

AMANDA.   Why can't you?

LAURA.   Because I'm sick. (*Crosses to L. end of day-bed and sits.*)

AMANDA.   You're sick! Am I sick? You and your brother have me puzzled to death. You can never act like normal children. Will you give me one good reason why you should be afraid to open a door? You go to that door. Laura Wingfield, you march straight to that door!

4. Fear of her mother triumphed over her fear of answering the door.

LAURA (*Crosses to door R.*).   Yes, Mother.   4.

AMANDA (*Stopping LAURA*).   I've got to put courage in you, honey, for living. (*Exits through living-room curtains, and exits R. into kitchen. LAURA opens door.*)

THE INTRUDER, by Maurice Maeterlinck, is shrouded in mystery. The old blind GRANDFATHER with his son (FATHER) and son-in-law (THE UNCLE) and three GRANDAUGHTERS await the coming of a NUN, the GRANDFATHER'S daughter, while the MOTHER lies at the point of death in an adjoining room.

GRANDFATHER	URSULA	SUGGESTIONS AND
FATHER	* YOUNGER DAUGHTER	STAGE DIRECTIONS
* UNCLE	* YOUNGEST DAUGHTER	

GRANDFATHER. I do not know what ails me; I feel uneasy. I wish your sister were here. 1.

UNCLE. She will come. She promised to.

GRANDFATHER. I wish this evening were over! 2.

(*The* THREE DAUGHTERS *come in again.*)

FATHER. Is he asleep?

URSULA. Yes, Father. Very sound.

UNCLE. What shall we do while we are waiting?

GRANDFATHER. Waiting for what?

UNCLE. Waiting for our sister. 3.

FATHER. You see nothing coming, Ursula?

URSULA (*at the window*). Nothing, Father.

FATHER. Not in the avenue? Can you see the avenue?

URSULA. Yes, Father, it is moonlight, and I can see the avenue as far as the cypress wood. 4.

GRANDFATHER. And do you not see anyone?

URSULA. No one, Grandfather.

GRANDFATHER. I cannot hear the nightingales any longer.

YOUNGER DAUGHTER. I think someone is coming into the garden, grandfather.

GRANDFATHER. Who is it?

YOUNGER DAU. I do not know; I can see no one.

UNCLE. Because there is no one there.

YOUNGER DAU. There must be some one in the garden; the nightingales have suddenly ceased singing.

GRANDFATHER. But I do not hear anyone coming.

YOUNGER DAU. Someone must be passing by the pond, because the swans are scared.

YOUNGEST DAU. All the fishes in the pond are diving suddenly. 5.

FATHER. You cannot see anyone?

YOUNGEST DAU. No one, father.

1. The THREE DAUGHTERS group to represent a single person. Emotions grow tense.

2. GRANDFATHER probably speaks in quavery voice, seems to tremble.

3. UNCLE and FATHER sit idly in their chairs. UNCLE is more agitated, cross.

4. THREE SISTERS may group in different arrangements, but always together. They symbolize one person.

5. DAUGHTERS might squint and shade their eyes from indoor light as they peer into semi-darkness.

FATHER.   But the pond lies in the moonlight.

YOUNGEST DAU.   Yes, I can see that the swans are scared.

UNCLE.   I am sure it is my sister who is scaring them. She must have come in by the little gate.

FATHER.   I cannot understand why the dogs do not bark. . . .

GRANDFATHER.   And yet there is no noise.   6.

6. GRANDFATHER'S comments carry an ominous tone that grows more and more frightening.

FATHER.   There is a silence of the grave.

GRANDFATHER.   It must be some stranger that scares them, for if it were one of the family, they would not be silent.

UNCLE.   How much longer are we going to discuss these nightingales?

GRANDFATHER.   Are all the windows open, Ursula?

URSULA.   The glass door is open, grandfather.

GRANDFATHER.   It seems to me that the cold is penetrating into the room.   7.

7. GRANDFATHER might shiver and draw, his shawl tightly about him.

YOUNGEST DAU.   There is a little wind in the garden, grandfather, and the rose leaves are falling.

FATHER.   Well, shut the door, it is late.

YOUNGEST DAU.   Yes, father. . . . I cannot shut the door.   8.

8. Someone offstage might slip an obstacle into door crack. All seem to push hard.

The OTHER DAUGHTERS.   We cannot shut the door.

GRANDFATHER.   Why, what is the matter with the door, my children?

UNCLE.   You need not say that in such an extraordinary voice. I will go help them.

URSULA.   We cannot manage to shut it quite.

UNCLE.   It is because of the damp. Let us all push together. There must be something in the way.

FATHER.   The carpenter will set it right tomorrow.

GRANDFATHER.   Is the carpenter coming tomorrow?

URSULA.   Yes, grandfather; he is coming to do some work in the cellar.

GRANDFATHER.   He will make a noise in the house.

URSULA.   I will tell him to work quietly. (*Suddenly the sound of a scythe being sharpened is heard outside.*)

GRANDFATHER (*with a shudder*).   Oh!   9.

UNCLE.   What is that?

YOUNGER DAU.   I don't know quite; I think it is the gardner. I cannot quite see; he is in the shadow of the house.

FATHER.   It is the gardner going to mow.

UNCLE.   He mows at night?

FATHER.   Is not tomorrow Sunday?— Yes—I noticed that the grass is getting very long around the house.

GRANDFATHER.   It seems to me that the scythe makes as much noise . . .

YOUNGEST DAU.   He is mowing near the house.

GRANDFATHER.   Can you see him, Ursula?   10.

URSULA.   No, grandfather. He stands in the dark.

GRANDFATHER.   I am afraid he will wake my daughter.

UNCLE.   We can scarcely hear him.

9. This *Oh!* can be full of fear.

10. GRANDFATHER'S voice full of fear, body leaning forward, hands shaking.

THE RUNNER STUMBLES, by Milan Stitt, is a sensitive play about a youthful, loving NUN who challenges the basic beliefs of a priest who is locked in the old traditions. In this scene, the conflict comes to a head as both the priest and the NUN try in their different ways to comfort ERNA, whose mother is dying. The scene is in ERNA'S parlor.

PRIEST (FATHER RIVARD)   NUN (SISTER RITA)
                          ERNA

SUGGESTIONS AND
STAGE DIRECTIONS

Notice the range of emotions: ERNA's sorrow, as she controls it and as she lets it go; the PRIEST's sterness and impatience; the NUN's eagerness, sympathy, and then frustration.

(NUN *enters. After a moment,* PRIEST *follows her. Silence, tension.*)

NUN (U. *small table*).   So this is Erna's. (*Silence. After a moment,* NUN *discovers a music box and begins playing it.* PRIEST *is startled and looks to see what the sound is.* PRIEST *crosses* U. L.) Music box. (PRIEST *turns off music box. Silence. He sits on settee.*)

PRIEST.   What you said last night. About me. It is not true.

NUN (*Sitting on chair*).   I never should— I'm sorry, Father. It was just—

PRIEST.   Let me say this before Erna comes back. Then it'll be over; you will forget last night. See, all this, it's your fault. And, I need your help.

NUN.   What is my fault?

PRIEST.   I can't get done what I should. Here at Erna's I am to comfort her. This is a normal, routine matter for a priest. But I'm so confused that, I know I need help. I have to if I'm to be a good priest. And I want to be. I must say what a good priest—

NUN.   I never said you weren't a good priest.

PRIEST.   Please, Sister. Hear me out. I can learn, or re-learn. I can change. I have already, just saying out loud that I am afraid is a start. I have to tell you that Erna's mother, well, she is going to die. The doctor told me. I have to tell Erna. I have to help her try. And I thought all night about what you think of me, and very early this morning I decided that you should be here, that you would help me make a new start. I thought that if I hear you talk with Erna, I would hear the way you would try to—   1.

1. Note the emotional difficulty he is having. He is confused, yet recognizes a need to change. This is awkward for him.

NUN.   You want me to help?

PRIEST.   Yes.

NUN.   Thank you, Father. (*Erna enters from* L. *She has a handkerchief and is trying not to cry, but is barely succeeding.*)

ERNA.   Mama's still sleeping. I checked.

NUN (*Sitting with* ERNA *on settee*).   My aunt's husband was sick something like your mother, Erna. The same. He stayed like your mother, just sleeping, for five days.

ERNA.   But he died. Mama's not going to die.

NUN.   But before. That was actually the hardest for me. I was terrified to be in his room, ashamed not to be.

ERNA.   I'm afraid she'll hear me crying.

NUN.   I know. I tried to keep it inside so my uncle wouldn't hear. Of course, he couldn't. I was much younger than you. I didn't know what was to become of me if he died.

PRIEST.   Sister, maybe Erna wouldn't want to hear about this?

ERNA.   Oh yes, Father. It's just the same. I have to be quiet too. And I don't know what'll happen either. I just don't. Mama and I, we take care of each other. (PRIEST *indicates* NUN *may continue.*)

NUN. When I was in his room, I remember loking out the window. It was spring. I had just planted my garden. And there was a little sparrow at the feeder, but I'd forgotten to put out crumbs for worrying. Suddenly the sparrow flew down to the garden and started eating the seeds I'd planted.

ERNA. That's awful.

NUN. He was hungry. I wondered how he knew to do that. Whatever would make him know there were seeds there? Then I remembered that God watches over all things, even the sparrows. I laughed. 2.

2. The NUN uses her imagination to recreate the scene and her emotional response of joy.

ERNA (*Crying openly*). Oh, Sister.

PRIEST. What Sister is saying is that God obviously was watching over her in her trouble. Just as He will watch over you and your mother too, Erna.

NUN. And, of course, that is all I wanted to say, Father.

ERNA. Mama's not going to die, is she?

PRIEST. Your mother's lived a good life. She's a good Catholic. She has nothing to fear. You don't need to cry.

ERNA (*Standing, embraced by* NUN). No. No. No. Mama can't die.

PRIEST (*Crossing behind* ERNA). Please, Erna. Listen to me. Crying won't help.

NUN. It can, Father. Just let her— 3.

3. The old conflict between the PRIEST and the NUN emerges again.

PRIEST. Erna, you must accept God's will.

ERNA. I don't want to be all alone. She can't die. (*Throwing herself in* NUN'S *arms, crying.*) What would happen to me out here? I'd be all alone.

PRIEST. Erna—

NUN. Father, perhaps, it would be better—

PRIEST. Your mother is in God's hands, isn't she? Don't cry, Erna.

ERNA (*Turning to* PRIEST). But I can't help it. When it starts, I just can't.

PRIEST. Pray for strength, say your rosary. "They who

wait upon the Lord shall renew their strength. They shall mount up with wings as eagles, they shall run and not be weary ..." See, if you try hard enough, you can resist the temptation to—

NUN.   To be human? People have to cry, Father. Before you said that you—

PRIEST.   Erna. Tears are personal destruction. Destruction of anything is an affront to God.

NUN.   But Jesus wept. God was not affronted when His only begot—   4.

PRIEST.   Erna, you must accept all of God's world. Not just that which pleases you . . .

ERNA.   I don't mean to, Father. When it starts, I just can't . . . I'm sorry.

4. Note all the lines that are cut off. This indicates a fairly rapid tempo for the argument. Cues must be picked up very quickly.

OH! SUSANNA, by F. Ryerson, C. Clements, and A. Ronell, is an authentic story of Stephen Foster, the great song writer. The scene is laid on the porch of the Foster Warehouse in an Ohio rivertown in June about 1840. JEANIE, recently from the deep South, and STEPHEN FOSTER fall deeply in love. JEANIE's father, DR. MCDOWELL, will not consent to her marriage to this happy-go-lucky ne'er-do-well song writer. STEPHEN leaves town to make good before returning to claim his love. JEANIE hears nothing from him, thinks he has deserted her, and becomes engaged to a former suiter, RICHARD. The wedding day is near. Friends and neighbors are busily sewing JEANIE's wedding garments. She is very downhearted.

RICHARD	JEANIE	SUGGESTIONS AND
*EXTRA BOYS	LAURA	STAGE DIRECTIONS
	AUNT GUSTA	
	SUSY (a tomboy)	Happiness, sadness,
	MELINDA	worry, sympathy, and
	GORA	flirtatiousness
	LILY	
	DORA	
	*EXTRA GIRLS	

LAURA, *at one side of the group, and* CORA *at the other, are working on quilts in a large flower design. The others are sewing on lingerie.* AUNT GUSTA, C., *is helping* MELINDA *make yards and yards of ruffling.*

They are all sewing, except JEANIE, *who sits on bench at* R. *in a sad abstraction, remembering only now and then to pick up her work.*

Several girls sewing on household supplies and wedding garments. Seated on benches, stools and bales of cotton.

Needles move to rhythm of the music.

SEWING BEE

Aunt Gusta, Melinda, Boys and Girls

Aunt Gusta.

Don't be idle! Never, never!
Be the soul of industry;
In the Garden of Endeavor,
Labor for the Sewing Bee!

Girls.

Twinkle, twinkle, little needle!
Ply your way for all to see;
Don't be idle, little needle,
Labor for the Sewing Bee!

Aunt Gusta.

Often often we too free are
With a male society;
There's no mischief here where we are
Labor for the Sewing Bee!

Girls.

Twinkle, twinkle, little needle!
Ply your way for all to see;
Don't be idle, little needle,
Labor for the Sewing Bee!

Melinda.

Rise up early in the dawning,
We must be exemplary;
You won't help your neighbor yawning,
Labor for the Sewing Bee!

Girls.

Twinkle, twinkle, little needle!
Ply your way for all to see;
Don't be idle, little needle.
Labor for the Sewing Bee!

(*During the last verse,* Aunt Gusta *nods and dozes off.
The* boys *enter cautiously, hoping to flirt with the* girls
while Gusta *is asleep. The sewing drops to the ground
and work is forgotten as the girls join the boys. The
latter become too ardent, the girls hold them off at
the points of their needles.* Aunt Gusta *wakes up,
sings loudly the last line.*)

Boys and Girls (*softly*).
Twinkle, twinkle, little needle!
Ply your way for all to see;
Don't be idle, little needle,
Labor for the Sewing Bee!

Aunt Gusta (*clapping her hands*).   Girls! Girls!

(*The* boys *hurry out. The* girls *run back to their work.*)

Melinda (*measuring ruffles*).   Seventy-one—two—four—six. Jeanie, do you think seventy-eight yards of ruffling will be enough for your second-under wedding petticoat?

Aunt Gusta (*as* Jeanie *does not answer*).   Sounds skimpy to me.

Laura.   Richard won't care what she wears. Will he, Jeanie? Jeanie!

Melinda.   She's in a trance.

Angelina.   Because she loves him so.

(*The* girls *giggle, sing a short parody on O'ER THE GREEN, tossing the lines back and forth as though making them up.*)

Lily.
Richard's coming o'er the green——

Cora.
Finer man was never seen——

Melinda.
He thinks so himself, I wean——

All the Girls.
How can she love him so?

Jeanie.   Please! Please, don't!

Lily.   Jeanie, darling, we're sorry.

Melinda.   We were only funnin'.

Susy (*Runs in from warehouse, flourishing a small four-page newspaper. She is older than when we last saw her; her skirts have lengthened until they show only a few inches of pantalette, but she is still a tomboy*). Girls! Have you seen the *Gazette?* All about Jeanie's wedding! What she's going to wear. Names of the bridesmaids. Everything!

GIRLS (*passing paper from one to the other, down the line*).

"Exquisite bridal accoutrements."

"White satin and lace——"

"Laura Lee and Dora Dell——"

"Pink sarcenet, with garlands of roses——"

Oh, doesn't it look wonderful in print?

SUSY. Don't you want to see it, Jeanie?

JEANIE. No, thank you. I've something in my eye.

AUNT GUSTA (*understandingly*). Take my handkerchief, honey. (*She stands between* JEANIE *and the* GIRLS.)

MELINDA. Oh, look——

LILY. There's something about Steve Foster!

GIRLS (ALL *glancing toward* JEANIE).

Hush!

Shh!

Be quiet!

JEANIE (*her pride hurt*). You needn't stop on my account. Here—I'll read it aloud. (*She takes the newspaper, reads firmly*) "A New York correspondent writes ye editor that our esteemed townsman, Stephen Foster, is not content with conquering the entire country with his *Oh! Susanna*——"

SUSY. *My* song!

JEANIE. "—*Old Black Joe* and *Kentucky Home*. He must needs conquer all female hearts. The wit and charm so well remembered——" (*Her voice breaks*) "—so well remembered——"

MELINDA (*quickly taking the paper*). "—remembered by his many friends in this locality have been causing bosoms to flutter not only in the purlieus of polite society——"

DORA (*reading excitedly over* MELINDA's *shoulder*). "—but also, it is whispered, among those fairer and frailer damsels who——"

AUNT GUSTA (*snatching the paper*). That's enough of that!

SUSY. But, Aunt Gusta, it only says "—who ornament our stages."

AUNT GUSTA. Never mind what it says! You need skinning—every last one of you! Get along now. Shoo!

(*The* GIRLS *tiptoe out* R., *hurriedly,* SUSY *with them.* AUNT GUSTA *speaks softly to* JEANIE, *who has returned to* C.) Don't go getting the dismals, child——

JEANIE. Oh, Aunt Gusta, why do I have to keep thinking about an old worthless who's never even bothered to write me a letter?

AUNT GUSTA. You're a woman, honey—so you haven't much sense.

JEANIE. And why does he have to be so worthless?

AUNT GUSTA. He's a man—so he hasn't any sense at all.

RICHARD (*calling, from off* R.). Jeanie!

JEANIE. It's Richard. I don't want to see him!

AUNT GUSTA. You'll be seeing him often when you're married.

(JEANIE *looks at her, then turns, runs into the warehouse.* RICHARD *enters from* R.)

RICHARD. Jeanie! Jeanie! (*To* AUNT GUSTA, *as the warehouse doors close*) What's the matter with her?

AUNT GUSTA. Plenty. (*Shakes newspaper under his nose.*) How much did you pay the editor to write that paragraph? Or maybe you wrote it yourself.

RICHARD. I'm afraid I don't understand you.

AUNT GUSTA. Well, I understand *you!* My nose tells me when an egg's bad, even if it's served up on silver.

RICHARD. Ha!

AUNT GUSTA. Ha! to you, sir! What did you do with all those letters Stephen wrote to Jeanie?

RICHARD.   What did *I* do!

AUNT GUSTA.   Yes, *you.* I've known there was a rat in the woodpile ever since the Postmistress turned up at church with a New York bonnet and two dollars for the collection plate.

JEANIE *(returning from warehouse).*   Richard—is it true? Did Stephen really write me? Did you steal his letters?

RICHARD.   If I did, it was for your own good.

JEANIE.   Oh!

"The Sewing Bee"

(Foster—Ronell)

GUSTA, MELINDA, GIRLS and BOYS

Music and Lyrics by
ANN RONELL

Build Your Emotions

CHAPTER 8

Character Study

The heart of good acting is creating *realistic* characters, those who seem to actually live the story in which the dramatist has placed them.

You need to see that person in action. When you build a character, the movements should be *right*; if the actions do not build this character, they are *wrong*. Create, for each role, a true "new life," and treat your character as a live human being.

Delay decisions on definite actions and voice. Instead, work gradually; let actions grow as you develop your part. It is good to work on character in your own home using voice and movement while going about your daily activities. Keep building your part in this way during all the weeks of your rehearsal.

Somebody has said, "No matter how important sincerity is in art, it is not sufficient. . . . . . For art, there must be expressive form." It is not enough for *you* to feel your own emotions; they are worthless unless they reach the audience.

Listening to another actor means more than merely looking at the speaker. Actors must not be resting while others are speaking lines; they should be alert all the time, not merely when they are to speak. In a chorus or crowd scene, each performer must determine his or her behavior and attitude toward other characters or events in the play.

Stanislavski advised: when you play a nasty character, search to find and show something good in him or her. Showing a character as having some good quality makes ugly, nasty actions more interesting; perhaps surprising.

THE DRAMATIST AND THE PLAY

When a dramatist dreams up an idea for a play, he usually thinks first of plot, a conflict, although sometimes the first thought is of a leading character. As the idea grows, the writer begins to people his play, hoping to create characters that are each distinct from all the others. The dramatist visualizes each, noting the appearance, characteristics, and moral and social attitudes that belong to only that individual.

A good dramatist describes or suggests characteristics and relationships and, through dialogue, helps the player understand that character too. However, some of the suggestions may be subtle or hidden, clear to the dramatist but hard for the player to find.

RESEARCH YOUR CHARACTER

You need to search in many ways to discover and become fully acquainted with your character. However, your duty is not finished when you learn to know your own character. You need to project that personality to other characters to make that personality distinctive. Others, in turn, need to help you know each of them. Your character helps create others' characters, as they do yours, and this leads to a blending of efforts for the play's success.

What the Author Writes. The author's descriptions provide one of the many avenues you have through which to learn all about the character you are to play. Some description may be found in introductory remarks, and other information is interspersed with the lines. The dramatist often tells—or hints—about a character's appearance, disposition, social status, relationships, and other characteristics.

The author often tells what the character looks like, about his social status, disposition, and relationships. Note these examples:

THE ENVOY (*Staggering to his feet: pulling a paper from his pocket and speaking with boisterous confidence*).   Get up, Molly. Up with you, Eth.
(From *Back to Methuselah*, by George Bernard Shaw)

(MR. STANLEY, *solid, substantial—the American businessman—is descending stairs* C.)

(*A moment's pause, and then a wheelchair is rolled through the door by the nurse. It is full of pillows, blankets, and* SHERIDAN WHITESIDE. SHERIDAN

WHITESIDE *is indeed portly and Falstaffian. He is wearing an elaborate velvet smoking-jacket and a very loud tie, and he looks like every caricature ever drawn of him. There is a hush as the chair rolls into the room* D.R. *Welcoming smiles break over every face. His fingers drum for a moment on the arm of the chair. He looks slowly around the room.*)

(From *The Man Who Came to Dinner,* by George S. Kaufman and Moss Hart)

What Other Characters Reveal. Some characters talk about others in such a way that they give you many hints, often clear mental pictures of their associates. Background or disposition may only be revealed through hints, as relationships are often revealed. Actions and treatment of other characters tells you about a character's social status, moral feelings, and other qualities.

Through all dialogue, your character and others build the audience's awareness of each character. You may need to read between the lines to grasp the author's full intentions in having characters act and speak as they do. You can understand how necessary it is to study the entire play, not just for your character's lines, but for creative ideas which make you the full acquaintance of the one whose mask you are wearing. Dialogue may be full of statements and *implications.*

The following examples will show how authors reveal a character's traits and appearance through dialogue.

POULENGEY (*Slowly*). . . . But there hasn't been a word that has anything to do with her being a woman. They have stopped swearing before her. There is something! Something! It may be worth trying.

ROBERT. Oh, come, Polly! pull yourself together. Common sense was never your strong point; but this is a little too much.

(From *Saint Joan,* by George Bernard Shaw)

MRS. ETTEEN. . . . Doctor Conrad, has science nothing to say?

CONRAD. Yes. Science tells that the trouble is that Frank is not an amoeba.

MRS. ETTEEN. What is an amoeba?

CONRAD. Our common ancestor. An early form of life which you will find in the nearest ditch.

MRS. ETTEEN. And where does Franklyn come in?

CONRAD. The amoeba can split himself into two amoebas, and the two can split themselves into four and so on. Well, Frank cannot split himself up into a dozen Franks so that there shall be a dozen Franks for every woman who wants him. There's only one of him; and Clara's got it. Hadn't you better make up your mind to that?

(From *A Glimpse of the Domesticity of Franklyn Barnabas*, by George Bernard Shaw)

How Characters Reveal Themselves. *A character reveals self* by the clothes the character selects and the care with which he or she wears them. These tell something of the character's social status and orderliness. He or she may be depicted as very neat even in badly worn garments, or be seen in dressy outfits inappropriate for the occasion.

Your character's treatment of others and their attitude toward him or her give you reason to find out why such feelings exist. Notice the actions, speech patterns, diction, response to others, all these tell you a great deal.

Your character's previous action, background, family relations—if the author mentions them—all help. Note especially the character's association with others in the play; find the purpose the dramatist had for including this character. We'll hope that the author has made known the reason for including this character so that you have help in enacting this likeness of a person.

It may be a challenge to you to create your characters in plays by authors who have given little help. In such plays, you will need to use a generous supply of imagination to fill in what the dramatist's construction lacks.

Notice, in the following, how characters reveal their attitudes and dispositions.

SPEED. Al, don't talk to him. He's dealing (*to* MURRAY) Murray, you wanna rest for a while? Go lie down, sweetheart.

MURRAY. You want speed or accuracy, make up your mind. (*He begins to deal slowly.* SPEED *puffs on his cigar angrily.*)

ROY. Hey, you want to do me a really big favor? Smoke toward New Jersey.

(SPEED *blows smoke at* ROY.)

(From *The Odd Couple*, by Neil Simon)

IMAGINE YOUR CHARACTER

Your imagination may keep searching for satisfactory movements, mannerisms, and costume to satisfy your need in playing a role; you want to make it interesting and just right for the play. We'll suppose that the author has given you little or no help for your characterization, and that your research hasn't helped much either.

Let's suppose that your character is the wife of a shopkeeper in an isolated Norwegian village. She is the town's gossip and has good scenes in the

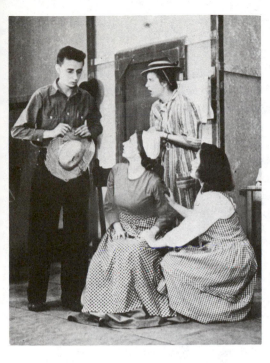

Papa Is All by Patterson Greene is a story of Pennsylvania Dutch people. It was presented by Grove City College, with Miriam A. Franklin as director. Good characterizations shown in facial expressions.

Oliver by Lionel Bart was presented by Wheaton College, directed by Morris Blauer and Gwendolyn Berndt Rostron. Notice position of hands and feet.

Camino Real is by Tennessee Williams. It was directed by Hugh G. McCausland for Washburn University. Costuming is a part of characterization.

Character Study 139

play. You try various walks, standing positions, and mannerisms such as twisting stray locks, tapping one foot, licking your lips, taking long strides. Use your imagination.

First, you *concentrate*, thinking of and imagining the kind of life your character lives in the cold Norwegian climate. She helps in the shop to keep the family clothed and fed. Think about all the aspects of her life. What should she wear? Is she tidy or untidy? You know that a usual image of Norwegians is sturdy, rosy-cheeked, and industrious.

You feel sure that she lives modestly and is interested in community life and its problems. You think that she would step briskly and never dawdle, as she has much to do. She would probably wear bulky, warm clothes. You imagine that she has developed some peculiar habits that are hers alone. Try to invent several that might suit her.

Character observation will help you in the portrayal of roles. Study the characteristics of three people who are strangers to you. A good place to watch people who are unaware of you is an intercity bus station. Describe each one vividly, imagining his or her disposition, likes and dislikes, and interests. Try to envision each one at home, at work, and relaxing.

Compare your character to somebody you know or have known. Visualize that person's appearance, movements, speech, and attitudes. Concentrating on and recalling that individual may help you to develop your character. Try to think of individuals you have seen at fairs, at bargain counters, at work in small shops.

You may *study similar characters* on TV or in movies. If you watch these entertainments with the one purpose in mind of finding a character you could place in your role, you have gained valuable help. You imagine actions, speech, mannerisms, that you hope will fit your character.

Another source of help can be found in old *photographs*. Search through old magazines in libraries, through family photographs. Our ancestors were sturdy folk, usually dressed very plainly when at work, who wore plain hairstyles. Both men and women wore unpressed clothes, except when they attended special occasions.

However, the character you are to enact may be a dressy man, immaculate in attire. You will wish to fit your walk, gestures, and speech to him. Can you see him sitting comfortably erect in a chair or sloppily lounging over it? It will be quite as difficult, but fully as necessary, to find mannerisms for *this* character.

If your character should speak with an accent, you have an interesting assignment. Make a careful study of the sounds you should use and practice carefully, using speech intonations and any characteristic accompanying actions. Almost all peoples who have grown up in foreign lands speak with an accent and the distinctive "tune" of the language. Find mannerisms that make your character distinctive and altogether believable. Keep practicing throughout the rehearsal weeks.

ACTING YOUR CHARACTER

The first performance is always hailed with excitement and nervous tension. It is a time when everything weaves together for the performance; the last-minute weaknesses have been corrected at final rehearsals.

All actors and crews should try to remain calm so that the play can move smoothly. Avoid talking except when a word is essential, and then only in a low whisper, *not undertone* (whispers do not carry; undertones do.) Actors also cooperate with crews by giving them full sway for stage work. The excitement of a first-night performance is contagious. Unless all work to be calm, the green-room and backstage will become noisy.

A performance provides entertainment and diversion for people. The theater depicts the life of other peoples, their prejudices, interests, and dominant attitudes. Listeners have come to enjoy those emotion-filled scenes. They find in them resemblances of people they know, but placed in peculiar and interesting situations.

First-night performances are generally considered choice. Actors give their best performances at that time. There may be a letdown later unless they continue to strive. You should not cheat audiences on the following nights because you are not as highly keyed up. Some audiences don't let you know their feelings because they send fewer empathic responses to you than other audiences. The quieter audiences are often those who enjoy a play more and remember it longer. If an audience *does not seem* to respond to you as much as others, therein lies a challenge for you. Work harder for them; give them your best.

Creating a character is one of the great challenges for the actor. Good characterizations have made many great names for actors and actresses since the beginning of acting for the stage.

In working up your role, *avoid hackneyed actions* and mannerisms. First, know your character's background and the situation in which you now find him or her. Give your character a distinctive personality, original actions, speech, to fit whatever kind of person he or she is, and develop a characterization that you can handle.

Study hard all aspects of creating a character. Make your character an individual with some *distinctive qualities*—more than a stereotyped waiter, butler, soldier, or maid. You are covering your real self with a mask that you must wear every moment you are on stage. Creating a distinctive character is a challenge for any actor.

Richard III by William Shakespeare was presented by Eastern Michigan University. Peter Muschamp, director. Splendid characterization.

Fiddler on the Roof by Joseph Stein, Jerry Bock, and Sheldon Harnick was presented by South Dakota State University. Ray Peterson directed. This well-known musical play carries fine characterization.

Exercises in Pantomine and Improvisation

1. Study the characters of three people who are strangers to you. A good place to watch people is in an intercity bus station. Describe each one vividly, imagining his or her disposition, likes, dislikes and interests. Try to envision each one at home, at work, in relaxation.

2. Impersonate your character in these locations.
   At a bargain necktie counter.
   In a bus depot, impatiently waiting.
   On a park bench, on a hot day.
   Aboard a crowded city bus.
   Trying to swat an annoying fly.
   With arms full of packages, trying to tie a shoelace on the street.

Don't make a peculiar character ridiculous or unbelievable. All your actions should be convincing to the audience. Give special attention to scenes in which your character is on stage but has no lines. Enjoy working on characterization.

Building any role demands thoughtful imagination and often extensive research. The following chapter, "Learning the Language," is simple enough to allow you to relax after the study and research of the previous chapters. You probably know and have been using many of these traditional theater terms. However, it is a good idea to get acquainted with new ones and use the language of the theater in your acting.

Excerpts for Practice

THE PRISONER OF SECOND AVENUE is Neil Simon's tribute to the plight of the little, middle-class guy who gets caught in the middle of society's pressures. At this point, MEL, the title character, has had a nervous breakdown. His brother and three sisters here meet to decide how they can help MEL and his wife, EDNA.

HARRY

PEARL
PAULINE
* JESSIE

SUGGESTIONS AND
STAGE DIRECTIONS

Each of these characters is comic in his or her own way. Try to discover the right combination of voice, body attitudes, gestures, and facial expressions that will make each character distinct.

HARRY (*thinks a moment*). Let me have some coffee. (PEARL *pours him a cup of coffee*) So let's face the facts . . . The man needs help. Who else can he turn to but us? This is my suggestion. We make Mel a loan. We all chip in X number of dollars a week, and then when he gets back on his feet, when he gets straightened out, gets a job again, then he can pay us all back. That's my suggestion. What do you all think?

(*There is a moment's silence.* PAULINE *whispers to to* PEARL. PEARL *nods.*)   1.

PEARL.   Pauline has a question.

HARRY.   What's the question?

PAULINE.   How much is X number of dollars?

HARRY.   X is X. We have to figure out what X is. We'll talk and we'll decide.

PAULINE.   I mean is it a big X or a little x?

HARRY.   It's not even an X. It's a blank until we fill X in with a figure.

PAULINE.   I'm not complaining. We have to do the right thing. But when you say it like that, "X number of dollars," it sounds like a lot of money . . . I have limited capital, you know.

JESSIE.   Everybody has limited capital. Nobody has *un*limited capital. · Pearl, do you have unlimited capital?

PEARL.   I wish I did. I'd give Mel X numbers of dollars in a minute.

PAULINE.   All I'm asking is, how much is X. I can't figure with letters, I have to know numbers.

JESSIE.   Harry, don't say X any more. We're not businesswomen, we don't know about X. Say a number that we can understand.   2.

HARRY.   I can't say a number until I figure out A, how much does Mel need a week, and B, how much are we willing to give. I can't even guess what X is until we figure out how much A and B come to.

PEARL.   All right, suppose we figure out what A is and what B is. And if we know that, then we'll figure what X is, right?

HARRY.   Right.

PEARL.   And now suppose everyone here agrees except one person. She thinks it's too much. She doesn't want to give X. She wants to give M or W, whatever. What do we do then?

1. Since HARRY is in charge (more or less), try having him standing and the three sisters seated, gracefully arranged.

2. There is a lot of comic mileage possible in this "X." Play with it. Use it in different ways.

HARRY.   Forget X. Forget I ever said X. (*He rubs his head and drinks some more coffee*) Let's figure what Mel needs to get over his nervous breakdown . . . His biggest expense is the doctor, right? Edna says he's the best and he has to go five times a week.

PAULINE.   Five times a week to the best doctor? I'm beginning to see what X is going to come to.

JESSIE.   Maybe it's not even a nervous breakdown. Doctors can be wrong, too. Remember your pains last year, Pearl?

PEARL.   It's true. They took out all my top teeth, then found out it was kidney stones.   3.

3. When these three get going, the tempo picks up and the cues close up. HARRY has to top them to break in.

HARRY.   I can't believe what I'm listening to . . . You're a hundred and sixty years old between the three of you and not one of you makes any sense . . . If you'll all be quiet for a minute, I'll settle this thing.

PEARL.   All right, we're quiet. Settle it, Harry.

HARRY.   The most important thing is that Mel gets well, agreed?

ALL THREE.   Agreed!

HARRY.   And that the only way he's going to get well is to see a doctor. Agreed?

ALL THREE.   Agreed.

HARRY.   And it is our obligation, as his only living relatives—not counting his wife, no disrespect intended—to bear the financial responsibility of that burden. Agreed?

ALL THREE.   Agreed.

HARRY.   And we'll all see this thing through to the end whether it takes a week or a month or a year or even five years. Agreed? (4) (*There is stony silence*) Okay. Our first disagreement.

4. HARRY, and perhaps the girls, should react in the rhythm of the previous "Agreeds" until it is realized that this question is different.

PAULINE.   No one's disagreeing. We're all in agreement. Except when you mention things like five years. I don't see any sense in curing Mel and ending up in the poorhouse. If, God forbid, that happened, would he be in any position to help us? He's not too able to begin with.

JESSIE. So what should we do, Harry? You know how to figure these things. What should we do?

HARRY. Well, obviously we can't afford to let Mel be sick forever. We've got to put a time limit on it. Agreed?

ALL THREE. Agreed.

HARRY. What do we give him to get better? Six months?

PAULINE. It shouldn't take six months. If that doctor's as good as Edna says, it shouldn't take six months.

(*The door to the bedroom is heard closing*)

PEARL. Shhh . . . She's coming.

PAULINE. We'll let Harry do the talking.

PEARL. And then we'll settle everything. Thank God, it's almost over.

This scene is from Robert Anderson's play I NEVER SANG FOR MY FATHER. GENE *has just picked up his parents at the train station on their return from a winter in Florida. They have now returned to their home in the suburbs of New York City.* GENE *begins by speaking to the audience.*

GENE   MARGARET (GENE'S mother)   SUGGESTIONS AND
TOM (GENE'S father)   STAGE DIRECTIONS

This short scene is a good exercise in playing credible old age. Play for age in body posture, voice (slower, less pitch variation), and movement (slower, more careful). But do not overdo it! Avoid the rickety, gravel-voiced stereotypes of old age that young actors often fall into.

GENE. (1) My Father's house was in a suburb of New York City, up in Westchester County. It had been a quiet town with elms and chestnut trees, lawns and old sprawling houses with a certain nondescript elegance. My Father had been mayor of this town, a long time ago. . . . Most of the elms and chestnut trees had gone, and the only elegance left was in the pretentious names of the developments and ugly

1. This speech is spoken directly to the audience. The actor should use imagination to picture the scene described.

apartment houses . . . Parkview Meadows Estates . . . only there was no meadow, and no park, and no view except of the neon signs of the chain stores . . . Some old houses remained, like slightly frowzy dowagers . . . The lawns were not well kept, and the houses were not painted as often as they should have been . . . but they remained. My Father's house was one of these . . . (TOM *and* MARGARET *have now started coming in from the back . . .*)

TOM. Just look at this town.

MARGARET. What, dear?

TOM (*Raises his voice in irritation*). Do you have that thing turned on?

MARGARET. Yes.

TOM. I said, "Just look at this town."

MARGARET. I know, dear, but time marches on.

TOM. Junky, ugly mess. (2) When we came here . . .

MARGARET. Don't get started on that. You can't play the show over again.

TOM. I can make a comment, can't I?

MARGARET. But you always dwell on the gloomy side. Look at the good things.

TOM. Like what? . . . I'll bet you Murphy didn't bring the battery back for the Buick. I wrote him. (*He heads for the garage.*)

MARGARET (*To* GENE). I don't know what we're going to do about that car. Your Father shouldn't be driving any more. But they just keep renewing his license by mail . . . (*She moves stiffly, looking at her garden and trees and lawn.*) (3) I must say, there's no place like home. Mmmmm. Just smell the grass.

GENE (*Taking his Mother's arm*). You all right?

MARGARET. It's just my mean old joints getting adjusted . . . I want to look at my garden . . . I think I see some crocuses . . . (*And she moves into shadows to see her garden.*)

TOM (*Coming back*). Well, he did bring it back.

GENE. Good.

2. TOM should really see before him specific elements of this "junky, ugly mess." The actor should visualize a *specific* mess, not a vague mess.

3. MARGARET, too, responds as though there were real trees, flowers, and lawn to examine. Again, use imagination.

TOM. Can't count on anyone these days. Where's your Mother?

GENE. She's walking around her garden.

TOM. What?

GENE. She's walking around her garden.   4.

4. Slower and more distinctly the second time.

TOM. You know, Gene, I don't mean to criticize, but I noticed you're mumbling a great deal. . . . It's getting very difficult to understand you.

GENE (*Friendly . . . hand on Dad's shoulder*).   I think you need a hearing-aid, Dad.

TOM. I can you hear perfectly well if people would only enunciate. "Mr. Garrison, if you would only E-NUN-CIATE . . ." Professor Aurelio, Night School. . . . Didn't you ever have to take any public speaking?

GENE. No, Dad.

TOM. All your education. Well . . . Where did you say your Mother was?

GENE. Walking around her garden.   5.

5. GENE makes sure this time that his father is able to hear.

This scene is from Lewis Carroll's fantasy ALICE IN WONDER-LAND, as adapted for the stage by Eva Le Gallienne and Florida Friebus. ALICE *has wandered into a wonderland by stepping through her looking glass. In one of her strange adventures,* ALICE *wakes to discover herself seated between* THE RED QUEEN *and* THE WHITE QUEEN. *She also finds a crown on her head, a sceptre in her lap, and a string of pearls around her neck.*

ALICE (a seven-and-a-half-year-old girl)
THE RED CHESS QUEEN (bossy)
THE WHITE CHESS QUEEN (anemic)

SUGGESTIONS AND STAGE DIRECTIONS

The two QUEENS are opposites, and both are fantasy creatures. Feel free to exaggerate their qualities in defining their characters. ALICE's normality should seem abnormal next to these two.

ALICE. What *is* this on my head? And how can it have got there without my knowing it? (*She lifts crown down into her lap and examines it.*) Well, this *is* grand. (*She replaces crown on her head.*) I never expected I should be a Queen so soon . . . and if I really am a Queen, I shall be able to manage it quite well in time. (*To the* RED QUEEN.) Would you tell me, please . . . 1.

RED QUEEN.   Speak when you're spoken to!

ALICE.   —But if everybody obeyed that rule, and if you only spoke when you were spoken to, and the other person always waited for *you* to begin, you see nobody would ever say anything, so that— 1.

RED QUEEN.   Ridiculous! Why, don't you see, child— (*She breaks off with a frown, and after thinking a minute, suddenly changes the subject of the conversation.*) What do you mean by "If you really are a Queen"? What right have you to call yourself so? You can't be a Queen till you've passed the proper examination. And the sooner we begin it, the better.

ALICE.   I only said "if"! (*The* Two QUEENS *look at each other.*)

RED QUEEN (*With a shudder*).   She *says* she only said "if"— 1.

WHITE QUEEN (*Moaning and wringing her hands*).   But she said a great deal more than that! Oh, ever so much more than that!

RED QUEEN.   So you did, you know. Always speak the truth—think before you speak—and write it down afterwards.

ALICE.   I'm sure I didn't mean— 1.

RED QUEEN (*Impatiently*).   That's just what I complain of! You *should* have meant! What do you suppose is the use of a child without any meaning? Even a joke should have some meaning—and a child's more important than a joke, I hope. You couldn't deny that, even if you tried with both hands.

ALICE.   I don't deny things with my *hands*.

RED QUEEN.   Nobody said you did. I said you couldn't if you tried.

WHITE QUEEN.   She's in that state of mind that she wants to deny *something*—only she doesn't know what to deny!

RED QUEEN.   A nasty, vicious temper. (*There is an un-*

1. All the interrupted lines at the beginning of the scene require quick handling of cues.

comfortable silence for a second or two. To WHITE QUEEN.) I invite you to Alice's dinner-party this afternoon.

WHITE QUEEN (*Weakly*). And I invite *you*.

ALICE. I didn't know I was to have a party at all, but if there is to be one, I think I ought to invite the guests.

RED QUEEN. We gave you the opportunity of doing it, but I daresay you've not had many lessons in manners yet?

ALICE. Manners are not taught in lessons. Lessons teach you to do sums and things of that sort.

WHITE QUEEN. Can you do Addition? What's one and one and one and one and one and one and one and one and one and one?

ALICE. I don't know. I lost count.

RED QUEEN. She can't do Addition. Can you do Subtraction? Take a bone from a dog: what remains?

ALICE. The bone wouldn't remain, of course, if I took it—and the dog wouldn't remain: it would come to bite me—and I'm sure I shouldn't remain!

RED QUEEN. Then you think nothing would remain?

ALICE. I think that's the answer.

RED QUEEN. Wrong, as usual. The dog's temper would remain.

ALICE. I don't see how—

RED QUEEN. Why, look here! The dog would lose its temper, wouldn't it?

ALICE. Perhaps it would.

RED QUEEN. Then if the dog went away, its temper would remain.

ALICE. They might go different ways. (*Aside.*) What dreadful nonsense we are talking!

BOTH QUEENS. She can't do sums a *bit*.

ALICE (*To* WHITE QUEEN). Can *you* do sums?

WHITE QUEEN (*Gasps and closes her eyes*). I can do Addition, if you give me time—but I can't do Subtraction under *any* circumstances!

RED QUEEN. Of course you know your A B C?

ALICE. To be sure I do.

WHITE QUEEN (*Whispers*). So do I. We'll often say it over together, dear. And I'll tell you a secret—I can read words of one letter! Isn't *that* grand? However, don't be discouraged. You'll come to it in time.

RED QUEEN. Can you answer useful questions? How is bread made?

ALICE. I know *that!* You take some flour—

WHITE QUEEN. Where do you pick the flower? In the garden or in the hedges?

ALICE. Well, it isn't *picked* at all. It's ground— 2.

WHITE QUEEN. How many acres of ground? You mustn't leave out so many things.

RED QUEEN. Fan her head! She'll be feverish after so much thinking. (*They fan her with their scepters.*) She's all right again now. Do you know Languages? What's the French for "Fiddle-de-dee"?

ALICE. Fiddle-de-dee's not English.

RED QUEEN. Who ever said it was?

ALICE. If you'll tell me what language "Fiddle-de-dee" is, I'll tell you the French for it!

RED QUEEN (*Drawing herself up*). Queens never make bargains.

ALICE (*Aside*). I wish Queens never asked questions.

WHITE QUEEN. Don't let us quarrel. What is the cause of lightning?

ALICE. The cause of lightning is the thunder—No, no! I meant the other way.

RED QUEEN. It's too late to correct it. When you've said a thing, that fixes it, and you must take the consequences.

2. The pace of the questions (and the scene) should be dizzying without affecting the diction.

This scene is from John M. Synge's short Irish tragedy, RIDERS TO THE SEA. The old woman MAURYA *has lost a husband and four sons to the sea and now fears that her fifth son,* MICHAEL, *has also drowned. In this scene, she attempts to persuade her last son,* BARTLEY, *not to go out to sea as he is planning to do.* BARTLEY *gives instructions to his two sisters.*

BARTLEY   MAURYA
                                   CATHLEEN
                                   NORA

SUGGESTIONS AND
STAGE DIRECTIONS

This scene requires a
sensitivity to the poetic
qualities of the Irish
dialect. The characters
are defined by their relationship to their mother.
Careful attention to the
props in this scene will
also help define char-
acter.

1. It is essential that you
think carefully about
the set and ground plan
so that all the action
is clear and all props
are well placed.

BARTLEY (*comes in and looks around the room.* (1) *Speaking sadly and quietly*).   Where is the bit of new rope, Cathleen, was bought in Connemara?

CATHLEEN (*coming down*).   Give it to him, Nora; it's on a nail by the white boards. I hung it up this morning, for the pig with the black feet was eating it.

NORA (*giving him a rope*).   Is that it, Bartley?

MAURYA.   You'd do right to leave that rope, Bartley, hanging by the boards. (BARTLEY *takes the rope.*) It will be wanting in this place, I'm telling you, if Michael is washed up tomorrow morning, or the next morning, or any morning in the week, for it's a deep grave we'll make him by the grace of God.

BARTLEY (*beginning to work with the rope*).   I've no halter the way I can ride down on the mare, and I must go now quickly. This is the one boat going for two weeks or beyond it, and the fare will be a good fare I heard them saying below.

MAURYA.   It's a hard thing they'll be saying below if the body is washed up and there's no man in it to make the coffin, and I after giving a big price for the finest white boards you'd find in Connemara. (*She looks around at the boards.*)

BARTLEY.   How would it be washed up, and we after looking each day for nine days, and a strong wind blowing a while back from the west and south?

MAURYA.   If it isn't found itself, that wind is raising the sea, and there was a star up against the moon, and it rising in the night. If it was a hundred horses, or a thousand horses you had itself, what is the price of a thousand horses against a son where there is one son only?

BARTLEY (*working at the halter,* (2) *to* CATHLEEN). Let you go down each day, and see the sheep aren't jumping in on the rye, and if the jobber comes you can sell the pig with the black feet if there is a good price going.

2. Use substitute props if you cannot find the real things.

MAURYA. How would the like of her get a good price for a pig?

BARTLEY (*to* CATHLEEN). If the west wind holds with the last bit of the moon, let you and Nora get up weed enough for another cock for the kelp—It's hard sot we'll be from this day with no one in it but one man to work.

MAURYA. It's hard set we'll be surely the day you're drown'd with the rest. What way will I live and the girls with me, and I an old woman looking for the grave?

(BARTLEY *lays down the halter; takes off his old coat, and puts on a newer one of the same flannel.*)

BARTLEY (*to* NORA). Is she coming to the pier?

NORA (*looking out*). She's passing the green head and letting fall her sails. 3.

3. NORA sees the ship through the window, the ship BARTLEY plans to take.

BARTLEY (*getting his purse and tobacco*). I'll have half an hour to go down, and you'll see me coming again in two days, or in three days, or maybe in four days if the wind is bad——

MAURYA (*turning round to the fire and putting her shawl over her head*). Isn't it a hard and cruel man won't hear a word from an old woman, and she's holding him from the sea?

CATHLEEN. It's the life of a young man to be going on the sea, and who would listen to an old woman with one thing and she saying it over?

BARTLEY (*taking the halter*). I must go now quickly. I'll ride down on the red mare, and the gray pony'll run behind me. (4) . . . The blessing of God on you. (4) . . . (*He goes out.*)

4. He pauses twice, waiting for MAURYA's blessing.

MAURYA (*crying out as he is in the door*). He's gone now, God spare us, and we'll not see him again. He's gone now and when the black night is falling I'll have no son left me in the world.

CATHLEEN. Why wouldn't you give him your blessing and he looking round in the door? Isn't sorrow enough is on everyone in this house without your sending him out with an unlucky word behind him and a hard word in his ear?

(MAURYA *takes up the tongs and begins raking the fire aimlessly without looking round.*)

NORA (*turning towards her*). You're taking away the turf from the cake.

CATHLEEN (*crying out*). The Son of God forgive us, we're after forgetting his bit of bread. (*She comes over to the fire.*)

NORA. And it's destroyed he'll be going till dark night, and he after eating nothing since the sun went up.

CATHLEEN (*turning the cake out of the oven*). It's destroyed he'll be, surely. . . . There's no sense left on any person in house where an old woman will be talking forever.

(MAURYA *sways herself on her stool.*)

CATHLEEN (*cuts off some of the bread and rolls it in a cloth; to* MAURYA). Let you go down now to the spring well and give him this and he passing. You'll see him then and the dark word will be broken and you can say 'God speed you,' the way he'll be easy in his mind.

MAURYA (*taking the bread*). . . . Will I be in it as soon as himself?

CATHLEEN. . . . If you go now quickly.

MAURYA (*standing up unsteadily*). . . . It's hard set I am to walk.

CATHLEEN (*looking at her anxiously*). . . . Give her the stick, Nora, or maybe she'll slip on the big stones.

NORA. What stick?

CATHLEEN. The stick Michael brought from Connemara.

MAURYA (*taking a stick* NORA *gives her*). . . . (5) In the big world the old people do be leaving things after them for their sons and children, but in this place it is the young men do be leaving things behind for them that do be old. (*She goes out slowly.*)

5. MAURYA studies the stick as she speaks.

THE MIKADO, by W. S. Gilbert and Arthur Sullivan, is a musical farce. The MIKADO, *emperor of Japan, has looked forward to his son,* NANKI-POO, *following him as emperor. However, a plan has been afoot to kill the heir apparent and thus usurp the throne for another.*

MIKADO of Japan   KATISHA, an elderly lady
* PISH-TUSH, a noble lord   YUM-YUM, one of three schoolgirls
* NANKI-POO, son of Mikado   PITTI-SING, a schoolgirl
KO-KO, husband of Katisha   * POOH-BAH, a noble lord
CHORUS MEMBERS, MEN   CHORUS MEMBERS, LADIES

SUGGESTIONS AND STAGE DIRECTIONS

These delightful characters always please the audience. Keep all light, humorous.

(*Flourish. Enter the* MIKADO, *attended by* PISH-TUSH *and Court.*)

MIK.   Now then, we've had a capital lunch, and we're quite ready. Have all the painful preparations been made?

PISH.   Your Majesty, all is prepared.

MIK.   Then produce the unfortunate gentleman and his two well-meaning but misguided accomplices.

(*Enter* KO-KO, KATISHA, POOH-BAH, *and* PITTI-SING. *They throw themselves at the* MIKADO's *feet.*)

KAT.   Mercy! Mercy for Ko-Ko! Mercy for Pitti-Sing! Mercy even for Pooh-Bah!

MIK.   I beg your pardon, I don't think I quite caught that remark.

POOH.   Mercy even for Pooh-Bah.

KAT.   Mercy! My husband that was to have been is dead, and I have just married this miserable object.

MIK.   Oh! You've not been long about it!

KO.   We were married before the Registrar.

POOH.   *I* am the Registrar.

MIK.   I see. But my difficulty is that, as you have slain the Heir Apparent——

(*Enter* NANKI-POO *and* YUM-YUM. *They kneel.*)

NANKI.   The Heir Apparent is *not* slain.

MIK.   Bless my heart, my son!

YUM.   And your daughter-in-law elected!

KAT.   (*seizing* KO-KO). Traitor, you have deceived me! 1.

1. KO-KO, kneeling next to his new wife, KATISHA, tries to protect himself as KATISHA takes her vengence on him. She strikes, chokes, and shakes him violently.

Character Study   **155**

MIK.   Yes, you are entitled to a little explanation, but I think he will give it better whole than in pieces.

KO.   Your Majesty, it's like this: It is true that I stated that I had killed Nanki-Poo—— 2.

MIK.   Yes, with most affecting particulars.

POOH.   Merely corroborative detail intended to give artistic verisimilitude to a bald and——

KO.   *Will* you refrain from putting in your oar? (3) (*To* MIKADO.) It's like this: When your Majesty says, "Let a thing be done," it's as good as done—practically, it *is* done—because your Majesty's will is law. Your Majesty says, "Kill a gentleman," and a gentleman is told off to be killed. Consequently, that gentleman is as good as dead—practically, he *is* dead—and if he is dead, why not say so?

MIK.   I see. Nothing could possibly be more satisfactory!

FINALE

PITTI.   For he's gone and married Yum-Yum—

ALL.   Yum-Yum!   4.

PATTI.   Your anger pray bury,
For all will be merry,
I think you had better succumb—

ALL.   Cumb—cumb!

PITTI.   And join our expressions of glee!

KO.   On this subject I pray you be dumb—

ALL.   Dumb—dumb!

KO.   Your notions, though many,
Are not worth a penny,
The word for your guidance is "Mum"—

ALL.   Mum—Mum!

KO.   You've a very good bargain in me.

ALL.   On this subject we pray you be dumb—
Dumb—dumb!
We think you had better succumb—
Cumb—cumb!
You'll find there are many
Who'll wed for a penny,
There are lots of good fish in the sea.

2. KO-KO, with pleading voice and hands, shuffles nearer MIKADO.

3. KO-KO might turn sharply and roar at POO-BAH, a shocking contrast to his pleading voice for MIKADO.

4. Chorus of MEN and LADIES in background might dance a simple uniform rhythmic step to the music.

YUM. *and* NANK.   The threatened cloud has passed
  away,
  And brightly shines the dawning day;
  What though the night may come too soon,
  We've years and years of afternoon!
ALL.   Then let the throng
  Our joy advance,
  With laughing song
  And merry dance,
  With joyous shout and ringing cheer,
  Inaugurate our new career!
  Then let the throng, etc.

CURTAIN

For He's Going to Marry Yum–Yum

Words by
W. S. GILBERT

Music by
ARTHUR SULLIVAN

PART THREE
Preparing for Performance

CHAPTER 9

Learning the Language

As you begin rehearsals with your director, there are terms and basic aspects of acting that you will wish to know. You can help your director if you understand the language of the stage.

ACTOR'S TRADITIONS

Stage Areas. The areas of the stage are labeled *left* and *right* from *upstage* looking toward the audience. They are your own left or right as you look toward the house.

The *stage areas* outlined on the accompanying diagram are only approx-

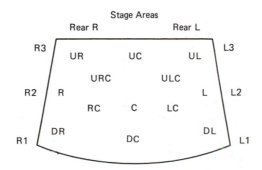

Stage Areas

imate. You may know, however, that *up left center* means a space on stage left, near center, as the actor faces the audience, and that it is farther upstage than downstage. *Center stage* is the strongest acting area; most acting pivots about it.

Body Positions. Body positions should look comfortable even though you may feel strained. Remember to *stand tall* and to take shorter steps than on the street because acting should look like life—steps look longer on the stage, although gestures look smaller. When you sit down on a sofa or chair, it is wise to back toward the seat until you feel it against your knee. When you rise, edge to the front of the seat, then, with one foot back, bear the weight on it to bring you to your feet.

A graceful female character, when seated, will cross her feet at the ankles, instead of crossing her knees. If the dialogue indicates that you are deeply concerned, keep an alive physical bearing. A "straight" character will remain poised. Other characters might be fidgety, toying nervously with some small object or constantly moving about. Movements should be in character and suitable to the scene.

Your *standing position* can help or hinder your performance. A *full front* position is seldom used, though in older plays it was very popular. *Full back* can be used for highly dramatic scenes. *Profile* position can be effective when there is a heated argument or when one actor is intently listening to another, but it is used sparingly. A *quarter* position is a quarter turn away from the audience, used in most scenes. Two characters share a scene in this position. The upstage foot is slightly in advance of the other foot, which

Quarter

Profile

Three-quarters
and Quarter

Full Front
Full Back

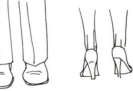

allows the audience to see the actor's face and action better. *Three-quarter* position gives the advantage to one character, used when the one in quarter position deserves dominance in the scene.

Giving Focus. "Giving focus" means arousing interest by any of several theatrical devices. Special visual interest is needed often to further the plot or make a character important, or give hints of some approaching danger or surprise.

Your *eyes* are agents that help spectators to see and *focus* on something important to the play. Your planned eye focus draws others to look at the spot or character to which you have led them. Almost anything can be made important by focusing on it, even unpleasant weather. Spoken lines are not essential to pointing up an important object. An audience may become curious, then suspect some danger—or delight, if the play is light-hearted.

Planting. By eye focus, casual actions, or a combination of both, you can "plant" by emphasizing ideas significant to the plot or by hinting at forebodings through bringing to mind some item that will play a part later in the play. There need be no lines at all. Suppose that Uncle Hank, who is to be robbed later in the play, takes out his wallet during the first act and counts his money. He has no lines and other characters take no notice. However, later, when he knows exactly what kind of bills were stolen, the audience will believe him because of this *plant.*

Characters can be *emphasized* in many different ways. Here is a limited list of methods.

1. Place character downstage center, upstage center, or with open space on all sides.
2. Players can be on contrasting levels: use of steps, platform, chair, throne, or table. Character may sit on floor with others standing, lie on couch with others above, stand while others are seated, or sit while others stand.
3. Spotlight space into which character will come. Center spot on character.
4. Clothes of character may be different, outstanding: bright color while others are drab, black while others wear white or light, or style very different.
5. Characters heard speaking offstage, whistle, or sound of horses' hoofs; then character enters, or there is auto horn or call. Character may pass window seen by audience, or knock on door.
6. Players hear somebody coming. They focus on entrance, may run to look through window, then primp or straighten room.
7. Characters suddenly stop whatever they are doing, seem greatly surprised. Focus on entering character.
8. Character framed in doorway, on stairs, in apex of a strong triangle, or on a level where lines of scenery converge.
9. Minor characters enter, group about entrance, are talkative, but suddenly become quiet, focus on entrance.
10. Provide long suspense-filled pause in dialogue, seem expectant.

GLOSSARY OF THEATER TERMS

Like many other trades and occupations, the theater has its own colorful language. Each expression originated to fulfill a need. Note these:

ABOVE   Upstage of (as in the direction, "Cross above the sofa").

AD LIB   To extemporize during a performance.

AMATEUR   One who works in the theater without pay.

AMBER   Soft yellow light used for stage lighting.

ANTICLIMAX   An event noticeably less important than preceding event, often directly following climax.

APRON   That part of stage projecting in front of curtain.

ASBESTOS: Fireproof curtain, located between stage and audience.

ASIDE   Line to audience or other character, not noticed by other characters on stage.

BACKSTAGE   Portion of theater not included in auditorium and stage proper.

BATTEN   Movable pipe above the stage, used for hanging scenery.

BELOW   Downstage of (as in "cross below the sofa").

BIT PART   Role with very few lines, if any, or little action.

BLANK   Mental fade-out causing lines or business to be forgotten.

BLEND   Actors move closer together, close gaps.

BOARD   Diagram of theater seating plan, used in box office.

BOMB   Theatrical dud.

BOOK   Play manuscript.

BOOKING   To hire companies or actors.

BORDERLIGHT   Strip of reflectors to light stage from overhead.

BUILD   To bring a scene to a climax by increasing volume, emphasis, pace, or intensity.

BURLESQUE   Exaggerated acting, often referred to as "ham."

BUSINESS   Stage action.

BYPLAY   Stage action that helps to characterize, usually side action or mannerisms.

CALL   Warning to actors to be ready for entrace.

CALLBOARD   Bulletin board backstage on which are posted important notices for actors and crews.

CATTLE CALL   The type of audition at which many actors are present.

CATWALK   Ledge near overhead lights, used by electricians.

CHARACTER PART   Role depicting unusual individual.

CHORUS   Group of singers, dancers, or speakers, working in unison.

CIVIC THEATER   Noncommercial theater.

CLEAR STAGE   Command to leave stage.

CLOSE IN   Move closer together.

CLOSE THE CUES   Shorten time spaces between cues and the following lines; pick up tempo. Also PICK UP CUES.

COME DOWN   Approach part of stage nearer audience.

COUNTER   Balancing move in opposite direction made by one actor to counter cross of another.

COVER   To attempt to hide mistakes in lines or action. Also, to block another character from audience's view.

CREPE HAIR   Wool-like substance used for making beards.

CROSS   Actor's movement from one part of stage to another; abbreviated by "X."

CUE   Last words of a speech, signaling another to speak or enter.

CUE SHEET   List of cues for stage noises, light changes. Notations in prompt copy.

CURTAIN GOING UP   Signal to cast that scene is ready to begin.

CURTAIN LINE   Imaginary line where front curtain hangs between audience and stage. Also, last line of play.

CYC   Cyclorama or backdrop.

DIRECTOR   One who plans and directs the play for production.

DOWNSTAGE   Toward the audience.

DRAMATIS PERSONAE   Latin, meaning persons in the play.

ENSEMBLE   Group of players acting together.

EQUITY   Actors' Equity Association, an actors' union.

FAKE   To seem to be doing something without doing it.

FEATURED   Billing secondary only to starting.

FLATS   Pieces of scenery for mounting, consisting of canvas or muslin stretched over a frame.

FLIES   Space directly above stage into which scenery is raised.

FLOP   Theater production that fails.

FOCUS   To center attention on something.

FOLK DRAMA   Play originating in legend or popular lore.

FOOTS   Footlights.

FOURTH WALL   Imaginary side of room toward audience.

FULL SET   Use of entire stage.

GAG   (Slang) Highly noticeable twist of comedy.

GIVE STAGE   Move to less important position.

GREASEPAINT   Mixture of grease and coloring, used in theatrical makeup.

GREEN ROOM   Lounge near stage used by actors, author, and director.

GRIPS   Stage hands.

GROUND CLOTH   Large canvas covering floor or acting areas to muffle footsteps.

GROUND ROW   Low flats set on stage floor for scenic background.

GROUPING   Placing of cast about stage.

HAM   Actor who is bad but thinks he is good.

HAND PROPS   Items that actors carry onstage for business.

HANDBILL   Printed sheet stating title, cast, date, theater, or play.

HARE'S FOOT   Good luck charm used to apply dry rouge.

HEADLINER   Star or leading player.

HEAVY   Usually villain of cast, or adult in serious role.

HOKUM   Sure-fire stock situation, good for laughs.

HOLD   Keep position without moving.

HORSEPLAY   Rude, boisterous playing.

HOUSE   Audience.

INGENUE   Young girl playing love interest.

IN THE RED   Losing money on show.

INTERVIEW AUDITION   Private audition, opposite of cattle-call.

JURY   First-night audience.

JUVENILE   Player of youthful male roles.

IMPROVISATION   Short bit with lines and action created by actor. Often used as rehearsal exercise.

IMPROVISE   Unprepared lines and action, often needed to cover.

KILL   To eliminate a piece of scenery or property from set, or to black out the lights.

KNOCKOUT   Sure-fire hit.

LEAD   Actor playing the most prominent or important part.

LEVELS   Acting areas placed higher than stage level.

LINES   Speeches of play.

MASQUE   Early dramatic presentation of mythology.

MILK IT DRY   (Slang) Squeeze the most laughs from line or expression.

MIME   Use of gestures and actions rather than words.

MONOLOGUE   Protracted speech by one person.

NOTICES   Reviews, clippings, dramatic criticism.

OFFSTAGE   Area of the stage not enclosed by set.

ONSTAGE   Portion of stage enclosed by set and visible to audience.

OPEN UP   Turn more toward audience.

OUT FRONT   Area occupied by audience.

OVERLAP   Picking up cue before previous speaker has finished.

PACE   Timing of lines and action.

PACES   Steps, as "Move two paces down right."

PACKING THE HOUSE   Filling theater for performance.

PANNING   Unfavorable reviewing.

PANTOMIME   Currently synonymous with mime; acting without words.

PIT   Orchestra area in modern theaters.

PICK UP CUES   To begin speaking immediately after last line of previous speaker.

PLACES   Signal for cast to take places for opening curtain.

PLANT   1. Person stationed in audience who has function in play.
2. Line, idea, or character that significantly foreshadows some important element coming later in play.

POINT-UP or **POINT**   To emphasize: play-up idea or character.

POSITION   Actor's place on stage as set by director.

PROMPT BOOK or **PROMPT SCRIPT**   Script marked with directions and cues for use of prompter.

PROPERTIES   ("PROPS") All objects on stage exclusive of scenery.

QUICK STUDY   One who can memorize a part quickly.

RAKE   Gradual slope of auditorium floor. Raked house or raked stage.

RAMP   Sloping walk leading to higher elevation.

REPERTORY   Collection of plays that may be readily performed because of familiarity to actors.

REP SHOW   Company playing repertory.

REVAMP   To rewrite scene or play by bringing it up to date.

REVOLVING STAGE   Turntable stage.

REVUE   Musical comedy, without plot.

RING DOWN   Close front curtain, often in emergency.

ROYALTY   Fee charged by publishers to present play.

RUN   Length of engagement.

RUN THROUGH   To rehearse play without stopping.

SCENE   Division of an act; usually refers to short section where there is change of characters.

SCHTICK   Bits of clichéd character business designed to get laughs.

SCRIPT   Typewritten or printed copy of play.

SHOE-STRING PRODUCTION   Production with minimum of financial expenditure.

SIDES   Pages of manuscript paper holding an actor's lines and cues.

SITTING ON THEIR HANDS   (Slang) Unresponsiveness of audience.

SITUATION   Plot.

SRO   Standing room only.

STAGE CALL   Meeting of cast and director on stage for instructions.

STAGE DIRECTIONS   Instructions in script of play.

STAGE HANDS   Helpers employed backstage.

STAGE LEFT   Actor's left when facing audience.

STAGE MANAGER   Person responsible for play in production; calls cues for actors, lights, sound, set changes.

STAGE RIGHT   Actor's right when facing audience.

STAGE STAFF   Helpers for technical aspects of production.

STAGE SUPERSTITIONS   *Bad luck:* (1) being wished good luck; (2) whistling in dressing room; (3) using old rabbit's foot for new makeup; (4) opening telegrams before first performance. *Good luck:* (1) pocketful of coins; (2) cat backstage; (3) wearing old shoes associated with hit; (4) wishing player bad luck ("Break a leg").

STAGE WHISPER   Whisper loud enough for audience to hear.

STEAL A SCENE   To call attention to yourself when it should be elsewhere.

STOCK   Company performing new play every week.

STRAIGHT MAKEUP   Makeup bringing out natural features.

STRIKE   Call given to stage crew to remove scenery or dismatle the entire production.

STROLLING PLAYERS   Traveling actors.

TABLEAU   Living picture posed by players.

TAG   Line at climax (pointing up preceding speech).

TAKE A CALL   Bow before audience.

TAKE STAGE   Move into stronger stage position.

TEASER   Shallow overhead drapery used to mask lighting equipment.

TECH DIRECTOR   Person responsible for all production crews.

TELESCOPING   Beginning to speak before other has finished, in order to build scene.

THE ROAD   Area outside New York played by touring companies.

THE STICKS   Small towns played by touring companies.

TOPPING CUES   Pitching voice higher or louder than cues.

TORMENTER   Flats or drapes at sides, upstage of act curtain, used to mask backstage.

TRAP   Opening in stage floor.

TROUPER   Seasoned actor who always works for play's best interest.

TURKEY   Theatrical flop or "bomb."

TURN IN, TURN OUT   Turn your body toward or away from others.

UNDERSTUDY   Actor capable of playing another's role in emergency.

UPSTAGE   Toward rear stage.

UPSTAGING   Moving upstage to gain audience's attention, thus compelling cast to turn.

WALK-ON   Minor role with few lines.

WARDROBE   Costumes and articles of dress for production.

WINGS   Space at either side of stage, behind the scene.

X   Abbreviation for "cross," as in XDL (cross down left.)

THEATER ARCHITECTURE

There are many types of stages, including the great out-of-doors. Let us consider three types. The *Proscenium arch stage* is found in more theaters than any other type. The audience sits all in one direction, facing the stage. The stage is closed at the back and on two sides. An *arena stage* has an open place at center for the acting, which the audience completely surrounds. A few open aisles are used by actors to go to and from dressing rooms. It is an intimate type of theater, as the actors play to an audience that surrounds them. A *thrust stage* (or *apron stage*) has one closed rear wall. The audience is seated on three sides. Scenery and props are changed in dimmed light, and there is no front curtain to draw.

If you play on stages of recent architectural design, you will need to rethink stage positions. When playing on an *arena* stage, some players will play with backs to spectators part of the time. It is helpful if actors change position frequently in order to face different directions. Three-quarter positions are practical for arena playing so that all the audience can see one face of a team of players.

Almost any area, small or large, can be a stage. Wagon beds were stages in the sixteenth and seventeenth centuries; barns have been theaters with stages since the 1930s. From the beginnings of theater down to the present, the great out-of-doors has been an acceptable, even favorite, space to present plays. Voices must be big or penetrating for outdoor theaters unless there is a good sounding board.

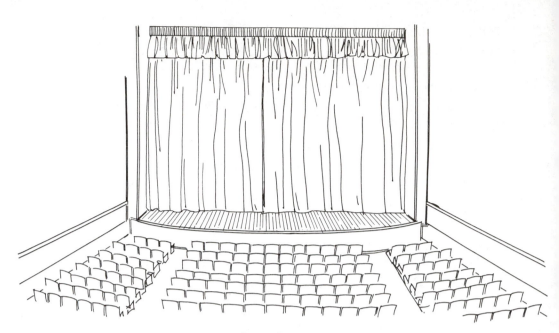

Proscenium stage.

Arena stage.

Thrust stage (or apron stage).

Many terms explained in this chapter were undoubtedly familiar to most of you before you read them. Activity in local and educational theaters is so much a part of people's lives today that you probably covered the material quickly.

Learning theater language leads naturally into the following section for study, "Blocking Stage Action." Since this is the director's job, actors should not interfere unless asked for suggestions. However, it would be a good study for you to block scenes before the director does, just to see how many different interpretations can be used.

CHAPTER 10

Blocking Stage Action

A director seeks to help the cast understand their interpretation of the script and to help each player find the relationship which his or her character has to other characters and to the play as a whole—not only psychologically, but in terms of physical positions and movements.

Directors think of movement mainly as crossing the stage, taking steps, entering, backing away, and going into groups or out of them. They must concern themselves with finding motivation for each move, and directing players to suit their movements to the characters they are playing. Directors like to plan effective groupings and stage pictures which involve line, mass, movement, color, emphasis, and action.

The first blocking rehearsal is usually slow and full of changes as the director moves characters from place to place, which helps him or her visualize general atmosphere. Study of characterization can come later. If time is not too limited, many directors will rehearse a segment of the play several times to help *set* movement in the minds of the cast.

In order to save rehearsal time, some directors plan stage movement with bits of pasteboard, or colored paper, pushing these "players" about on a cardboard "stage" to work out smoothness and effects. However, this cannot be as satisfactory as working onstage.

MOVEMENT

Movement and *business* are very closely related, but they are not quite the same. A director who says he or she is going to work out the business for a play is referring to planning specific actions for the players and their movements about the stage. Business should be set in advance of performances and fully rehearsed. This inspiration that comes with an audience often suggests possible embellishments. Never use these ideas unless you are sure they are entirely appropriate, will not confuse any other player, and will have the approval of the director. After a play is set, it should stay set except for necessary changes.

Many people have a hand in planning stage movement—dramatist, director, and members of the cast if their director has invited suggestions. "No movement without a purpose" is a good rule to remember.

Purposes of Movement. The purposes of movement are many. A few of them are:

To set the mood	To add force, power, and speed
To dress stage appropriately	To free players' tensions
To open space for others	To reveal feelings such as anxiety,
To characterize	nervousness, sorrow, and delight
To emphasize importance	To secure appropriate rhythm
To dress the stage	To show relationship

Do's and Dont's of Movement

DO:	*DON'T:*
Cooperate to maintain balance	Sidle
Move in the rhythm of the play	Stand in a semi-circle
Speak and move in character	Stand in a straight line
Use full playing space of stage	Stand equal distance apart
Group in twos, threes, fours, fives	Bunch
Help maintain stage pictures	Get out of character
Keep your relationship with others	Cover or be covered
Give stage smoothly	
Listen with your mind	

Don't stand in a semicircle.

Don't stand in a straight line across the stage.

Don't bunch.

Principles of Movement. The following principles of movement have been developed through stage experience. They are not rules—acting in the theater defies rules, and principles need to be modified at times to fit the needs of directors and actors. Observe these principles—except when they need to be broken.

1. You usually *cross toward* the objective point. If grace and beauty in the scene are desired, cross in a curved line.
2. Always move in *character*.
3. In general, cross on your own lines.
4. Your speech may be broken while you cross behind others.
5. When two cross together, the speaker usually walks upstage and slightly in advance of the other, turning head downstage to speak.
6. When several enter in a group, *the speaker enters first*.
7. To open an area for an important character, move smoothly.
8. *Countercross.* When a character in U.L.C. crosses stage to an area on stage R., a character at R. may countercross to some area on L. to retain good balance.
9. *Movements* on stage seem *stronger* than the same movement offstage. A step looks like a stride; a slump looks droopier; a sway appears broader. Avoid curved backbone, rounded shoulders, and careless walk, except for roles that require them for characterization.
10. You may address a part of your speech to a character across the stage, then walk toward that one as you speak.
11. Relationship often dictates a cross. Characters should be close together for heated arguments, happy friendships, and secretive dialogue, but apart for small differences.
12. There are some emphatic *dont's*: Don't stand in a straight line; don't bunch; don't stand in a semicircle.
13. A player may *drift, edge, walk*, or *ease* into place, depending upon mood, character, and atmosphere. Appropriate rhythm must be maintained—walk fast when speaking rapidly, slowly when speaking slowly. *Don't mix slow and fast paces.*
14. Cross at the correct instant so that speech is completed exactly with movement. Rehearse carefully to time all to the finish.
15. A cross either before or after the line can emphasize it. (Example: Henry may say, "Frank, this time my car makes the trip"; then turn and walk briskly out. Or Henry may walk to the door, pick up his briefcase, turn, speak his line, and go out. If he should walk while speaking, the line would lose its force.)
16. Usually turn toward rather than away from audience, unless this involves a wide awkward turn. If so, turn easiest way.
17. When sitting down, either turn and go to the chair or step back until its edge is against the back of your knee.
18. Backing a step or two toward an exit just before leaving shortens the distance to walk. You may speak, turn, walk to the door, finish your speech.
19. *Taking stage* and *giving stage* should become second nature. The actor on

whom interest is centered usually *takes stage*—that is, moves into a more desirable position; others near that spot *give stage* by backing away, or walking to another place.

20. "Assume your character and walk twenty paces before reaching your stage entrance," is an old principle and a good one. *Any* entrance is important. Make it seem right. Players often weaken their entrances by coming on stage so late that they cannot reach the planned location to speak their line on cue. They don't assume their character until it is time to speak, whereas they should get in character before entering.

GROUPING

To know the principles and *purpose* of grouping helps actors relate to other characters and to the work of the director. Work for effective groupings. One purpose of artistic stage grouping is to generate a pleasing psychological effect, a kind of pleasure people go to the theater for. The director works for contrasts in keeping with the mood of the play: bright spots contrasting with shadows, and contrasts in mass, in spaces, in colors, in forms.

Effective contrasts are used in Maeterlinck's *The Intruder*. The three sisters, dressed alike in white and always grouped together, lend contrast to the fearful old grandfather in his somber gray shawl and black skullcap. Dark, somber colors suggest foreboding, worry, or sadness, whereas bright or gay colors suggest happiness and bright spirits.

There are several *purposes* of effective grouping. *Relationships* are indicated through groupings of characters. They are usually close together for bright, happy scenes, but also for fierce disapproval and conflicts. Minor differences may be played by keeping characters across stage from each other.

Grouping can *emphasize* the importance of a *character* or characters, or the importance of a subject. The important character or discussion of the important subject can be played in a prominent position. Psychologically, characters who talk together secretly must be close together, even though their whispers must be heard by those in the back of the house.

One of the chief purposes of effective grouping is to give *visual pleasure* to the audience. Just as a painter works for pleasing line, balance, color, and light and dark contrasts, so the theater artist works to give aesthetic pleasure through stage arrangements. An actor can help through an understanding of stage balance. All mass, including stage setting, furniture, and characters, contributes to *stage balance*. However, not only mass, but also importance of characters, is involved in balance. Balance of characters really means balance of interest. One dominant character on one side of the stage can balance a dozen minor characters on the other side.

Movement is a prime consideration in *stage balance*. Drama is action, so

Picnic by William Inge was presented by Eastern Michigan University, and directed by Parker R. Zellers. This is an effective arrangement, natural and pictorial.

The Imaginary Invalid by Moliere. Play presented by Brandeis University; directed by Daniel Gidron. Photograph by Ralph Norman. Fine grouping points to center of interest.

stage balance is constantly changing. This often involves *counter-cross-ing*—when a character goes across stage, an empty spot is left which another character can move across to fill or to balance in some other way. It is really only a shifting of positions. The cross should be motivated if possible, or at any rate be unobtrusive.

Counter-crosses share in effecting groupings. Visualize this, for example. Hank and Tom are at a table L., playing chess. Allen moves from his easy chair at R. to watch the game. Then Mike comes from U.L., down to pick up a newspaper and lounge in the easy chair vacated by Allen. This is a counter-cross which Mike motivated by picking up the paper. Countercrossing is difficult and subtle until it is practiced.

When two or three players are involved in dialogue, be careful that you do not "upstage" your playing partner, by taking a position upstage of that

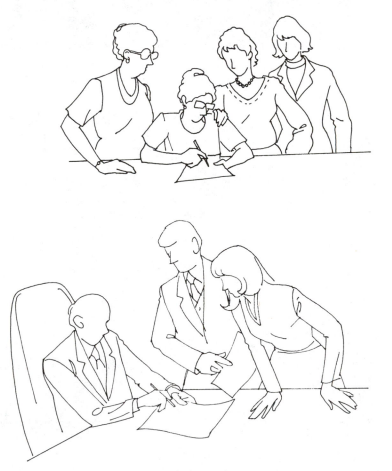

Grouping for stage pictures.

character so that your face is toward the audience and he is in a three-quarters position with his face largely turned away from them.

A character usually holds a single position for only a short time. The audience needs to see change of positions and movements. Also, in all speech and action keep to the mood of the play but use variety and contrast—speed up to slow down, shift position if seated, change from soft to loud voice.

Stage Pictures. Stage pictures are largely a matter of grouping, tied in with stage furnishings, color, movement, and balance. An irregular line is, in general, more pleasing than a straight line, a square, a blob, or large mass. This principle carries over strongly into theater, where actors together with stage settings can have important psychological effects on their audience.

The use of triangles is pleasing to the human eye. Your own share in maintaining stage pictures involves your posture, position in relation to other characters, and movement. Keep movement in mind but also think of triangular shapes when you shift position. Players who sidle or edge out of place can quickly destroy the effect. Become conscious of grouping, always watching to keep the arrangements interesting, and using triangles as the basis for many pictorial effects.

STAGE SPECTACLE

Lights, color, stage setting, movements, and characters may all be involved in making up stage spectacle. The director and designer have visualized and planned the oversize picture and have adjusted their plan to the acting space available. If a large group is in a scene, they can create a beautiful spectacle with effective lighting and good colorful or drab, beautiful or ugly costumes.

A spectacle may be almost entirely the result of stage scenery, or it may involve a large number of actors working in unified rhythm. Although your director may describe quite vividly the plans and how scenes are to be played on the playing space, you may have a problem adjusting to steps, levels, entrances, groupings, and movement when the set is finally in place and being used; also move with care, appropriately, in your costume.

Lighting must be adjusted and rehearsed many times with the actors. You need to be patient and cooperative. You won't need to try your costumes at the same time; that will come later. However, it is helpful to improvise if you are to wear something that you are not used to.

Most spectacles involve action, which you and your director will need many rehearsals to work on. Some spectacles use dance or action routines in which all perform the same action simultaneously, as in *The Volga Boatman*, in which all the men pull oars together simultaneously. Other spectacle scenes use only the same basic action, as when all raise arms or point but not

Camino Real by Tennessee Williams was given by Washburn University, and directed by Hugh G. Mc-Causland. Here a very large cast faces away from the audience. One character is emphasized.

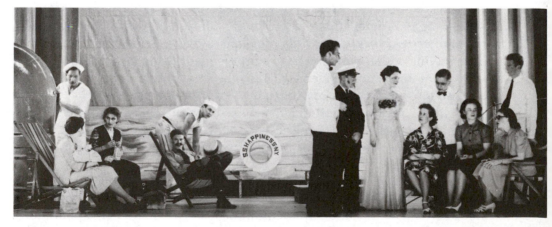

Excursion by Victor Wolfson shows a number of passengers on an excursion boat trip. There are diversified interests in the excursion. One actress is counter focusing. Presented at Grove City College. Miriam A. Franklin, director.

in exactly the same way. However, the action is synchronized into an all-over pattern. For example, in *The Eternal Road* by Franz Werfel, staged by Max Reinhardt, many Jews toil for Pharaoh in small groups. Their actions blend, creating a rhythm peculiar to the play. Slaves perform, symbolically, different tasks: men lifting bricks and stacking them, women with enormous palm fans waving them over and around a princess, a group pulling a heavy load with a rope. Directors look over papers, and slave masters watch workers from an elevated platform. All these small groups blend into one large picture.

GROUP ACTIONS

Here is an important principle which needs to be repeated often: In a large group, when dialogue shifts from one character to another, the next speaker should "signal" the audience in some way to let them know who is speaking. The signal may be a noticeable hand gesture, a head movement, leaning forward, or taking a step or two. Other players may help by focusing noticeably on the speaking character. It is very annoying to the audience to hear an actor speaking and be unable to find the speaker until the speech is almost finished. Everybody wants to *see*, as well as *hear*, the play. You must *listen* carefully to *catch cues* from other onstage groups.

Some large groups on stage are involved in ensemble action. This can be very effective if all work together. The action may have individual differences, although all may use the same action, as in all raising arms

Arrange even small groups on different levels.

A stage having different levels offers opportunity for pictorial effects.

together, all swaying at the same time, all bowing together. When such a scene is planned, be sure that you act according to the mood of the play. If all are raising hands in supplication, all hands should look as if they were pleading; a simultaneous bowing should show real respect. Some large groups are divided into segments, each with a different appropriate action. Notice the illustration of the sailors on a ship.

Maintain spaces between groups. Separate groups use appropriate business for ensemble effect.

Using stage levels offers greater opportunity for interesting grouping.

Those in the rear of a group must guard against being covered.

Dramatic positions enhance pictorial effects.

STAGE BUSINESS

In the language of the theater, stage business includes movements about the stage, the use of various props, and all the other movements and gestures that the audience sees. You may say "I don't care," by merely shrugging your shoulders, or "Come on, let's move in closer," with a suggestive jerk of your head. Shakespeare observed in *A Winter's Tale*, "There was speech in their dumbness, language in their very gesture."

All business should be carefully rehearsed. You may not have real props to work with before dress rehearsal, but you can rehearse with fakes. Use a pile of books for a typewriter, an eraser for a gun, or some notepaper for dishes.

Business needs to be *opened up* so that the audience can see all of it—better yet, so they *can't miss it*. Conversely, some business needs to be covered, such as lighting a kerosene lamp that is really electrified.

Gesture. Gesture is a part of stage business. It refers to moving a part of your body to help express a thought, feeling, point out an idea or place, emphasize, or assist in the development of character. Any hand gesture should start from the shoulder. Some actors tend to hug their ribs with their elbows, using only the forearm to gesture. That's not enough. Even a small hand action should use the whole arm.

When you gesture, carry the movement out to the tip of your fingers. It's irritating to watch a gesture that stops at the wrist. If the idea is important enough to use gesture, your whole hand should show the feeling.

It is an art to complete a piece of business at exactly the right instant. Some must finish exactly on the last syllable of the last word. Practice dropping into a chair on the last word of this speech: "After a day like this, boy, am I tired!" Business and lines need to correlate. When movement plays a part in a line, first, think in character; second, look at the spot; third, go to it; finally, speak the line. *Remember: thought—look—action—words.*

Definite and Indefinite Business. *Definite* and *indefinite* business have slightly different meanings. If the play itself suggests specific action, it is known as *definite* business. Such business may come ahead, on, or following the line: "It's getting late, I'll bring some coffee."

Indefinite business is action added by the director or actors to aid characterization, create atmosphere, or show state of mind. Some examples could be constantly tapping a foot, twirling a mustache, getting up, taking a step or two and sitting down again. It could be turning the pages of a magazine, rolling it, squinting through the roll, tapping it on the arm of a chair. Pieces of clothing may be toyed with in indefinite business: hats, ruffles, a handkerchief, glasses. If the play is a costume play, plan ahead of time what actions might be suitable.

Many beginning players don't know what to do with their *hands*; they feel heavy and any action feels unnatural. To overcome this feeling, carry some kind of item for use in indefinite action. Also, use your hands *more* than enough until they do not feel unnatural when gesturing.

Blocking stage action continues during the weeks of rehearsal, with making changes here and there, adding new action, smoothing out movement on stage, and working to see that timing is right. It is only in the last rehearsals that movement and business are set and no changes are desirable. Never put any new action or movement into the play on inspiration that comes when you are before the audience. Such action should have approval of your director. If changes or adjustments are needed, they should be planned and rehearsed between productions.

Blocking stage action is a slow, tedious procedure that demands many tries and retries. Story development and relationships are shown through action. Group arrangements change to lend variety and create pleasing stage pictures. Some characters are placed for strength, others to support the leads. All action demands patience and cooperation.

OCCASIONAL ACTION

Occasionally an actor must perform so that an action looks real but is performed in a certain way to avoid injury or to become accustomed to an unfamiliar action. Here are some suggestions.

Falling. Take a stage fall a little at a time. In falling to one side, drop from ankle, to knee, to hip, to shoulder. In falling forward, crumple down, breaking the fall by knees, hands, shoulder. In falling backward, place one foot back to support your body as you drop, and then go on down. Sometimes you can fall behind a piece of furniture to hide the technique. After a stabbing or shooting, the victim may stagger a few steps and then crumple down.

Embraces. Amateurs often rehearse love scenes too little, and then the performance is not convincing. Learn to gaze into each other's eyes, to press cheeks together, and to kiss when this is called for. Kisses can be covered in most plays to avoid lipstick blotches; the woman's face upstage, the man's head bent over hers. A kiss should be comparably short; lovers in tight embrace are often more effective.

Struggling and Fighting. John Wayne described fist fights this way: "... one actor eventually throwing a haymaker that just misses the opponent's chin, while the foe flips backward in a picturesque sprawl."*

Reader's Digest, September 1970.

You may strike between the actor's chest and his upstage arm. Use the same technique in sword fights—the blade passes between body and upstage arm. When a shooting takes place on stage, the killer stands downstage of the person shot; thus, the gun is pointed away from the audience. Practice fully any fight, with arms, face, and body showing tension. After rehearsing fully, *don't change anything.*

Slaps. A slap can be faked by a hand open-palm thrust up to a quarter-inch from the face, then suddenly stop. At that instant, the receiver throws his head to one side, as if he has been struck. Exactly on time he claps his hands together to make the sound of a slap. The audience is watching only the slap, not the hands. This little scene provides for such action:

JENNIE.   You're always playing tricks—hateful tricks! (*She jerks her hand away from him.*)

DENNIS.   Now you know you like holding hands.

JENNIE.   Do I? I hadn't noticed!

DENNIS (*grasping her hand again*).   Jennie, don't try to be haughty.

JENNIE.   Let go my hand!

DENNIS.   I love to see you bristle!

JENNIE (*furiously*).   Let go my hand!

DENNIS.   You know you like it.

JENNIE.   You brute! (*She gives him a sound slap. He grabs her and kisses her.*)

Fainting. You must know how to relax—*completely!* In a faint, your head, arms, legs, eyelids, fingers—all parts of the body—go limp and drop of their own weight. If a shoe drops, or hairdo gets mussed, okay! You are unconscious.

Bowing, Kneeling, Curtseying. When you, as a man, make a courtly bow, hold your back straight, bend from hips; your hand may be held in front of your waist. A lady's courtly bow drops low, weight on the back foot, the other foot forward for support. Often the sides of a full skirt are held out from the sides. In modern life, people make slight bows with head and shoulders. *Kneeling* should be done by bending the downstage knee to the floor and resting the weight on it. It is easy to rise from this position.

Eating and Drinking. It is better to actually eat and drink than to pantomine the action. Time your small bites or sips so that action will not interfere with lines. Take some lessons from television. Use foods that are not dry: raw apples, canned peaches, perhaps spaghetti, bread and butter. Most of these can be cut into inconspicuous bites. Water is probably the safest drink, or tea, coffee, grape or orange juice, or Koolaid may be used. When drinking a hot beverage, make it *look hot* by the way you hold your cup and sip cautiously.

Smoking. Whether a character is smoking a cigarette, pipe, or cigar, he must remove it from his lips while speaking. Time the action so that it does not interfere with lines. If you are interpreting a crude character you may speak while smoking, but your lines must be understood by all.

Drunkenness. A drunk scene can easily be overacted. Alcohol paralyzes brain cells so that one cannot control movements or speech. Be sure to decide on the right stage of drunkenness: blurred speech with loose actions; loud-mouthed and quarrelsome; slap-happy; or dead drunk, oblivious to everything.

Dying. Usually dying is played slowly, with shortness of breath, lines broken, voice weak. Lines must be projected by stage whisper to be heard. A death scene can be made more effective by the actions of the other characters on stage than by the dying character's actions.

Improvisations for Unusual Actions

Falling

1. You met with an accident a few weeks ago which caused your knee to weaken. As your young son tries to drive the family car through a narrow opening, you stand facing him and backing away as you guide his driving. You back into an object which causes your knee to give way, and you fall.

2. You have been stacking firewood on the back porch. As you are carrying in a large armload you stumble over a roller skate and fall forward.

3. You and a friend are taking a brisk walk through a timbered area. The friend stumbles over a fallen tree branch. As you reach to help her, you, too, fall and sprain your ankle.

Struggling and Fighting

4. A friend of yours has drawn a cartoon of you and your first date. You and she are looking at it and laughing when your young brother decides that he, too, wants to see it. You and he scuffle as he tries to take the paper away from you.

5. A fellow classmate boasts to a group of you that he could take any one of the group down. You call his bluff and the struggle begins.

Fainting

6. A young girl becomes so excited while watching a football game that she faints and has to be carried from the stadium.

7. A traffic officer comes to a woman's house to tell her that her husband and eldest child have been killed in an automobile collision. She faints. He catches her and carries her to a sofa.

Curtseying and Bowing

8. At a formal ball in the nineteenth century, the guests are bidding good-night to other guests and to their host and hostess. They mill about speaking to one another before making final adieus.

Eating and Drinking

9. Four upper-classmen are in a booth at the College Inn. They are eating sandwiches and drinking coffee as they argue about the best methods for bringing freshmen to a full appreciation of the college.

10. A family of six are at the dinner table. The two high school members are eager to tell about the rumpus at school that day; the two younger children are bubbling with enthusiasm over the magician who came to school and performed. Parents ask questions, make comments, and try to tone down the hubbub so that one at a time can be heard.

11. Henry and Fran are at breakfast. Henry reads the morning paper aloud to his wife much of the time. She asks questions, makes comments, and eats. She replenishes her husband's coffee and hot cakes.

12. After rehearsal for a play, a few of the crew and cast sit about the stage with coffee pot, cups, and doughnuts. They talk about plans for improvement, best scenes, when they can work for improvement of the set, and other production problems. Coffee is boiling hot; the doughnuts are covered with sugar.

Smoking a Pipe

13. Three men meet in committee to plan for the basketball season. They speak of hazards and shortcomings discovered in their last season, and try to seek remedies. All smoke pipes.

Excerpts for Practice

In this scene from the delightful comedy by Shakespeare A MIDSUM-MER NIGHT'S DREAM, a group of awkward, uneducated craftsmen have been rehearsing a play called "Pyramus and Thisby," which they hope to present before the noble THESEUS, DUKE OF ATHENS, *on his wedding day. To their joy, their play is chosen from the list of possible entertainments. For the sake of this exercise, these characters may be played by any combination of men and women.*

PROLOGUE
THESEUS
PHILOSTRATE
PETER QUINCE (PROLOGUE)
SNOUT (WALL)
BOTTOM (PYRAMUS)
FLUTE (THISBY)
SNUG (LION)
STARVELING (MOONSHINE)

SUGGESTIONS AND
STAGE DIRECTIONS
There are immense
comic possibilities in
this farcical scene. Con-
trast the noble speech
and manner of
THESEUS and
PHILOSTRATE with
the bungling styles of
the tradesmen. Experi-
ment to make each of
the characters distinct,
and do not be afraid to
exaggerate for comic ef-
fect.

THESEUS.   I will hear the play; Go bring them in; (*Exit*
PHILOSTRATE.)
For never any thing can be amiss,
When simpleness and duty tender it.

Enter PHIL.   So please your Grace, the Prologue is address'd.

THE.   Let him approach.

(*Enter* PYRAMUS, THISBY, *and* WALL [Lion].)

PROLOGUE.   Gentles, perchance you wonder at this
show;
But wonder on till truth make all things plain;
This man is Pyramus, if you would know;   1.
This beauteous lady Thisby, is certain.
This man, with lime and rough-cast, doth present
Wall, that vile Wall, which did these lovers sunder;
And through Wall's chink, poor souls, they are
content
To whisper. At the which let no man wonder.
This man, with lantern, dog, and bush of thorn,   2.
Presenteth Moonshine, for if you will know,
By moonshine did these lovers think no scorn
To meet at Ninus' tomb, there, there to woo.
This grisly beast, (2) which Lion hight by name,
The trusty Thisby, coming first by night,
Did scare away, or rather did affright;
And as she fled, her mantel she did fall,
Which Lion vile with bloody mouth did stain.
Anon comes Pyramus, sweet youth and tall,
And finds his trusty Thisby's mantle slain

1. The actors present
themselves in a straight
line for introductions.

2. Certainly much of
this scene is visual. Use
appropriately comic
costumes and props.

Whereat, with blade, with bloody blameful blade,
He bravely broach'd his boiling bloody breast;   3.
And Thisby, tarrying in mulberry shade,
His dagger drew, and died. For all the rest,
Let Lion, Moonshine, Wall, and lovers twain
At large discourse, while here they do remain.

(Exit PROLOGUE, PYRAMUS, THISBY, AND LION.)

THE.   I wonder if the lion be to speak.

PHIL.   No wonder, my lord; one lion may, when many
asses do.

WALL.   In this same enterlude it doth befall
That I, one (*Snout*) by name, present a wall;
And such a wall, as I would have you think,
That had in it a crannied hole or chink,   4.
Through which the lovers, Pyramus and Thisby,
Did whisper often, very secretly.
This loam, this rough-cast, and this stone doth show
That I am that same wall; the truth is so;
And this the cranny is, right and sinister,
Through which the fearful lovers are to whisper.

PHIL.   It is the wittiest partition that ever I heard
discourse, my lord.

(Enter PYRAMUS.)

THE.   Pyramus draws near the wall. Silence!

PYR.   O Grim-look'd night! O night with hue so
black!   5.
O night, which ever art when day is not!
O night, O night! alack, alack, alack,
I fear my Thisby's promise is forgot!
And thou, O wall, O sweet and lovely wall,
That stand'st between her father's ground and mine!
Thou wall, O wall, O sweet and lovely wall,
Show me thy chink, to blink through with mine eyne!

(Wall indicates chink.)

Thanks, courteous wall; Jove shield thee well for this!
But what see I? No Thisby do I see.
O wicked wall, through whom I see no bliss!
Curs'd be thy stones for thus deceiving me!

THE.   The wall methinks, being sensible, should curse
again.

3. Exaggerate the allite-
ration here and else-
where.

4. Hold up fingers to
form a hole.

5. PYRAMUS' style is
bombastic, as evidenced
by all the exclamation
marks!

PYR.   No, in truth, sir, he should not.   6.   "Deceiving me" is Thisby's cue. She is to enter now, and I am to spy her through the wall. You shall see it will fall pat as I told you. Yonder she comes.

6. PYRAMUS breaks character and goes to THESEUS.

(*Enter* THISBY.)

THIS.   O wall, full often hast thou heard my moans,
For parting my fair Pyramus and me!
My cherry lips have often kiss'd thy stones,
Thy stones with lime and hair knit up in thee.

PYR.   I see a voice! Now will I to the chink,
To spy and I can hear my Thisby's face,
Thisby!

THIS.   My love thou art, my love I think.

PYR.   Think what thou wilt, I am thy lover's grace;
And, like Limander, am I trusty still.

THIS   And I like Helen, till the fates me kill.

PYR   Not Shafalus to Procrus was so true.

THIS.   As Shafalus to Procrus I to you.

PYR.   O, kiss me through the hole of this vile wall!   7.

7. They kiss WALL'S fingers, of course, who may then wipe off their slobber in disgust.

THIS.   I kiss the wall's hole, not your lips at all.

PYR.   Wilt thou at Ninny's tomb meet me straightway?

THIS.   'Tide life, 'tide death, I come without delay.

(*Exit* PYR. *and* THIS.)

WALL.   Thus have I, Wall, my part discharged so;
And being done, thus Wall away doth go. (*Exit.*)

PHIL.   This is the silliest stuff that ever I heard.

THE.   Here come two noble beasts in a man and a lion.

(*Enter* LION *and* MOONSHINE.)

LION.   You, whose gentle hearts do fear.   8.
The smallest monstrous mouse that creeps on floor,
May now, perchance, both quake and tremble here,
When lion rough in wildest rage doth roar.
Then know that I, as Snug the Joiner, am
A lion fell, or else no lion's dam;
For, if I should, as lion, come in strife
Into this place, 'twere pity on my life.

8. SNUG, who plays the LION, is actually very weak in voice and body.

THE.   A very gentle beast, and of a good conscience.

PHIL.   The very best at a beast, my lord, that e'er I saw.

MOON.   This lanthorn doth the horned moon present—

PHIL.   He should have worn the horns on his head.

MOON.   This lanthorn doth the horned moon present;
Myself the man i' th' moon do seem to be.

THE.   This is the greatest error of all the rest.
The man should be put into the lanthorn. How is it
else the man i' th' moon?

PHIL.   He dares not come there for the candle. Proceed
moon.

MOON.   All that I have to say is to tell you that the
lanthorn is the moon, I the man i' th' moon, this
thorn-bush, my thorn-bush, and this dog my dog. 9.

9. MOON is impatient at the interruptions, and blurts out the rest of the speech quickly.

THE.   Why, all these should be in the lanthorn; for all
these are in the moon. But silence! Here comes
Thisby.

(*Enter* THISBY.)

THIS.   This is old Ninny's tomb. Where is my love?

LION.   O! (LION *roars.* THISBY *runs off.*)

PHIL.   Well roar'd, Lion.

THE.   Well run, Thisby.

PHIL.   Well shone, Moon. Truly, the moon shines with
a good grace.

(LION *shakes* THISBY'S *mantle.*)   10.

10. Put mantle in mouth and shake head, growling.

THE.   Well mous'd, Lion.

(*Enter* PYRAMUS.)

PYR.   Sweet Moon, I thank thee for thy sunny beams.
I thank thee, Moon, for shining now so bright;
For by thy gracious golden glittering gleams,
I trust to take of truest Thisby sight.
But stay! O spite!
But mark, poor Knight
What dreadful dole is here!
Eyes, do you see?
How can it be?
O dainty duck! O dear!
Thy mantle good,
What, stained with blood?
Approach, ye Furies fell!

O Fates, come, come,
Cut thread and thrum,
Quail, crush, conclude and quell!

THE. This passion, and the death of a dear friend,
would go near to make a man look sad.

PYR. O, wherefore, Nature, didst thou lions frame?
Since lion vile hath here deflow'r'd my dear;
Which is— no, no— which was the fairest dame
That lived, that lov'd, that lik'd, that looked with
cheer.
Come, tears, confound,
Out, sword, and wound
The pap of Pyramus;
Ay, that left pap,
Where heart doth hop. (*stabs himself*)
Thus die I, thus, thus, thus.   11.
Now I am dead,
Now I am fled;
My soul is in the sky.
Tongue, lose thy light,
Moon, take thy flight. (*Exit* MOON.)
Now die, die, die, die. (12.) (*Dies.*)

PHIL. How chance Moonshine is gone before
Thisby comes back and finds her lover?

(*Enter* THISBY)

THE. She will find him by starlight. Here she comes,
and her passion ends the play.

THIS. Asleep, my love?
What, dead, my dove?
O Pyramus, arise!
Speak, speak! Quite dumb?
Dead, dead? A tomb
Must cover thy sweet eyes.
These lily lips,
This cherry nose,
These yellow cowslip cheeks,   13.
Are gone, are gone!
Lovers, make moan;
His eyes were green as leeks.
O Sisters Three,
Come, come to me,

11. PYRAMUS takes the short wooden sword from his belt and "stabs" himself between his left arm and left side. Repeat this on each "thus."

12. Make each one of these different, and make the death flamboyant. PYRAMUS is a ham

13. Tweak each of these items in turn.

With hands as pale as milk;
Lay them in gore,
Since you have shore
With shears his thread of silk.
Tongue, not a word!
Come, trusty sword,
Come, blade, my breast imbrue! (*Stabs herself.*)
And farewell, friends;
Thus Thisby ends;
Adieu, adieu, adieu. (*Dies.*)   14.

THE.   Moonshine and Lion are left to bury the dead.

PHIL.   Ay, and Wall too.

PYR (*starting up*).   No, I assure you, the wall is down that parted their fathers. Will it please you to see the epilogue?

THE.   No epilogue, I pray you; for your play needs no excuse. Never excuse; for when the players are all dead, there need none to be blam'd. Marry, if he that writ it had play'd Pyramus, and hang'd himself in Thisby's garter, it would have been a fine tragedy; and so it is, truly, and very notably discharg'd.   15.

This scene is from the prologue to ANDROCLES AND THE LION, by George Bernard Shaw. The time of the play is the first century A.D. AN-DROCLES, *a Christian, and his wife,* MEGAERA, *have been travelling through the forest.*

ANDROCLES   MEGAERA
A LION (male or female)

SUGGESTIONS AND
STAGE DIRECTIONS

Be sure to provide some set pieces, such as rocks, stump, log, bushes, around which the action can be blocked. Furniture may be used for these.

MEGAERA.   How is any woman to keep her house clean when you bring in every stray cat and lost cur and lame duck in the whole countryside? You took the bread out of my mouth to feed them: you know you did: dont attempt to deny it.

ANDROCLES.   Only when they were hungry and you were getting too stout, dearie.

MEGEARA.   Yes, insult me, do. (*Rising*) Oh! I wont bear it another moment. You used to sit and talk to those dumb brute beasts for hours, when you hadnt a word for me.

ANDROCLES.   They never answered back, darling.

(*He rises and again shoulders the bundle*).

MEGAERA.   Well, if youre fonder of animals than of your own wife, you can live with them here in the jungle. Ive had enough of them and enough of you. I'm going back. I'm going home.

ANDROCLES   (*barring the way back*). No dearie: dont take on like that. We cant go back. Weve sold everything: we should starve; and I should be sent to Rome and thrown to the lions—

MEGAERA.   Serve you right! I wish the lions joy of you. (*Screaming*) Are you going to get out of my way and let me go home?

ANDROCLES.   No, dear—

MEGAERA.   Then Ill make my way through the forest; and when I'm eaten by the wild beasts youll know what a wife youve lost. (*She dashes into the jungle and nearly falls over the sleeping lion.*) Oh! Oh! Andy! Andy! (*She totters back and collapses into the arms of* ANDROCLES, *who crushed by her weight,* (1) *falls on his bundle*).

1. Some indication of their comparative size, which makes ANDY seem even more put upon. It is not essential for this exercise, however, that she be larger than he.

ANDROCLES (*extracting himself from beneath her and slapping her hands in great anxiety*).   What is it, my precious, my pet? Whats the matter? (*He raises her head. Speechless with terror, she points in the direction of the sleeping lion. He steals cautiously towards the spot indicated by* MEGAERA. *She rises with an effort and totters after him*).

MEGAERA.   No, Andy: youll be killed. Come back.

(*The lion utters a long snoring sigh.* ANDROCLES *sees the lion and recoils fainting into the arms of* MEGAERA, *who falls back on the bundle. They roll apart and lie staring in terror at one another* (2). *The lion is heard groaning heavily in the jungle*).

2. Practice these actions until they are smooth, safe, and appropriately comic. The lion can be on the far side of the stage instead of offstage.

ANDROCLES (*whispering*).   Did you see? A lion.

MEGEARA(*despairing*). The gods have sent him to punish us because youre a Christian. Take me away, Andy. Save me.

ANDROCLES. (*rising*). Meggy: theres one chance for you. Itll take him pretty nigh twenty minutes to eat me (I'm rather stringy and tough) and you can escape in less time than that.

MEGAERA. Oh, dont talk about eating. (*The lion rises with a great groan and limps towards them*). Oh! (*She faints*).

ANDROCLES (*quaking, but keeping between the lion and* MEGAERA). Dont you come near my wife, do you hear? (*The lion groans. Androcles can hardly stand for trembling*). Meggy: run. Run for your life. If I take my eye off him, its all up. (*The lion holds up his wounded paw and flaps it piteously before* AN-DROCLES). Oh, hes lame, poor old chap! Hes got a thorn in his paw. A frightfully big thorn. (*Full of sympathy*) Oh, poor old man! Did um get an awful thorn into um's tootsums wootsums? Has it made um too sick to eat a nice little Christian man for um's breakfast? Oh, a nice little Christian man will get um's thorn out for um; and then um shall eat the nice Christian man and the nice Christian man's nice big tender wifey pifey. (*The lion responds by moans of self-pity*). Yes, yes, yes, yes, yes. Now, now (*taking the paw in his hand*) (3) um is not to bite and not to scratch, not even if it hurts a very, very little. Now make velvet paws. That right (*He pulls gingerly at the thorn. The lion with an angry yell of pain, jerks back his paw so abruptly that* ANDROCLES *is thrown on his back*). Steadeee! Oh, did the nasty cruel little Christian man hurt the sore paw? (*The lion moans assentingly but apologetically*). Well, one more little pull and it will be all over. Just one little, little, leetle pull; and then um will live happily ever after. (*He gives the thorn another pull. The lion roars and snaps his jaws with a terrifying clash*). Oh, mustnt frighten um's good kind doctor, um's affectionate nursey. That didn't hurt at all: not a bit. Just one more. Just to shew how the brave big lion can bear pain, not like the little

3. The actor playing the LION can make some appropriate gesture, tensing and relaxing his claws.

crybaby Christian man. Oopsh! (*The thorn comes out. The lion yells with pain, and shakes his paw wildly*). Thats it! (*Holding up the thorn*). Now its out. Now lick um's paw to take away the nasty inflammation. See? (*He licks his own hand. The lion nods intelligently and licks his paw industriously*). Clever little liony-piony! Understands um's dear old friend Andy Wandy. (*The lion licks his face*). Yes, kissums Andy Wandy. (*The lion, wagging his tail violently, rises on his hind legs and embraces Androcles, who makes a wry face and cries*). Velvet paws! Velvet paws! (*The lion draws in his claws*) (3) Thats right. (*He embraces the lion, who finally takes the end of his tail in one paw, places that tight around* ANDROCLES' *waist,* (4) *resting it on his hip.* ANDROCLES *takes the other paw in his hand, stretches out his arm, and the two waltz rapturously, round and round and finally away through the jungle*).

4. Use a length of rope long enough to suit this action for the LION'S tail.

MEGAERA (*who has revived during the waltz*).   Oh, you coward, you havnt danced with me for years; and now you go off dancing with a great brute beast that you havnt known for ten minutes and that wants to eat your own wife. Coward! Coward! Coward! (*She rushes off after them into the jungle*).

THE GREEN PASTURES is a fantasy by Marc Connelly. An elderly Negro preacher has been teaching his Sunday-school classes of young boys and girls. The children visualize the joys of heaven as the pleasures they themselves most enjoy here upon earth. In the following scene the angels appear to be happy Negroes at a fish fry.

The principal singers are marching two by two in a small area at the right of the stage. Two MAMMY ANGELS *are attending to the frying beside the kettle. Behind the table a* MAN ANGEL *is skinning fish and passing them to the cooks. Another is ladling out the custard. A* MAMMY ANGEL *is putting fish on bread for a brood of cherubs, and during the first scene they seat themselves on a grassy bank upstage. Another* MAMMY ANGEL *is clapping her hands disapprovingly and beckoning a laughing* BOY CHERUB *down from a cloud a little out of her reach. Another* MAMMY ANGEL *is solicitously slapping the back of a* GIRL CHERUB *who has a large fish sandwich in her hand and a bone in her throat. There is much movement about the table, and during the first few minutes several individuals go up to the table to help themselves to the food and drink.*

FIRST MAN ANGEL,
  skinning fish
*SECOND MAN ANGEL,
  ladling custard
*BOY CHERUB,
  on cloud
*EXTRAS, singing,
  marching
*EXTRAS, milling
  about

FIRST COOK, frying fish
*SECOND COOK,
  frying fish
*MAMMY ANGEL,
  putting fish on
  bread
MAMMY ANGEL,
  scolding boy on
  cloud
STOUT ANGEL
SLENDER ANGEL
*GIRL CHERUB, with
  bone in throat
*BROOD OF CHERUBS

This scene offers a
splendid opportunity for
practicing movement
with a large group

FIRST MAN ANGEL.   Well, it jest so happen dat minny fishin' is de doggondest fool way of fishin' dey is. You kin try minny fishin' to de cows come home an' all you catch'll be de backache. De trouble wid you, sister, is you jest got minny fishin' on de brain. 1.

SECOND COOK.   Go right on, loud mouf. You tell me de news. My, my! You jest de wisest person in de worl'. First you, den de Lawd God.

FIRST MAN ANGEL (*to the custard ladler*).   You cain't tell dem nothin'. (*Walks away to the custard churn.*) Does you try to 'splain some simple fac' dey git man-deaf. 2.

FIRST MAMMY ANGEL (*to* CHERUB *on the cloud*).   Now you heerd me. [*The* CHERUB *assumes several mocking poses, as she speaks.*] You fly down yere. You wanter be put down in de sin book? (*She goes to the table, gets a drink for herself and points out the* CHERUB *to one of the men behind the table.*) Dat baby must got imp blood in him he so vexin'. (*She returns to her position under the cloud.*) You want me to fly up dere an' slap you down? Now, I tol' you. [*The* CHERUB *starts to come down.*]

STOUT ANGEL (*to the* CHERUB *with the bone in her throat*).   I tol' you you was too little fo' cat fish. What you wanter git a bone in yo' froat fo'? (*She slaps the* CHERUB'S *back.*) 3.

SLENDER ANGEL (*leisurely eating a sandwich as she watches the back-slapping*).   What de trouble wid Leonetta?

1. Many are on stage other than those having lines. They must keep acting, talking, moving, and always listening to the lines, without seeming to.

2. During these lines the CHERUBS eat, talk to each other, and play in childish ways, but without attracting attention to themselves.

3. It is *essential* that, as dialogue shifts from one group to another, the character speaking move or gesture broadly enough so that spectators can locate the speaker immediately.

STOUT ANGEL. She got a catfish bone down her froat. (*To the* CHERUB.) Doggone, I tol' you to eat grinnel instead.

SLENDER ANGEL. Ef'n she do git all dat et, she gonter have de bellyache.

STOUT ANGEL. Ain't I tol' her dat? (*To* CHERUB). Come on now; let go dat bone. (*She slaps* CHERUB'S *back again. The bone is dislodged and the* CHERUB *grins her relief.*) Dat's good.

SLENDER ANGEL (*comfortingly*). Now she all right. 4.

STOUT ANGEL. Go on an' play wid you' cousins. [*The* CHERUB *joins the* CHERUBS *sitting on the embankment. The concurrency of scenes ends here.*] I ain't see you lately, Lily. How you been?

SLENDER ANGEL. Me, I'm fine. I been visitin' my mammy. She waitin' on de welcome table over by de throne of grace.

STOUT ANGEL. She always was pretty holy.

SLENDER ANGEL. Yes, ma'am. She like it dere. I guess de Lawd's took quite a fancy to her.

STOUT ANGEL. Well, dat's natural. I declare yo' mammy one of de finest lady angels I know. 5.

SLENDER ANGEL. She claim you de best one she know.

STOUT ANGEL. Well, when you come right down to it, I suppose we is all pretty near perfec'.

SLENDER ANGEL. Yes, ma'am. Why is dat, Mis' Jenny?

STOUT ANGEL. I s'pose it's caize de Lawd he don' 'low us 'sociatin' wid de devil any mo' so dat dey cain' be no mo' sinnin'.

SLENDER ANGEL. Po' ol' Satan. Whutevah become of him?

STOUT ANGEL. De Lawd put him some place I s'pose.

SLENDER ANGEL. But dey ain't any place but Heaven, is dey?

STOUT ANGEL. De Lawd could make a place, couldn't he?

SLENDER ANGEL. Dat's de truth. Dey's one thing confuses me though.

4. Since there is much talk in the various groups, each speaker must speak out enough to *top* all other noises.

5. A character appears to take no notice of groups except the one of which he is a part, but he must listen to all lines in order to coordinate and pick up cues.

STOUT ANGEL.   What's dat?

SLENDER ANGEL.   I do a great deal of travelin' an' I ain't never come across any place but Heaven anywhere. So if de Lawd kick Satan out of Heaven jest whereat did he go? Dat's my question.

The scene is located in Japan in MADAME BUTTERFLY'S *little house. It is spring and the first robin has just been seen.* MADAME BUTTERFLY *is anxiously awaiting the return of the American seaman she married, who promised he would return to her when the robins nest again.* SHARPLESS, *the American Consul, is urging her to marry another. (This scene is from David Belasco and John Luther Long's MADAME BUTTERFLY.)*

SHARPLESS	MADAME BUTTERFLY	SUGGESTIONS AND
*NAKODO	*SUZUKI	STAGE DIRECTIONS
*A SMALL CHILD		

Japanese dialect. This scene also carries widely diversified emotions: anger, rage, love, fear, pride, confidence, and unbounded joy.

SHARPLESS (*folding the letter*).   No use—you can't understand. Madame Butterfly, suppose this waiting should never end; what would become of you? 1.

1. SHARPLESS is really trying to help MADAME BUTTERFLY at first.

MADAME BUTTERFLY.   Me? I could dance, mebby, or—die?

SHARPLESS.   Don't be foolish. I advise you to consider the rich Yamadori's offer.

MADAME BUTTERFLY (*astonished*).   *You* say those? You, 'Merican consul?—when you know that me, I am marry?

SHARPLESS.   You heard Yamadori: It is not binding.

MADAME BUTTERFLY.   Yamadori lies! 2.

2. Sudden anger expressed after a pause. Her anger grows to quiet rage in next speech.

SHARPLESS.   His offer is an unusual opportunity for a girl who—for any Japanese girl in your circumstances.

MADAME BUTTERFLY (*enraged—she claps her hands*). Suzuki! The excellent gentleman—(*bowing sarcastically*) who have done us the honor to call—he wish to go hurriedly. His shoes—hasten them!

(SUZUKI, *who has entered carrying a jar, gets* SHARPLESS' *clogs and gives them to him—then passes off with her jar.*)

SHARPLESS (*holding the clogs awkwardly*).   I'm really very sorry. 3.

MADAME BUTTERFLY.   No, no, don't be angery. But jus' now you tol' me—O, gods! You mean—(*Looks at him pitifully.*) I not Lef-ten-ant B. F. Pik-ker-ton's wive—Me? 4.

SHARPLESS.   Hardly.

MADAME BUTTERFLY.   O, I—(*She sways slightly.* SHARPLESS *goes to her assistance, but she recovers and fans herself.*) Tha's all right. I got liddle heart illness. I can't . . . I can't someways give up thingin' he'll come back to me. You thing tha's all over? All finish? (*Dropping her fan.* SHARPLESS *nods assent.*) Oh, no! Loave don' forget some thin's or wha's use of loave? (*She claps her hands—beckoning off.*) Loave's got remember . . . (*pointing*) some thin's!

(*A child enters.*)

SHARPLESS.   A child . . . Pinkerton's? . . .

MADAME BUTTERFLY (*showing a picture of Pinkerton's and brightening*).   Look! Look! (*Holding it up beside the child's face.*) Tha's jus' his face, same hair, same blue eye. . . .

SHARPLESS.   Does Lieutenant Pinkerton know?

MADAME BUTTERFLY.   No, he come after he go. (5) (*Looking at the child with pride.*) You thing fath-er naever comes back—tha's wha *you* thing? He do! You write him ledder; tell him 'bout one bes' mos' nize bebby aever seen. . . . Ha—ha! I bed all moaneys he goin' come mos' one million mile for see those chil'. Surely this is tie—bebby. Sa-ey, you didn't mean what you said 'bout me not bein' marry? You make liddle joke? (*Moved,* SHARPLESS *nods his head in assent, to the great relief of* MADAME BUTTERFLY.) Ha! (*She lays the baby's hand in* SHARPLESS'.) Shake hand consul 'Merican way.   6.

SHARPLESS (*shaking hand with the child*).   Hm . . . hm . . . what's your name?

MADAME BUTTERFLY.   Trouble. Japanese bebby always change it name. I was thinkin' some day w'en he come back, change it to Joy. 7.

3. SHARPLESS is trying to say gently that PINKERTON has betrayed BUTTERFLY.

4. Another sharp change of MADAME BUTTERFLY's attitude. She is beginning to realize the full implication of SHARPLESS' words.

5. A fourth emotion now comes over her—pride—with it confidence, which carries through several lines.

6. MADAME BUTTERFLY makes a conscious effort to have everything American—flag, handshake, cigarettes, even her wink.

7. Now SHARPLESS would probably react noticeably to this ironical name.

SHARPLESS. Yes . . . yes . . . I'll let him know. (*Glad to escape, he takes an abrupt departure.*)

SUZUKI (*in the distance, wailing*). Ay . . . ay . . . ay. . . . 8.

8. This wail is a plaintive sing-song cry.

MADAME BUTTERFLY. Tha's wail. . . .

SUZUKI (*nearer*). O, Cho-Cho-San! (MADAME BUTTERFLY *goes to the door to meet* SUZUKI.) Cho-Cho-San!

MADAME BUTTERFLY. Speak!

SUZUKI. We are shamed through the town. The Nakodo——

NAKODO (*appearing*). I but said the child——(*He points to the baby, whom* MADAME BUTTERFLY *instinctively shelters in her arms.*) was a badge of shame to his father. In his country, there are homes for such unfortunates and they never rise above the stigma of their class. They are shunned and cursed from birth.

MADAME BUTTERFLY (*who has listened stolidly—now with a savage cry, pushing him away from her until he loses his balance and falls to the floor*). You lie! 9.

9. Good opportunity here to practice stage fall. Do it correctly.

NAKODO (*on the floor*). But Yamadori——

MADAME BUTTERFLY (*touching her father's sword*). Lies! Lies! Lies! Say again, I kill! Go . . . (*The* NAKODO *goes quickly.*) Bebby, he lies. . . . Yaes, it's lie. . . . When your fath-er knows how they speak, he will take us 'way from bad people to his own country. I am finish here. (*Taking the American flag from the tobacco jar and giving it to the child.*) Tha' your country—your flag. Now wave like fath-er say w'en excite—wave like "hell!" (*Waves the child's hand.*) Ha'rh Ha'rh! (*A ship's gun is heard.*) Ah! (MADAME BUTTERFLY *and* SUZUKI *start for the balcony.* MADAME BUTTERFLY *runs back for the child as the gun is heard again; then returning to the shoji, looks through the glasses.*) Look! Look! Warship! Wait . . . can't see name. . . . 10.

10. Again MADAME BUTTERFLY is enraged. Then suddenly comes joy, followed by elation.

SUZUKI. Let me——

MADAME BUTTERFLY. No! Ah! Name is "Con-nec-ti-cut"! His ship! He's come back! He's come back! (*Laughing, she embraces* SUZUKI—*then sinks to the floor.*) He's come back! Those robins nes' again an' we didn' know! O, bebby, bebby—your fath-er come back! Your fath-ers' come back! O! O! (*Shaking a bough of cherry blossoms, which fall on them both.*) This is the bes' nize momen' since you was borned. Now your name's Joy! Suzuki; the Moon Goddess sent that bebby straight from Bridge of Heaven to make me courage to wait so long. 11.

11. This part must have a tremendous build up to contrast with the tragic end of the play.

The story of *Madame Butterfly* has been told many times and in many forms of literature. In the original story, Madame Butterfly's lover never returned to her. The following song, "Someday Soon," expresses her feelings as she waits for him.

Someday Soon

Words and Music by
JAMES RIVERS

Longingly

Oh, gen - tle ba - by,___ you are so trust - ing. ___ My dear - est one, ___ let me share your faith! ___ Yes, some - day soon ___ we will be to - geth - er, and hap - pi - ness ___ will melt the pain. ___ And hap - pi - ness ___ will melt the pain.

Look, small one ___ for your fa - ther's ves - sel. It can't be far! ___ It can't be far! ___ He's com - ing soon, ___ and we'll be to - geth - er, and hap - pi - ness ___ will melt the pain. Hap - pi - ness ___ will melt the pain.

CHAPTER 11

The Director and the Cast

THE AUDITION

The audition for an amateur play is usually a simple reading of parts. It is hoped that you can be somewhat familiar with the play and the role or roles you are to read. Sometimes when you wish to audition for a role, you are asked to present a selection that you are familiar with, or even have memorized. It is especially helpful if you can have an opportunity to read the script beforehand and study those roles for which you are best suited. Many times this is not possible, so those persons who do not read or act readily on first sight are at a disadvantage.

If an aspirant must read the lines "cold," the director may wish to ask him or her to read the selection a second time immediately following the first reading. If a director is undecided, he or she will often ask certain contestants to work on scenes and return for further auditions.

Realize that acting involves not only body and voice but also mind and emotions, and that all these are blended in creating a character. Consider your own capabilities: your size, voice, general appearance, the time you have to devote to study of a part and to rehearsal, and also your ability to express suitable emotions.

When planning to audition for an upcoming play, some may find it helpful to read lines with another person. This can help an actor to pick up cues rapidly, and to respond to another's feelings and to the situation and mood of the scene. Such preparation seems to help an actor pay closer attention to the other character's feelings.

After you decide which part or parts you'd like to try, reread and restudy the script. If at all possible, find all words, actions, and implications that other characters and the playwright give about your chosen character. Weigh all of your own characteristics that would help you fit the role.

Perhaps you are in a community where competition is very keen, where many will be auditioning. In theaters using extensive auditions or in semi-professional theaters, there are special preparations for auditions.

When a notice is sent out, or the director announces, that a certain play is to be produced and that auditions will be held soon, you can, if possible, get a copy of the script, read it thoughtfully, and decide which part you'd like to try for.

Go over the lines of the character a number of times; get the feel of the part. Also become familiar with the sound of others' lines. In every scene, understand the relationships of your chosen character with others. As you study, try to give appropriate timing and emotional expression to the lines. Don't race them.

After you have built your interpretation as much as you can alone, ask a friend to read lines of other characters in certain scenes. Such practice will give you real help, especially if the friend reads with understanding and feeling. However, don't set a definite interpretation. Your director will have his or her own ideas that you will want to follow.

When the "cattle call" for auditions comes, you will feel ready for it. Your efficiency will depend somewhat—perhaps a great deal—on the person reading the other parts. If the companion reader comes alive, you will be able to interpret better than you could if a dull, monotonous, expressionless voice spoke the lines.

Many auditions are by cattle call only. An announcement informs those who wish to participate to come between certain hours on one or more days. In the audition, you may need to read with no knowledge of the time of the play or the situation about which it was built.

You are at a disadvantage if this gives you your only opportunity. The director will probably consider your appearance, voice, availability for rehearsals, and interpretation of lines. He or she may have told you something about the character's age, disposition, or background, but that's about all. Some directors choose their casts from these auditions.

After these free-for-all tryouts, some directors may ask you to return for

You Can't Take It With You by George S. Kaufman and Moss Hart was presented by the University of Kansas, and was directed by Jack Wright. Grouping, background, and actions all create the confusion that the play is planned to show.

A Sleep of Prisoners by Christopher Fry was presented by Crossroad Theatre Company of Grove City College with Susan Constantine directing. This scene shows the diverse action needed, along with the untidy setting, to create the right atmosphere.

The Director and the Cast   **207**

another reading alone, after you have read the play. This will give you an opportunity to show your ability to read with meaning.

Do not decide that there is only one interpretation for the role. Your director may see the character as an entirely different kind of person, or see you fitting a different part. Try different feelings and expressions suggested by your director, who is thinking of the play as a whole. By exploring different characterizations, you will be closer to the interpretation that ties the play together.

When this is completed and you feel that you have done your best, then *relax*. There is no more you can do until the cast is announced. Take a breather now, because if you are cast, nerve strain will surely follow. Make plans to schedule your many other responsibilities so that you can carry them and also allow time for work on the play.

THE DIRECTOR'S RESPONSIBILITIES

Throughout a play's production the director, cast, and technical staff work together hand in hand, each in his or her own field. There may be doubling of duties: an actor may be on scene crew, or the assistant director may play a small part in the play.

If you are new to the theater experience, you may not understand the duties of a director. He or she *studies the play*, including background for setting, characters, and construction from preparation for spectators to complication, to crisis, to resolution. Throughout this the director plans contrasts in characters, settings, voices, and other effects.

The director *decides on the interpretation* to be given the script. In some cases he or she may change the author's concept by changing the setting or language, may even cut scenes, or may modernize the play. Whatever concept the director gives the play, he or she will need to have it thoroughly in mind and prepared in order to explain to the actors. As the play progresses, the director will work for appropriate volume, tempo, and mood to build contrasts and dramatic effects.

Most directors will wish to consult with the actors on some phases of the production. Directors often find that actors' suggestions are very helpful and inspiring in making clear his own interpretation. Directors work to inspire confidence in cast and crews.

The work of the director is to *coordinate all* effects into a whole, blending into a single spirit the embodiment of the author's dream. The play itself, actors, the director, and crews work as an ensemble. You cooperate to make the production a real teamwork.

The director works with committees to choose appropriate colors, staging, and costume styles; variety in these add interesting effects. Additional aspects of production that the director may be responsible for are music and dance. Occasionally the director may be responsible for box-office receipts to finance the play.

SOME HELPS FOR DIRECTORS

Many directors use *an assistant* who is entirely reliable and understands play production. The assistant may play a minor acting role, help to provide substitute props and costumes for early rehearsals, run errands, help players with difficult scenes, and take over directing when the director must meet with committees or is busy with other matters.

For the sake of convenience, a director may divide a play into *segments*. This is practical because it allows more time to scenes that need help, those

Blithe Spirit by Noel Coward was presented by Washburn University, and was directed by Miriam A. Franklin. Grouping centers on leading action. The two spirits of characters help to create triangles in arrangement.

that seem difficult. Another advantage is that it brings together only those actors in certain scenes. Yet in segment rehearsals the actors can help the director unify the whole play.

There may be times when you need to miss a rehearsal; it may be essential. The director needs to know this as soon as possible so that rehearsal schedules can be adjusted. Directors are charitable to actors' needs and will cooperate when possible—that is, when your absence will not jeopardize the needs of a rehearsal or of the play's production. Do not expect to be excused except for essentials.

You must realize that, when you accept a role in a play, you will have to make sacrifices. Your time belongs to the play, and *other interests must be put aside.* Do not think that, because your part is small or because you have your lines memorized, you are not needed at every rehearsal. It is not only the director who needs you; other actors in the scenes rely on you. If you are not at rehearsal, it is like a page missing from a book. You are important. Treat your bit or big part with high regard.

Sometimes you are asked to use certain props or wear costumes that seem awkward. Bring them to rehearsals to become familiar with them. You may not see the need to practice with them. Your director wants nothing left incomplete and added only at dress rehearsals. When drinking coffee, use something to rehearse the scene that looks right. Remember to hold the *hot* cup and sip the coffee as if it were boiling hot. If you are to walk with the help of a cane, use a stick and act as if you really need its help.

SOME HELPS FOR ACTORS

You have an opportunity to receive valuable suggestions about acting if you listen to all instructions that the director gives, not only those for scenes you are in, but *directions to others* as well. Carry more than one sharp pencil and an eraser tied to your play script. Don't use ink. If the director changes business, you can mark the changes easily with pencil.

Your director may wish you to *assume the responsibility* of making small stage movements without being directed to. When you have a piece of business or are to cross to another location, you should try to find some plausible motivation for the action. You may know, without being asked, that you should balance stage when Tom goes off. You are to fill the spot to maintain balance. You may move across to pick up an imaginary pencil, look at a newspaper he left behind, or examine a foliage plant. You may move to the spot inconspicuously, listening to dialogue with both eyes and ears. The audience, intent on listening, will not notice you.

A director usually *gives special help* to those players with minor parts.

Small roles can dominate the whole acting group and take the glitter out of imaginary crowns of the stars. An adage of the theater is "There are no small parts, only small actors." Even if yours is a bit part, you have the challenge of making your part come alive.

COOPERATION IS HELP FOR ALL

Acting offers a big responsibility with many facets that must be brought together.

Players can help the development of a fine play if each is willing, eager, and responsive to needs of the play. Give every other actor his or her *share* of the *limelight;* never use tricks to give yourself undue prominence. Cooperation, with all helping in a production, is a *must* for fine theater.

There are many ways you can *cooperate* with others. While on stage, each person who is not speaking should pay appropriate attention to the speaker and lines, and should react as their character would without calling attention to their own acting. Instead, attention should be directed to the main interest at the moment. A few suggestions:

1. Come to rehearsals on time, even as much as thirty minutes ahead. During your wait, study your characterization.
2. Carry two sharp pencils, one with an eraser.
3. Work even a bit part to perfection.
4. Use your own script or sides. Don't borrow.
5. Take criticism gratefully and gracefully.
6. Be critical of your own acting. Keep improving.
7. Offstage, keep happy without being rowdy or thoughtlessly distracting others.
8. Be in place for your entrance, and in character, fully three minutes ahead of time. Assume responsibility for your entrance.
9. While waiting for your cue, don't talk to others. Get into the feel of your role, think your character's thoughts, stand and move like your character.
10. Onstage, stay in character while listening.
11. When off stage during rehearsals and performances, speak only in an unvoiced whisper. A *voiced* whisper or undertone carries; an *unvoiced* whisper does not.
12. Even if the green room is on a lower level, keep voices soft, to avoid disturbing others who are trying to concentrate.
13. Speak no lines on stage except your own lines.
14. Make no movement on stage except with the director's approval.
15. Listen intently to all the director's comments to others.
16. Don't direct fellow actors.

17. When listening to rehearsals from the auditorium, tell the director if you are unable to understand an actor's lines.

18. If something goes wrong, don't let disappointment get the better of you.

19. Never bring intoxicants to the theater. Do nothing before arriving that might hinder you from doing your best or interfere with your natural portrayal of a character.

20. Keep uppermost in your mind your desire to produce high-grade theater.

SHOWMANSHIP

Showmanship has three pertinent meanings. *Loyalty*, as implied in the slogan, "The show must go on," is an integral part of showmanship, the heartbeat of the theater. It has been the watchword of hundreds of troopers playing in cold houses, under leaky tents, or among competing noises. They have fought through snowstorms, plowed through blinding rains and deep mud, taken lengthy detours to bypass flooded areas, and even ridden railroad handcars to make their dates. They have played when hot with fever, or with raucous, nearly-gone voices. They have doubled parts in order to save the show when a member of the cast was too ill to appear. "The show must go on" is like an oath to a seasoned actor. This kind of loyalty involves showmanship.

However, being loyal to the show, or showmanship, doesn't always entail hardships. More often it involves cooperating happily with others, continuously *working for the good of the play*. There is another meaning to showmanship: it connotes a *sense of exhibition*. Actors have a product to sell—entertainment. They strive to display their product effectively so that the audience will leave the theater happily entertained or deeply moved. Showmanship is essential to good theater.

TEAMWORK

Good teamwork helps every play—"Each for all and all for each." You should not depend on rehearsals with the whole group to work up your role, although you will work with them to synchronize the parts and to blend the play into a whole.

During rehearsals listen to the lines of your co-actors. Actually *hear with your mind* what each says, then have your character react appropriately. Blend their speeches and yours into a rhythmic pattern. Keep pace and mood constant until a change is needed. Cooperate with the crews, who often have to work fast; thoughtless actors can cause delays in their efforts

The rule, *Interpret with the whole body adjusted to the voice*, is a good one to follow. As each player's tempo becomes convincing, a pleasing rhythmic movement will develop, and by teamwork, all parts will synchronize into an artistic unit.

The following monologues from plays give you an opportunity to prepare the kind of exercise that might be used for an audition in which an example of your ability to act is required.

"Glad to see you, Raymond!"
"Glad to see you, **RAYMOND!**"
"**Glad to see you, RAYMOND!**"

From *The Saturday Evening Post,* February 5, 1949.
Courtesy of Boris Drucker.

While reading the next chapter, where you will consider the work of the stage staffs and crews, think of some play that you have known: the setting for it, lights, costumes, props. Keep these in mind. Think of some unusual presentation, such as having children, robots, or fantastic characters act the roles. You may think of yourself as the director of a theatrical experiment. This exercise will help you to create varied costumes, props, and scenery as you direct an imaginary production throughout the next chapter.

Excerpts for Practice

This monologue by CHRISTY MAHON, *from THE PLAYBOY OF THE WESTERN WORLD by John Millington Synge, provides an excellent opportunity for using the imagination, working with props, and speaking the Irish dialect. Be sure to take time with the props, and be sure to enjoy and take time with the words and phrases.*

SUGGESTIONS AND
STAGE DIRECTIONS

CHRISTY (*to himself, counting jugs on dresser*).   Half a hundred beyond. Ten there. A score that's above. Eighty jugs. Six cups and a broken one. Two plates. A power of glasses. Bottles, a school-master'd be hard set to count, and enough in them, I'm thinking, to drunken all the wealth and wisdom of the County Clare. (1) (*He puts down the boot carefully.*) There's her boots now, nice and decent for her evening use, and isn't it grand brushes she has? (*He puts them down and goes by degrees to the looking-glass.*) Well, this'd be a fine place to be my whole life talking out with swearing Christians, in place of my old dogs and cat, and I stalking around, smoking my pipe and drinking my fill, and never a day's work but drawing a cork an odd time, or wiping a glass, or rinsing out a shiny tumbler for a decent man. (*He takes the looking-glass from the wall and puts it on the back of a chair; then sits down in front of it and begins washing his face.*) Didn't I know rightly I was handsome, though it was the divil's own mirror we had beyond, would twist a squint across an angel's brow; and I'll be growing fine from this day, the way I'll have a soft lovely skin on me and won't be the like of the clumsy young fellows do be ploughing all times in the earth and dung. (*He starts.*) Is she coming again? (*He looks out.*) Stranger girls. God help me, where'll I hide my-myself away and my long neck naked to the world? (2) (*He looks out.*) I'd best go to the room maybe till I'm dressed again.

1. Note the importance of the props in this scene. Place them so that the audience is able to see CHRISTY's face at all times. For this exercise, the props can be imaginary.

2. This sudden change from confidence to fear is characteristic of CHRISTY, and should be comic.

In THE GLASS MENAGERIE, by Tennessee Williams, AMANDA WINGFIELD *and her two grown children,* TOM *and* LAURA, *live in a small tenement apartment in St. Louis.* AMANDA *was raised in the deep South, and her memories of her younger days provide a vivid contrast to the gloom of her family's present situation.*

AMANDA
*LAURA (can be cut)

AMANDA   I found an old dress in the trunk. But what do you know? I had to do a lot to it but it broke my heart when I had to let it out. Now, Laura, just look at your mother. Oh, no! Laura, come look at me now! (*Enters dining-room* L. *door. Comes down through living-room curtain to living-room* C.)

This speech provides an excellent opportunity for concentration, imagination, use of the body, use of costumes, and use of props. Remember that AMANDA still has a southern accent. Though she is a tired, middle-aged woman, she here discovers some of her youthful zest. The trick is to show both in the same speech.

LAURA (*re-enters from fire-escape landing. Sits on* L. *arm of armchair*).   Oh, Mother, how lovely! (1) (*Amanda wears a girlish frock. She carries a bunch of jonquils.*)

1. These lines may be cut if scene is done without LAURA.

AMANDA (*standing* C., *holding flowers.*)   It used to be. It used to be. It had a lot of flowers on it, but they got awful tired so I had to take them all off. I led the cotillion in this dress years ago. I won the cake-walk twice at Sunset Hill, and I wore it to the Governor's ball in Jackson. You should have seen your mother. You should have seen your mother how she just sashayed around (*Crossing around* L. *of day-bed back to* C.) the ballroom (2) just like that. I had it on the day I met your father. I had malaria fever, too. The change of climate from East Tennessee to the Delta—weakened my resistance. Not enough to be dangerous, just enough to make me restless and giddy. Oh, it was lovely. Invitations poured in from all over. My mother said, "You can't go any place because you have a fever. You have to stay in bed." I said I wouldn't and I took quinine and kept on going and going. Dances every evening and long rides in the country in the afternoon and picnics. That country—that country—so lovely—so lovely in May, all lacy with dogwood and simply flooded with jonquils. (3) My mother said, "You can't bring any more

2. Do so.

3. Take time to visualize all this in your memory; then, the tempo accelerates.

jonquils in this house." I said, "I will," and I kept on bringing them in anyhow. Whenever I saw them I said, "Wait a minute, I see jonquils," and I'd make my gentlemen callers get out of the carriage and help me gather some. To tell you the truth, Laura, it got to be a kind of a joke. "Look out," they'd say, "here comes that girl and we'll have to spend the afternoon picking jonquils." My mother said, "You can't bring any more jonquils in the house, there aren't any more vases to hold them." "That's quite all right," I said, "I can hold some myself." Malaria fever, your father and jonquils. (AMANDA *puts jonquils in* LAURA'S *lap and goes out on to fire-escape landing.*)

The following two monologues from Shakespeare's MACBETH provide excellent opportunities for concentration and use of the imagination. Enter into these soliloquies with your whole self: body, voice, emotions, and mind, and so contact the soul of the character.

LADY MACBETH *has just received word of the* WITCHES' *prophecies to her husband, one of which is that he shall be king. Then word comes that* KING DUNCAN *is planning to spend the night at their castle, and she begins to plot against his life.*

LADY MACBETH.   The raven himself is hoarse
That croaks the fatal entrance of Duncan 1.
Under my battlements. Come, you spirits
That tend on mortal thoughts, unsex me here,
And fill me, from the crown to the toe, top-full
Of direst cruelty! Make thick my blood, 2.
Stop up th' access and passage to remorse,
That no compunctious visitings of nature
Shake my fell purpose, nor keep peace between
Th' effect and it! Come to my woman's breasts,
And take my milk for gall, you murd'ring ministers,
Wherever in your sightless substances
You wait on nature's mischief! Come, thick night,
And pall thee in the dunnest smoke of hell,
That my keen knife see not the would it makes,
Nor heaven peep through the blanket of the dark,
To cry "Hold, hold!"

1. The messenger who brought the news was hoarse from breathlessness.

2. Take time to savor and relish these images. Build intensity as the speech progresses.

MACBETH *has been spurred on by his ambition and his wife to murder* KING DUNCAN *so that he can become king. But* MACBETH *has vacillated between fear and resolve. His mind is tormented, as we see in this speech.*

MACBETH.   Is this a dagger which I see before me,
  The handle toward my hand? Come, let me clutch
  thee. 1.
  I have thee not, and yet I see thee still.
  Art thou not, fatal vision, sensible
  To feeling as to sight, or art thou but
  A dagger of the mind, a false creation,
  Proceeding from the heat-oppressèd brain?
  I see thee yet, in form as palpable
  As this which now I draw.
  Thou marshal'st me the way that I was going; 2.
  And such an instrument I was to use.
  Mine eyes are made the fools o' th' other senses,
  Or else worth all the rest. I see thee still;
  And on thy blade and dudgeon gouts of blood, 3.
  Which was not so before. There's no such thing.
  It is the bloody business which informs
  Thus to mine eyes.

1. The actor must "see" an imaginary dagger floating in the air in front of him. Take time to relate to it and to discover that you cannot grab it.

2. The dagger begins to move. As it does, the actor's eyes and body must begin to follow it.

3. Really imagine this, and react fully.

*In THE ODD COUPLE, author Neil Simon presents one of his most famous comic situations. Two recently divorced men—*FELIX, *neat as a pin, and* OSCAR, *a slob—attempt to share an apartment. At this point,* OSCAR *has invited the* PIGEON *sisters to dinner.* FELIX *is petrified.*

*FELIX   GWENDOLYN   SUGGESTIONS AND
OSCAR   CECILY   STAGE DIRECTIONS

Timing is absolutely essential in playing comedy effectively. It is important to cultivate an ear for knowing precisely how long a pause should be to get best comic response. Use English accent and mannerisms for girls.

FELIX.   I'm through! 1.

OSCAR.   Then smile. (OSCAR *smiles and opens the door. The girls poke their heads through the door. They are in their young thirties and somewhat attractive. They are undoubtedly British*) Well, hello.

1. FELIX is through worrying about what is coming and braces himself to have a good time.

GWENDOLYN (*To* OSCAR). Hallo!

CECILY (*To* OSCAR). Hallo.

GWENDOLYN. I do hope we're not late.

OSCAR. No, no. You timed it perfectly. Come on in. (*He points to them as they enter*) Er, Felix, I'd like you to meet two very good friends of mine, Gwendolyn and Cecily . . .

CECILY (*Pointing out his mistake*). Cecily and Gwendolyn. 2.

OSCAR. Oh, yes, Cecily and Gwendolyn . . . er (*Trying to remember their last name*) Er . . . Don't tell me. Robin? No, no. Cardinal?

GWENDOLYN. Wrong both times. It's Pigeon!

OSCAR. Pigeon. Right. Cecily and Gwendolyn Pigeon.

GWENDOLYN (*To* FELIX). You don't spell it like Walter Pidgeon. You spell it like "Coo-Coo" Pigeon.

OSCAR. We'll remember that if it comes up. Cecily and Gwendolyn, I'd like you to meet my room-mate, and our chef for the evening, Felix Ungar.

CECILY (*Holding her hand out*). Heh d'yew dew?

FELIX (*Moving to her and shaking her hand*). How do you do?

GWENDOLYN (*Holding her hand out*). Heh d'yew dew?

FELIX (*Stepping up on the landing and shaking her hand*). How do you do? 3.

(*This puts him nose to nose with* OSCAR, *and there is an awkward pause as they look at each other*)

OSCAR. Well, we did that beautifully. Why don't we sit down and make ourselves comfortable?

(FELIX *steps aside and ushers the girls down into the room. There is ad libbing and a bit of confusion and milling about as they all squeeze between the arm-chair and the couch, and the* PIGEONS *finally seat themselves on the couch.* OSCAR *sits in the armchair, and* FELIX *sneaks past him to the love seat. Finally all have settled down*) 4.

CECILY. This is ever so nice, isn't it, Gwen?

2. OSCAR has them reversed. He can laugh generously at his mistake and perhaps invite the glum FELIX to join in.

3. FELIX is obviously very stiff.

4. FELIX finds a seat furthest from the girls. OSCAR is between them and FELIX.

GWENDOLYN (*Looking around*).   Lovely. And much nicer than our flat. Do you have help?

OSCAR.   Er, yes. I have a man who comes in every night.

CECILY.   Aren't you the lucky one?
(CECILY, GWENDOLYN *and* OSCAR *all laugh at her joke.* OSCAR *looks over at* FELIX *but there is no response*)

OSCAR (*Rubs his hands together*).   Well, isn't this nice? I was telling Felix yesterday about how we happened to meet.

GWENDOLYN.   Oh? Who's Felix?

OSCAR (*A little embarrassed, he points to* FELIX).   He is!

GWENDOLYN.   Oh, yes, of course. I'm so sorry.

(FELIX *nods that it's all right*)

CECILY.   You know it happened to us again this morning.

OSCAR.   What did?

GWENDOLYN.   Stuck in the elevator again.

OSCAR.   Really? Just the two of you?

CECILY.   And poor old Mr. Kessler from the third floor. We were there half an hour.

OSCAR.   No kidding? What happened?

GWENDOLYN.   Nothing much, I'm afraid.
(CECILY *and* GWENDOLYN *both laugh at her latest joke, joined by* OSCAR. *He once again looks over at* FELIX, *but there is no response*) 5.

> 5. In each case, FELIX's dour face kills OSCAR's laughter.

OSCAR (*Rubs his hands again*).   Well, this really is nice.

CECILY.   And ever so much cooler than our place.

GWENDOLYN.   It's like equatorial Africa on our side of the building.

CECILY.   Last night it was so bad Gwen and I sat there in nature's own cooling ourselves in front of the open fridge. Can you imagine such a thing?

OSCAR.   Er, I'm working on it.

GWENDOLYN.   Actually, it's impossible to get a night's sleep. Cec and I really don't know what to do.

Oscar.   Why don't you sleep with an air conditioner?

Gwendolyn.   We haven't got one.

Oscar.   I know. But we have.

Gwendolyn.   Oh, you! I told you about that one, didn't I, Cec?

Felix.   They say it may rain Friday.

(*They all stare at* Felix)

Gwendolyn.   Oh?

Cecily.   That should cool things off a bit.

Oscar.   I wouldn't be surprised.

Felix.   Although sometimes it gets hotter after it rains.

Gwendolyn.   Yes, it does, doesn't it?

(*They continue to stare at* Felix)

Felix (*jumps up and, picking up the ladle, starts for the kitchen*).   Dinner is served! 6.

6. The stares, the silences, and his nerves: FELIX cannot bear them any longer.

In LADY WINDERMERE'S FAN, by Oscar Wilde, Lady Windermere *believes her husband faithless. She steals away alone to* Lord Darlington's *rooms prepared to go away with him.* Mrs. Erlynne, *the woman* Lady Windermere *accuses, finds her there and urges her to go back to her husband, whom* Mrs. Erlynne *knows to be guiltless.*

LADY WINDERMERE
MRS. ERLYNNE (LADY WINDERMERE'S mother, but unknown by LADY WINDERMERE)

SUGGESTIONS AND STAGE DIRECTIONS

Lady Windermere.   You talk as if you had a heart. Women like you have no hearts. Heart is not in you. You are bought and sold.

Mrs. Erlynne (*starts, with a gesture of pain. Then restrains herself, and comes over to where* Lady Windermere *is sitting. As she speaks, she stretches out her hands towards her, but does not dare to touch her*).   Believe what you choose about me, I am not worth a moment's sorrow. (1) But don't spoil your beautiful young life on my account! One pays for one's sin, and then one pays again, and all one's life one pays. You must never know that. (2) I may have wrecked my own life, but I will not let you wreck yours. You—why, you are a mere girl, you would be lost. You haven't got the kind of brains that enables a

1. With Lady Windermere seated, Mrs. Erlynne dominates the scene.

2. Should be played in or near center stage.

woman to get back. You have neither the wit nor the courage. You couldn't stand dishonor. No! Go back, Lady Windermere, to the husband who loves you, whom you love. You have a child, Lady Windermere. Go back to that child who even now, in pain or in joy, may be calling to you. (LADY WINDERMERE *rises*.) (3) God gave you that child. He will require from you that you make his life fine, that you watch over him. What answer will you make to God if his life is ruined through you? Back to your house, Lady Windermere —your husband loves you. He has never swerved for a moment from the love he bears you. But even if he had a thousand loves, you must stay with your child. If he was harsh to you, you must stay with your child. If he ill-treated you, you must stay with your child. If he abandoned you, your place is with your child.

3. LADY WINDER-MERE may edge away, but MRS ERLYNNE follows, keeping the same distance between them.

(LADY WINDERMERE *bursts into tears, rushes to her.*)

LADY WINDERMERE (*holding out her hands, helplessly, as a child might do*).   Take me home. Take me home.

MRS. ERLYNNE (*is about to embrace her. Then restrains herself. There is a look of wonderful joy in her face*). Come! Where is your cloak? Here. Put it on. Come at once! (*They go to the door.*)

MY FAIR LADY, a musical by Alan J. Lerner and Frederick Loewe, is considered by many to be the highest point yet reached by musical theater. It is based on the play PYGMALION, by George Bernard Shaw, which in turn was based on a Greek legend. HENRY HIGGINS has been attempting to transform the slovenly speech of ELIZA DOOLITTLE into the dulcet speech of the aristocracy. HIGGINS and his friend PICKERING have taken ELIZA to the races, a high-society function. The others suppose that ELIZA is of their own social stratum.

HENRY HIGGINS	ELIZA DOOLITTLE
*COL. PICKERING	MRS. HIGGINS (Henry's
FREDDY HILL	mother)
*LORD BOXINGTON	MRS. EYNSFORD-HILL
	LADY BOXINGTON

SUGGESTIONS AND STAGE DIRECTIONS

Be sure ELIZA is in position to get focus. Change focus at end as all stand to watch the race.

FREDDY.   The first race was very exciting, Miss Doolittle. I'm so sorry you missed it. 1.

MRS. HIGGINS (*Hurriedly*).   Will it rain do you think?

1. ELIZA has just arrived and been introduced to the group.

ELIZA. The rain in Spain stays mainly in the plain. 2.

(HIGGINS *irresistibly does a quick fandango step which is so bizarre that the others have nothing to do but pretend it didn't happen*)

But in Hertford, Hereford and Hampshire hurricanes hardly ever happen. 2.

FREDDY. Ha, ha, how awfully funny.

ELIZA. What is wrong with that, young man? I bet I got it right.

FREDDY. Smashing!

MRS. EYNSFORD-HILL. I do hope we won't have any un-seasonably cold spells. It brings on so much influenza, and our whole family is susceptible to it.

ELIZA (*Darkly*). My aunt died of influenza, so they said. (MRS. EYNSFORD-HILL *clicks her tongue sympathetically*) But it's my belief they done the old woman in. 3.

(HIGGINS *and* PICKERING *look at each other accusingly as if each blames the other for having taught* ELIZA *this last unrehearsed phrase*)

MRS. HIGGINS (*Puzzled*). Done her in?

ELIZA. Yes, Lord love you! Why should she die of influ-enza when she come through diphtheria right enough the year before? Fairly blue with it she was. They all thought she was dead; but my father, he kept ladling gin down her throat. 3.

(HIGGINS, *for want of something to do, balances his tea cup on his head and takes several steps without spilling it. Quite a feat*) 4.

Then she came to so sudden that she bit the bowl off the spoon.

MRS. EYNSFORD-HILL (*Startled*). Dear me!

ELIZA (*Piling up the indictment*). Now, what call would a woman with that strength in her have to die of influenza, and what become of her new straw hat that should have come to me? Somebody pinched it.

(HIGGINS *fans himself with a silver tray off the tea cart*) 4.

2. These are some of the pronunciation exercises HIGGINS has given ELIZA. She finds them them appropriate to in-sert in the conversation.

3. These kinds of phrases are all the funnier as ELIZA speaks them in a proper British accent, not her old Cockney.

4. HIGGINS' ridicu-lous actions illustrate his comic nervousness in this situation and lend a farcical air to the scene.

And what I say is, them as pinched it, done her in.

LORD BOXINGTON (*Nervously loud*).   Done her in? Done her in, did you say?

HIGGINS (*Hastily*).   Oh, that's the new small talk. To do a person in means to kill them.

MRS. EYNSFORD-HILL (*To* ELIZA, *horrified*).   You surely don't believe your aunt was killed?

ELIZA.   Do I not! Them she lived with would have killed her for a hatpin, let alone a hat.

MRS. EYNSFORD-HILL.   But it can't have been right for your father to pour spirits down her throat like that. It might have killed her.

ELIZA.   Not her. Gin was mother's milk to her. (PICKERING *stiffens.* HIGGINS *decides to leave, tips his hat to all, and starts off.* (5) *However, his uncontrollable curiosity holds him at the last moment to hear what else* ELIZA *has to say*) Besides, he'd poured so much down his own throat that he knew the good of it.

5. PICKERING and HIGGINS are more and more sure that ELIZA is going to reveal by her speech that she is really a lower-class Cockney. This is the central tension of the scene.

LORD BOXINGTON.   Do you mean that he drank?

ELIZA.   Drank! My word! Something chronic. (*To* FREDDY, *who is in convulsions of suppressed laughter*) Here! What are you sniggering at?

FREDDY.   The new small talk. You do it so awfully well.

ELIZA.   If I was doing it proper, what was you laughing at? (*To* HIGGINS) Have I said anything I oughtn't?

MRS. HIGGINS (*Interposing*).   Not at all, my dear.

ELIZA.   Well, that's a mercy, anyhow. (*Expansively*) What I always say is . . .

(PICKERING *jumps to his feet. He and* HIGGINS *make a number of desperate signals and strange sounds to prevent her from going on*) 5.

PICKERING (*Rushing to* ELIZA).   I don't suppose there's enough time before the next race to place a bet? (*To* ELIZA) Come, my dear.

(ELIZA *rises*)

MRS. HIGGINS.   I'm afraid not, Colonel Pickering.

(*They all rise as several of the ladies and gentlemen enter to take their positions for the next race*) 6.

FREDDY.   I have a bet on number seven. I should be so happy if you would take it. You'll enjoy the race ever so much more. (*He offers her a race ticket. She accepts*)

ELIZA.   That's very kind of you.

(FREDDY *leads* ELIZA *to a vantage point directly center*)

FREDDY.   His name is Dover.

ELIZA (*Repeating the name*)   Dover.

LADIES *and* GENTLEMEN *and* ALL (*except Higgins*)
There they are again
Lining up to run.
Now they're holding steady,
They are ready
For it.
Look! It has begun!

(*Again the mummified silence. The one exception is* ELIZA. *Clenching her fists with excitement, she leans forward. Oblivious to the deportment of those around her, she begins to cheer her horse on*) 7.

ELIZA (*at first softly*).   Come on, come on, Dover!

(*The* LADIES *and* GENTLEMEN *slowly turn to stare at her and look at each other in wonder*) 8.

Come on, come on, Dover!

(*Her voice crescendoes. The* LADIES *and* GENTLEMEN *move perceptively away from this ugly exhibition of natural behavior*) 8.

Come on Dover!!! Move your bloomin' arse!!! 9.

(*An agonizing moan rises up from the crowd.* (8) *The moment she says it she realizes what she has done and brings her hand to her mouth as if trying to push the words back in. Several women gracefully faint, and are caught by their escorts.* LORD *and* LADY BOXINGTON *are staggered.* PICKERING *flies from the scene running faster than Dover.* HIGGINS, *of course, roars with laughter*) 10.

6. They all come forward a few feet to an imaginary railing of some sort. The "extras" may be cut for this exercise.

7. The eyes of the crowd move in unison, following the progress of the horses from one far side to the other. ELIZA's body responses are in stark contrast to the reserved dignity of the others.

8. These reactions are also performed in unison.

9. ELIZA finally lapses back into her Cockney dialect, at its most colorful.

10. All this action occurs simultaneously and should give the impression of pandemonium breaking loose.

THE MERRY WIDOW *is a musical play by Charles George, with music by Franz Lehar. The scene is in a lounge of a smart seaside resort hotel where there is much small talk among guests. Men are greatly attracted by* ADELE, *the charming and stunning Merry Widow.*

"BERTIE" PRESTON (an elderly playboy)
MONTGOMERY NELSON attractive at 30)

ADELE TALBOT (the Merry Widow)
CLARISSA PRESTON (Bertie's wife)
BEATRICE KILLGARDEN (attractive columnist)

MONTY (*going to Bertie*).   And, Bertie, you old dog! How are you?

BERTIE (*as they shake hands*).   In the pink, brother! In the pink! (*He flexes his muscles and shakes his legs. General laughter.*)

CLARISSA (*to Beatrice*).   You know Mrs. Talbot? 1.

BEATRICE (*bowing*).   We've met!

ADELE (*trying to recall*).   Really?

BEATRICE.   When you and Mr. Talbot were on your world-wide honeymoon.

ADELE (*charmingly*).   Well—we visited so many places and met ever so many people that it's something of a jumble. So do forgive me if I don't recall exactly—

BEATRICE (*going to Adele*).   This was in Altruria. Of course, you remember Altruria? 2.

ADELE (*obviously affected by the memory*).   Why—yes—certainly.

MONTY.   Where in the world is Altruria?

BERTIE.   It's one of those central European kingdoms that pop up after a good spring rain. (*General laughter except from Adele.*)

BEATRICE.   It's a quaint little country. Its people are very friendly—extremely friendly—if you recall, Mrs. Talbot.

ADELE (*trying to smile*).   Yes—that's quite true. 3.

1. Characters are grouped near center stage, each face in view of audience.

2. General shifting of positions, ADELE to one side, apart from others.

3. ADELE gives an affected smile.

The Director and the Cast   **225**

BEATRICE. You and your late husband were dining in one of those picturesque cafes in the town of Vilia. At the table next to yours were two gentlemen; one young, handsome and debonair; the other slightly older. Before the evening was over, all of you had become friends. Now I am *sure* you remember. 4.

4. ADELE may be seated, BEATRICE stands near her.

ADELE. You're quite right. I *do* remember!

BEATRICE. I've often wondered if the younger gentleman revealed his true identity to you and Mr. Talbot. Perhaps you didn't know that he was the playboy Prince Nikalas.

CLARISSA. A Prince? How thrilling!

ADELE. Oh, yes! We knew! And now, if you'll excuse me—(*She starts up C. Monty follows quickly.*) No, Monty! I'll join you a little later, if you don't mind.

MONTY (*concerned*). Certainly, if you wish. But is anything wrong?

ADELE (*forcing a light laugh*). No, not at all. Just a woman's usual excuse—a slight headache. (*She is gone out C. off R.*)

CLARISSA. She seemed upset. No doubt the memory of her honeymoon. (*At this remark, Monty comes down R.*)

BERTIE. Those memories can be very disturbing. (*Coughs, significantly.*)

BEATRICE. Memories are an eternal earthly Paradise from which there is no awakening.

BERTIE. Or a Hell from which there is no escape.

CLARISSA (*going to him at L.*). Bertie, darling! What a thing to say! What will Miss Killgarden think? (*Laughs very forced as she caresses Bertie, much to his dislike.*) 5.

5. Perhaps CLARISSA strokes his bald head, or pats his cheek.

BEATRICE (*observing this*). By the way, have any of you met Mr. Popenstein?

MONTY (*Bertie joins with Monty to ad lib.*) Popenstein? No, I don't believe so, etc. ad lib. (*Clarissa is silent.*) (*Ad lib in full voice.*) 6.

6. Characters move about the room, perhaps admiring knick-knacks.

BEATRICE. He's become quite a personage since his arrival here, especially with the ladies. He attracts them as smorgasbord attracts a glutton.

MONTY (*amusedly*).   I wonder what technique he uses?

BEATRICE.   In Europe, it's called continental charm. In America, it's called a good line. (*Laughter from the two men.*) Of course, you have met him, Mrs. Preston?

CLARISSA (*uncomfortable*).   Why—yes—I believe so.

BEATRICE.   I'm sure none of our sex has missed him—except perhaps Mrs. Talbot, who is newly arrived. But she'll meet him—that's certain.

CLARISSA.   Which reminds me—there is something I must ask Adele—so before it slips my mind, I'll join her. (*Goes up C.*) If you'll excuse me.

OTHERS.   Of course! Certainly! (*And from Bertie*) Why not? (*Clarissa exits C. off R.*)

BERTIE (*to Beatrice*).   This fellow—Popenstein—you say he's quite successful with the ladies?

BEATRICE (*wryly amused*).   Sure-fire!

BERTIE.   I must cultivate him and study his method. (*General laughter.*)

BEATRICE.   You're an incurable optimist, aren't you, Mr. Preston?

BERTIE.   I decline to be a pessimist where lovely women are concerned. Why spoil a good time?

MONTY.   Have you ever married, Miss Killgarden? 7.

7. MONTY and BEATRICE stand near each other.

BEATRICE.   Not yet, and I doubt if ever I shall.

MONTY.   A man-hater?

BEATRICE.   Not at all. I admire men—I've even fancied myself in love with one or two. That is the Lucy Lovejoy who writes the advice to the lovelorn column. But the real Beatrice Killgarden who writes the gossip column nullifies everything Lucy has expressed.

BERTIE.   I see! In one column, you *justify* love; in the other, you *crucify* it.

BEATRICE.   (*She is between them for the musical number.*) Exactly!

Love Is

BERTIE, MONTY and BEATRICE

Lyric by
CHARLES GEORGE

Music by
FRANZ LEHAR

VALSE Vivace

Love is glad - ness, Love is mad - ness, Love is
ques - tion, of di - ges - tion, And it's
thet - ic, It's pa - thet - ic, It has

just a touch of Spring. El - e - vat - ing, En - er -
not hard to di - gest. Stim - u - lat - ing, Nau - se -
such en - tranc - ing charm. Love's ex - ces - sive, Too ex -

vat - ing, Love's the best of ev - 'ry thing. Love is
at - ing, But we seek it out with zest. Love's a
ces - sive, It will do more good than harm. Love's hyp -

cheer - ing, Dom - i - neer - ing, It's the kick that makes you
trea - sure, Doubt - ful plea - sure, If that's true the fault's not
not - ic, It's neu - rot - ic, When it hits you, It's a

fizz. It's de - press - ing, And dis - tress - ing, Do you
his. That's what he tells, Love for me smells, Do you
whizz. Love is phon - ey, Just ba - lon - ey, Do you

1.2. Men **3.**

know just what love is?_____ Love's a
know just what love is?_____ Love's as -
know just what love is?_____

CHAPTER 12

Performing with Sets, Props, and Costumes

In a way, you are a magician. You can make a stage seem like any place, in any time. The stage is your environment. You must work with various playing spaces, props, costumes, lights, stage furnishings, and entrances and exits to perform your magic.

THE SET

The modern scenery trend is to experiment, blending a combination of scenery designs and styles. Action must be fitted to the stage set. The *thrust* is one of the newest and most popular stage designs, in which the audience is seated in a horseshoe arrangement around three sides of the stage. There is a type of low scenery that allows the audience to see all the action and all the players.

Designers use steps and levels, low screens, and low set pieces of furnishings such as benches, stools, low tables, lamps, and even sturdy wood blocks, all arranged on the various playing areas. These give merely a suggestion of the location which is pinpointed by the lines in the play.

Use the stage environment to help you create an imaginary world. Use the stage furnishings as an aid to imagination. Make the audience imagine with you that the stage and set pieces are what the author has willed them to be. Actors, like children, must learn to pretend.

As soon as your set pieces or their equivalents are in place, you can practice your entrances and exits through doors, curtains, or imaginary openings, which may take you from spotlights into darkness or even into another playing area out of audience attention.

Proscenium stages are used in more theaters than any other kind. Spectators are seated facing the front of a conventional stage, an arrangement which has many *advantages* as well as *disadvantages.* There is less of the close-up give-and-take feeling than with an arena or thrust stage; empathy diminishes with distance. You will find audience emotions more difficult to stir when you act behind far-off footlights.

There are many advantages to conventional stages. Scenery can be tall or heavy because it can be removed between acts, out of sight of the audience. A front curtain shuts out all stage movement before the opening of the play, after closing, and between acts. With thrust and arena stages most scene and prop changes must be made on a darkened stage, with audience watching stage hands' dimmed movements.

A spectacle act or setting can be more effective when viewed from the distance of the conventional stage. Such stages are usually larger, making room for larger casts and for the division of the stage into numerous segments by scenery or by lights.

In *arena stages,* the audience is seated on all sides of the playing space. When playing on arena stage, you will change positions often to give the audience an opportunity to see the faces and actions of all members of the cast. Some of the actors should be facing different directions at all times during the play. Even if a segment of the audience cannot see the full face of the speakers, they will get views of other players.

Furnishings and scenery must be kept low; scenery is almost nonexistent. Because arena audiences are near the stage, voices carry to them more easily than to larger audiences, but actions should still be large so that every person is able to see them. Stages are practical and attractive when there are various levels for action.

Every actor must become thoroughly familiar with his or her movements on every section of the stage, as designed for a particular play. To make this possible, the playing areas of the stage should be ready well in advance of the opening date. The stage may give you less playing space than you had planned on. Don't go too close to open edges on an upper level, not for

Dinny and the Witches by William Gibson was presented by University of Missouri, with John Robert Lloyd as director. These costumes are the kind any costume mistress can put together. Very effective.

The Yellow Jacket by George Cochrane and Joseph Henry Benrino is made especially effective by the authentic Chinese costumes. Scenery and props also enhance the effect. Presented at Grove City College; Miriam A. Franklin, director.

your safety alone, but for the fear you generate in spectators, who may cringe for your safety and lose interest in the play.

Sight lines for each playing space are very important. It is your responsibility to be within view of the audience with every line you speak. In order that actors may become familiar with sight lines, it is necessary for the stage set to be ready about three weeks ahead of opening night.

On a conventional stage and many others, you need practice in *opening and closing doors.* As you open a door from the outside when entering the stage, use your upstage hand and take your first step with the upstage foot. This will turn your face somewhat toward your audience. In exits, you usually open the door with your upstage hand, move partially through the door, and reach back to close the door with the downstage hand, while you speak your exit line.

PROPERTIES

In a modern stage setting when you must use sofas, deep chairs, or ottomans, it is a good idea to sit forward throughout the scene or use plump cushions at your back to make it easier to rise to your feet. It is better if the prop crew realizes the problem and will substitute benches, straight-backed chairs, or knee-high stools for modern overstuffed furnishings. Tall people may have no problem with deep seats.

Hand props are almost essential for working up a part when they are necessary to the scene. You may use a piece of pasteboard for a hand mirror, a paper cup for a tea cup, or a couple of books to represent a leafy house plant. But to change, after a time, to a real prop is not easy.

You try to feel and sense the real activity with the hand prop: the fragrance and beauty of a rose must be projected by you to the spectators, and the primping behind a pasteboard must seem real so that it will carry the sensory image of a hand mirror.

One very difficult piece of business to project is the feeling of temperature. Say you come indoors on a cold day, take off your heavy gloves to warm your hands, and take off your big coat, shivering. You must make the viewers feel the atmosphere that you are projecting to them. When drinking coffee or tea, you act as if the cup is very hot and the beverage is ready to burn your tongue. If the action is well played, the viewers will feel the same sensory effects that you are imagining. When you pull off gloves after a frigid walk, the audience should shiver as you shiver. Use your imagination to telegraph imagery to your audience. Study films and TV for examples.

COSTUMES

Costumes suitable for your character may *look* easy to use. However, if you play a great-grandparent, a child, or an elegant historical character, you may find that getting used to an appropriate costume requires diligent practice. In real life, mothers and teenage daughters often wear the same clothes or trade them back and forth. However, the audience may not accept as believable a young girl playing the part of a mother who wears teenage clothes. In order to be convincing, the girl will need to dress a bit more like a matron.

The wearing of your real costume will usually be delayed until the final rehearsals. Try to imagine your costume so that it will feel fairly comfortable when you wear it. Observe movements and mannerisms of characters that you see on film and TV.

Practice how you think a character would move and act when wearing a heavy brocade silk or velvet, great sleeves, a bustle, or a hoop skirt. A man needs to practice movements of one wearing tight knee-length breeches, ruffled cuffs, elegant wigs, or Prince Albert coats. A man may have trouble carrying a large lace handkerchief throughout a scene. Women may have difficulty feeling at home in antique work clothes: long house dresses, long tie-around aprons, dumpy heavy broad-toed shoes. Use of makeshift costumes in early rehearsals may help.

Costumes create the visual appearance of characters. They show social status, as when coarse, open-weave homespun or a very wrinkled costume is worn by a character of meager means or perhaps a careless, untidy character. They help create a mood, as when bright gay colors are used in farce or somber shades in heavy tragedy. Colors or texture can help emphasize a character who wears striking black among bright colors or bright plaid among plain colors. Glisteny silks can also be used for emphasis. Both men's and women's costumes can follow the same color principles.

STAGE LIGHTS

Stage lighting has changed and advanced rapidly in the past two decades to become very important. The actor needs to become aware of spotlights as they focus on different stage areas.

Light changes are used to create many illusions, as when a window shade is raised and light floods a room, seemingly from that window. Actors need to take care when "lighting" a kerosene lamp; the action needs to be masked so that the audience does not see the electricity suddenly come on

The Mouse Trap by Agatha Christie
was directed by Robert W. Myers
for the Mount Pleasant Players.
Careful costuming, as well as stage
levels, helps in this production.

The Miracle Worker by William Gibson is nicely staged in this scene. The screen door
separating outdoors from indoors is splendidly planned. The pump, old bucket, and old
chair all help. Production by South Dakota State University; James L. Johnson, director.

with a spot turned on the lamp. Of course, they know what is taking place, but they want to believe that the play is a reality.

If you are in an important scene at a particular time, you will need to move into a *spotlighted* area. On the other hand, if your character is not important in that scene, you should give stage to the character who should be seen. Near every spotlight there are shaded areas. Scenes must not be played in shadow unless the story requires that kind of mystery. Every spoken line should come from a character who can be seen clearly and located quickly by spectators.

Light can divide a stage into sections, with shadow between them to form the *partitions* between different rooms, or house and garden, or between playing areas of a stage. Entrances and steps are usually spotlighted when scenes are played there. When you enter a stage, time your steps so that you are in the lighted area for your line, after having assumed your character backstage.

It is necessary that your lighting equipment be properly placed and in the hands of a competent *lighting staff*. Young people enjoy working with lighting equipment, even if they have had no training and experience. With good rehearsal, they will do well. Both crew and actors need light rehearsals; they should begin well in advance of dress rehearsals.

COOPERATION

The value of cooperation cannot be stressed too much. It is a quality you will wish to make a habit of in all your theater experiences. So many people, each with his or her own special duties, are involved in the many branches of a production that conflicts may be expected to arise. Your director will do his or her best to weave all into a unified and happy production team, but sometimes thoughtlessness causes difficulties and hard feelings.

It would be impossible to cite all the many ways to cooperate, but here is a short list.

1. When crews need the stage, keep out of their way. They have work to do, and in record time.
2. Respect crews as authorities in their fields. This is true for rehearsals as well as performances.
3. Don't use offstage props for any purpose. Furniture and set pieces are not intended to hold gloves, scripts, etc.
4. Don't give directions to crews. Leave that to head crewpersons.
5. Be tactful, tireless, and uncomplaining

In short: Work with others as you would have them work with you.

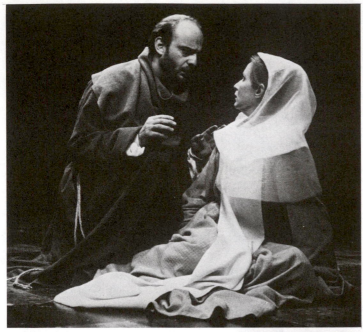

Measure for Measure by William Shakespeare is effectively costumed and the characters well positioned in this scene from the Yale Repertory Theatre production. Directed by John Madden, photographed by Kirsten Beck/Gerry Goodstein Studios.

The Prince, the Wolf, and the Firebird by Jackson Lacey. The play was given by Eastern Michigan University, and directed by Thelma L. McDaniel. Rich and effective costumes.

You have studied many aspects of rehearsal. With these admonitions in mind, you now come to the exciting moment of acting before an audience. As you study the next chapter, you may visualize yourself in a play, doing the thing you want most to do—acting. It will be exciting; however, there are many things to keep in mind, some new and some already discussed, as you study how to give your performance.

Excerpts for Practice

YOU CAN'T TAKE IT WITH YOU, by Moss Hart and George Kaufman, is a play about a zany household, the VANDERHOF-SYCAMORES. *The house is filled with eccentric characters who have found a haven for doing exactly what they want to do without the push to make money at a "normal" job. As the play begins,* ESSIE *comes in from the kitchen where she and* RHEBA, *the maid, have been making candy.* PENNY, ESSIE's *mother, is busy writing her eleventh play.* PENNY's *husband,* PAUL, *makes fireworks in the basement with* MR. DEPINNA, *who came to deliver ice several years ago and decided to stay.*

PAUL SYCAMORE   ESSIE
                  PENNY
                  RHEBA

SUGGESTIONS AND
STAGE DIRECTIONS

The variety of eccentric characters offers plenty of opportunities for character study. Do not be afraid to take some of the character traits to the extreme for comic effect.

ESSIE (*fanning herself*).   My, that kitchen's hot.

PENNY (*finishing a bit of typing*).   (1) What, Essie?

ESSIE.   I say the kitchen's awful hot. That new candy I'm making—it just won't ever get cool.

PENNEY.   Do you have to make candy today, Essie? It's such a hot day.

ESSIE.   Well, I got all those new orders. Ed went out and got a bunch of new orders.

PENNY.   My, if it keeps on I suppose you'll be opening up a store.

ESSIE.   That's what Ed was saying last night, but I said No, I want to be a dancer. (*Bracing herself against the table, she manipulates her legs, ballet fashion.*)   1.

PENNY.   The only trouble with dancing is, it takes so long. You've been studying such a long time.

1. Each of the characters begins to define him or herself in relation to some prop (typewriter, table as ballet bar, tablecloth and table service, firecracker, sky rockets). Relate to props carefully and comfortably.

ESSIE (*slowly drawing a leg up behind her as she talks*). Only—eight—years. After all, mother, you've been writing plays for eight years. We started about the same time, didn't we?

PENNY. Yes, but you shouldn't count my first two years, because I was learning to type.

(*From the kitchen comes a colored maid named* RHEBA—*a very black girl somewhere in her thirties. She carries a white tablecloth, and presently starts to spread it over the table.*) 1.

RHEBA (*as she enters*). I think the candy's hardening up now, Miss Essie.

ESSIE. Oh, thanks, Rheba. I'll bring some in, mother— I want you to try it. (*She goes into the kitchen.*)

(PENNY *returns to her work as* RHEBA *busies herself with the table.*)

RHEBA. Finish the second act, Mrs. Sycamore?

PENNY. Oh, no, Rheba. I've just got Cynthia entering the monastery.

RHEBA. Monastery? How'd she get there? She was at the El Morocco, wasn't she?

PENNY. Well, she gets tired of the El Morocco, and there's this monastery, so she goes there.

RHEBA. Do they let her in?

PENNY. Yes, I made it Visitors' Day, so of course anybody can come.

RHEBA. Oh.

PENNY. So she arrives on Visitors' Day, and—just stays.

RHEBA. All night?

PENNY. Oh, yes. She stays six years.

RHEBA. (*as she goes into the kitchen*). Six years? My, I bet she busts that monastery wide open.

PENNY. . . . I'm going back to my war play, Essie. What do you think?

ESSIE. Oh, are you, mother?

PENNY. Yes, I sort of got myself into a monastery and I can't get out.

ESSIE. Oh, well, it'll come to you, mother. Remember how you got out of that brothel. . . . Hello, boys. (*This little greeting is idly tossed toward the snake solarium, a glass structure looking something like a goldfish aquarium, but containing, believe it or not, snakes.*) The snakes look hungry. Did Rheba feed them?

PENNY (*as* RHEBA *re-enters*). I don't know. Rheba, did you feed the snakes yet?

RHEBA. No, Donald's coming and he always brings flies with him.

PENNY. Well, try to feed them before Grandpa gets home. You know how fussy he is about them.

RHEBA. Yes'm.

PENNY (*handing her the kittens*). And take Groucho and Harpo into the kitchen with you. . . . I think I'll have another Love Dream. (MR. SYCAMORE *emerges from the cellar again.*)

PAUL. Mr. De Pinna was right about the balloon. It was too close to the powder.

ESSIE (*practicing a dance step*). Want a Love Dream, father? They're on the table.

PAUL. No, thanks. I gotta wash.

PENNY. I'm going back to the war play, Paul.

PAUL. Oh that's nice. We're putting some red stars after the blue stars, then come the bombs and *then* the balloon. That ought to do it. (*He goes up the stairs.*)

ESSIE (*another dance step*). Mr. Kolenkhov says I'm his most promising pupil.

PENNY (*absorbed in her own troubles*). You know, with forty monks and one girl, something ought to happen.

BAREFOOT IN THE PARK is a charming Neil Simon play about the first frustrating week in the lives of a young married couple, PAUL and CORIE. In this scene, CORIE's mother, who is coming to dinner, has just succeeded in finding their tiny apartment—an exhausting chore.

| PAUL | CORIE
MOTHER | SUGGESTIONS AND
STAGE DIRECTIONS |

PAUL (*He opens the door*). Hello, Mom.

(MOTHER *collapses in and* PAUL *and* CORIE *rush to support her.* (1) *They quickly lead her to the armchair at right of the couch*)

CORIE. Hello, sweetheart, how are you? (*She kisses* MOTHER, *who gasps for air*) Are you all right? (MOTHER *nods*) You want some water?

(MOTHER *shakes her head "No" as* PAUL *and* CORIE *lower her into the chair. She drops her pocketbook on the floor*)

MOTHER. Paul . . . in my pocketbook . . . are some pink pills.

PAUL (*Picks up her bag, closes the door, and begins to look for the pills*). Pink pills . . . 2.

(CORIE *helps* MOTHER *take off her coat*)

MOTHER. I'll be all right . . . Just a little out of breath . . .

(CORIE *crosses to the coffee table and pours a drink*)

I had to park the car six blocks away . . . then it started to rain so I ran the last two blocks . . . then my heel got caught in the subway grating . . . so I pulled my foot out and stepped in a puddle . . . then a cab went by and splashed my stockings . . . if the hardware store downstairs was open . . . I was going to buy a knife and kill myself. 3.

(PAUL *gives her a pill, and* CORIE *gives her a drink*)

CORIE. Here, Mom. Drink this down.

PAUL. Here's the pill . . .

(MOTHER *takes the pill, drinks, and coughs*)

MOTHER. A martini? To wash down a pill?

CORIE. It'll make you feel better.

MOTHER. I *had* a martini at home. It made me sick . . . That's why I'm taking the pill . . .

(CORIE *puts the drink down on the table*)

PAUL (*Sitting on the end table*). You must be exhausted.

A clear ground plan is essential for the blocking of this scene. Be sure to set all the furniture early in rehearsal and determine where the bedroom will be. Use of all props will also have to be carefully blocked

1. This reaction must be rehearsed so that it looks precarious but is really safe.

2. The actor playing PAUL could have some fun here wading through the contents of MOTHER's purse, but should not steal focus.

3. She relives for them the emotional nightmare she has endured to get there. Perhaps she gets more frantic as she speaks.

MOTHER. I'd just like to crawl into bed and cry myself to sleep.

CORIE (*Offering her the tray of hors d'oeuvres*). Here. Mom, have an hors d'oeuvre.

MOTHER. No, thank you, dear.

CORIE. It's just blue cheese and sour cream.

MOTHER (*Holds her stomach*). I wish you hadn't said that.

PAUL. She doesn't feel like it, Corie . . . (CORIE *puts the tray down and sits on the couch.* PAUL *turns to* MOTHER) Maybe you'd like to lie down?

CORIE (*Panicky*). Now? She can't lie down now.

MOTHER. Corie's right. I can't lie down without my board . . . (*She puts her gloves into a pocket of her coat*) Right now all I want to do is see the apartment.

PAUL (*Sitting on the couch*). That's right. You haven't seen it with its clothes on, have you?

MOTHER (*Rises and moves to the left*). Oh, Corie . . . Corie . . .

CORIE. She doesn't like it.

MOTHER (*Exhausted, she sinks into the armchair at left of the couch*). Like it? It's magnificent . . . and in less than a week. My goodness, how did you manage? Where did you get your ideas from?

PAUL. We have a decorator who comes in through the window once a week.

CORIE (*Crossing to the bedroom*). Come take a look at the bedroom.

MOTHER (*Crossing to the bedroom*). Yes, that's what I want to do . . . look at the bedroom. Were you able to get the bed in? (*She looks into the room*) Oh, it just fits, doesn't it? 4.

PAUL (*Moves to the stairs*). (5) Just. We have to turn in unison.

MOTHER. It looks very snug . . . and did you find a way to get to the closet?

CORIE. Oh, we decided not to use the closet for a while.

4. If you have no door to look through, imagine one. All should agree on exactly how the room looks. Visualize the items.

5. A few stairs leading to bedroom. Cut them for this exercise.

MOTHER. Really? Don't you need the space?

PAUL. Not as much as we need the clothes. It flooded.

MOTHER. The closet flooded?

CORIE. It was an accident. Mr. Velasco left his bathtub running.

MOTHER (*Moving down the stairs*). Mr. Velasco . . . Oh, the man upstairs . . .

PAUL (*Taking her arm*). Oh, then you know about Mr. Velasco?

MOTHER. Oh, yes. Corie had me on the phone for two hours.

PAUL. Did you know he's been married three times?

MOTHER. Yes . . . (*She turns back to* CORIE) If I were you, dear, I'd sleep with a gun. (*She sits in the bentwood armchair*)

PAUL. Well, there's just one thing I want to say about this evening . . .

CORIE (*Quickly, as she crosses to the coffee table*). Er . . . not before you have a drink. (*She hands* MOTHER *the martini*) Come on, Mother. To toast our new home.

MOTHER (*Holding the glass*). Well, I can't refuse that.

CORIE (*Making a toast*). To the wonderful new life that's ahead of us all.

PAUL (*Holds up his glass*). And to the best sport I've ever seen. Your mother.

FATHER OF THE BRIDE, by Caroline Francke and Edward Streeter, is a comedy with some splendid roles. On the day of the wedding, a great deal of confusion and disagreement have stirred the BANKS *household. Last minute problems arise as the* BANKS FAMILY *is getting ready to go to the church for the ceremony.*

MR. BANKS	MRS. BANKS	SUGGESTIONS AND
BEN, age 18	KAY, the bride	STAGE DIRECTIONS
TOMMY, age 15	MRS. PULITZKI, dressmaker	

BANKS. You are the only ushers who know our family and you are responsible for seating them.

BEN. I know, Pops.

MRS. BANKS.   And I should be there, too.

BANKS.   Your mother is dependent on you . . . she should be there before us.   1.

BEN.   But, Pops, we did the best we could.

MRS. BANKS (*calling off* L.).   Hurry, Tommy.

TOMMY (*calling off* L.).   I am, Mom. Just putting it on.

MRS. BANKS.   Shouldn't your car be here, too, Stanley?

BANKS.   Yes—is Kay ready?

MRS. BANKS.   I thought she was ready when I came down. (*Calling.*) Kay——

MRS. PULITSKI (*calling*).   We're coming, Mrs. Banks.— Now slowly, Miss Kay—especially when you turn— slowly— (KAY *enters* L. *in full array: train, veil, bouquet, gloves. Moves to the same rhythm as though she were walking down the aisle—hesitating on every step. She pauses just as she enters and waits for* MRS. PULITSKI *to turn her train for her.* MRS. PULITSKI *follows her in* L.)

BANKS.   Kay!

MRS. BANKS.   Darling, you're lovely!

KAY.   Am I, Mother? Am I all right?   2.

BEN.   I'll say you're all right!

KAY.   Thanks, Ben.

BANKS (*in awe*).   You're beautiful!   3.

KAY.   Oh, I'm glad—if it's true. Shouldn't we be going? Shouldn't the boys have gone?

BANKS.   Yes—to both—(*He bellows off* L.) (3) TOM-MY!

TOMMY (*calling off*).   I am all ready—It's just that I can't find any cuff links.   3.

BANKS (*yelling*).   COME DOWN AS YOU ARE—THIS MINUTE!

KAY.   Where's our car, Pops?

BANKS.   It should be here, dear—(TOMMY *careens, enters* L. *completely slicked, but with his cuffs flapping. Holds out his arms and stares at the offending wrists.*)

TOMMY (*panting*).   I had 'em—only yesterday!   4.

1. Although no business is outlined by authors here, there should be a sense of hurry, confusion and impatience: hurry to see if the car is ready, hurry to the door to call TOMMY, hurry toward the door through which KAY will enter.

2. KAY would probably stand apart, perhaps up-stage of the others. She might be near her entrance at L., others R. She can balance, esthetically, all the others.

3. Agonizing pause.

4. Now, step up the tempo. Lines and action will seem faster in contrast to the preceding slow tempo.

BANKS.　God! Help me not to kill that boy!

MRS. BANKS.　Can't you roll them up, dear?

KAY.　Tommy—my wedding day!

TOMMY.　Oh, Gee, Kay, I didn't mean to do anything to your wedding day. It's just I can't find them.

MRS. PULITSKI.　Come here, Tommy.—One good thing about a dressmaker—she's always got pins. (*Goes to work on* TOMMY's *cuffs with pins*.)

MRS. BANKS.　Oh, Thank Goodness!

BANKS.　Go get the car started, Ben. You better start, Ellie.　5.

5. The rush continues with all except KAY and her mother.

KAY (*going to* MRS. BANKS).　Mother!

MRS. BANKS (*taking* KAY *in her arms and kissing her*). Darling!

MRS. PULITSKI.　Be careful of the veil—please—(*To* TOMMY.) There.

MRS. BANKS (*almost off* L.).　You better come with us, Mrs. Pulitski—(TOMMY *goes to* BANKS *and stands before him.* OTHERS *go off* L.)

TOMMY.　I'm sorry, Pops——

BANKS.　GO—GO—Son—do your best.

TOMMY (*running* L., *and off*).　Right, Pop—see you in church, Kay!

KAY.　Pop, I wish they'd come.

BANKS (*Going to window* R.).　I told that man——

KAY.　Buckley will die if we're late.

BANKS.　We won't be darling—no wedding is on the dot.　6.

6. Again the scene moves into slow tempo.

KAY.　Pops?

BANKS.　What is it, Kay?

KAY.　Something awful! What will I do?

BANKS.　Kitten, what is it?

KAY.　I feel like crying.

BANKS.　On your wedding day?—But why, Kitten?

KAY (*holding hand to her face*).　And if I do I'll ruin my face, and my veil and my dress——

BANKS. Is something troubling you? Is something wrong?

KAY (*sobbing*). Yes.

BANKS. What, my dear?—Tell Pop. 7.

7. BANKS, wanting to take KAY in his arms to reassure her, is restrained by wedding finery that dare not be rumpled.

KAY (*wailing*). I don't want to go!

BANKS. You don't want to go?

KAY (*nodding, through sobs*). To get married.

BANKS. But, Kay—it's a little late to feel like that.

KAY (*still weeping*). I know.

BANKS. There's nothing to be afraid of in marriage.

KAY. Oh! I'm not afraid of that. I'm not afraid of marriage—I'm just afraid of getting married—Pop—Have you got a handkerchief—Oh—my poor face!

BANKS (*producing handkerchief*). You're afraid of the people?

8. KAY will speak some of these lines with a tear in her voice and behind her father's handkerchief. She must take great care to project all lines: enunciate carefully and face front.

KAY (*wailing anew*). Yes! 8.

BANKS. But darling—You look so beautiful—How could you be afraid?

KAY. Suppose I trip on my train or fall down, or something?

BANKS (*wiping her eyes with his handkerchief*). Oh! Kitten—you had me scared. Is that all?

KAY. Is that all!

BANKS (*giving her handkerchief*). (9) Blow, Kitten! Listen, when you were a little girl and had a nightmare who took you out of bed and held you till you felt all right?

9. The audience should see this as a sweet, loving scene, but not at all laughable.

KAY. You did. (*Blows nose.*)

BANKS. And when you fell down and skinned your knee who told you stories until you felt better?

KAY (*calmer, starting to smile*). *You* did.

BANKS. And when you swallowed the peach pit, who swung you by the heels?

KAY (*laughing*). You did. And you hit me hard on the back.

BANKS. Well, I'm going to be right there. You're going to be holding my arm and nothing is going to happen.

KAY (*holding on to him*).   OH! Pops!—You're wonderful. How could anyone be scared with you! You're
NEVER scared, are you? You aren't scared of *anything.* (*Car horn outside honks insistently.*)

BANKS.   Of course not. (*Horn again.*) There's our car. 10.

KAY.   How's my face?

BANKS.   More beautiful than ever.

KAY.   You always know just what to do and what to say.

BANKS.   Ready?

KAY (*laughing*).   Let's go knock 'em dead. (*She takes
his arm. He hums wedding march and they go out
L. together.*)

10. Again the tempo
suddenly speeds up.
Atmosphere is happy
again.

---

*PAINT YOUR WAGON, a musical play by Alan Jay Lerner and Fred-
erick Loewe, takes place in a mining camp in California during the
1850s. There were few women and many men in the camps.* JOLIO *is a
young Mexican miner who lives in seclusion two miles from camp,
where he can save his finds from others. At camp,* JENNIFER *has kindly
doctored his injured toe with ointment from the camp store, which has
a 2-foot-high porch.*

JOLIO   JENNIFER   SUGGESTIONS AND
                                                           STAGE DIRECTIONS

JOLIO (*He starts to put on his boot*).   *Que cosa!* My toe
feels good. What's this medicine called?   1.

JENNIFER (*Looking at the bottle*).   I don't know.

JOLIO.   It's not written on the bottle?

JENNIFER.   Sure.

JOLIO.   What's it say?

JENNIFER.   You'll have to wait a couple of years before
I can tell you that.   2.

JOLIO.   What do you mean?

JENNIFER (*Flaring up suddenly*).   I can't read, that's
what I mean.   3.

JOLIO.   I'm sorry.

JENNIFER.   At least right now I can't. But next winter
I'm goin' East to school.

1. JOLIO may sit on
porch edge, foot out
along edge. JENNIFER
stands to treat the toe.

2. JENNIFER sits on
porch edge, looking at
bottle, then turns face
away.

3. She snaps, facing
JOLIO.

JOLIO. You're lucky. To read and write, that's what I want more than anything in the world.

JENNIFER. You can't read neither? That's wonderful!

JOLIO. No. I am an idiot, like you. But I'm not going to be forever, I can tell you. Someday me and all my little brothers and sisters, we all read and write like geniuses. I dig enough gold to buy back our land for us to live on. You ever hear of Palos Verdes?   4.

4. Give each some kind of indefinite business such as swinging feet, lacing boots, etc.

JENNIFER. No.

JOLIO. It's a place in California. Hills like green clouds, looking down over the sea. That's where I build my rancho.

JENNIFER. Sounds perfeckly wonderful. 'Cept it ain't gonna happen.   5.

5. Good opportunity here for thoughtful pauses, slow tempo.

JOLIO. Why not?

JENNIFER. I heard too many men tellin' tales about what they was goin' to do when they left here. And none of 'em ever do it.

JOLIO. Well I, Señorita Jennifer, I, Jolio Federico Juan Valenzuelo Valveras, I am going to do exactly what I say. Bring family, rancho, Palos Verdes, everything! Everybody's got to dream about something, even if it's only about gold, like these gringos here. And some people get what they want. Why not me? Why not you?   6.

6. JENNIFER may enjoy hearing about JOLIO's dreams, but her smile may suggest doubt.

(The music begins under)

I tell you, one day I write you and ask you to come visit me. And you'll write me that you will. And I'll take you all around my rancho, and tell you about my trip to Spain. And then . . .

(JENNIFER *smiles at all this*)

JOLIO. Don't smile. All this is going to happen. And I have never been so sure in my whole life as I am right this minute. So what do you think of that?

JENNIFER. Why right this minute?

JOLIO. (*He stares at her for a moment, making the discovery of why it all does seem suddenly real*).   Because you listen.

(*Sings*)   7.

("*I Talk to the Trees*")
I talk to the trees
But they don't listen to me.
I talk to the stars
But they never hear me.

The breeze hasn't time
To stop and hear what I say.
I talk to them all in vain.
But suddenly my words
Reach someone else's ears;
Touch someone else's heartstrings, too.

I tell you my dreams   8.
And while you're list'ning to me,
I suddenly see them come true.

I can see us on an April night
Sipping brandy underneath the stars.
Reading poems in the candle light
To the strumming of guitars.

I will tell you all the books I've read;
And the way I met the King of France.
Then I'll send the servants off to bed;
And I'll ask you for a dance.

(*He bows to her, inviting her to dance. She has never danced before with a man, and though she tries, and enjoys it, she not only trips all over herself, but unfortunately all over him. However, he is gallant and he carries it off with a gracious smile as if she were the nimblest of partners. When the dance ends, they are standing facing each other, caught in the emotion of which they are both aware*)

But suddenly my words
Reach someone else's ear;
Touch someone else's heartstrings, too.

I tell you my dreams
And while you're list'ning to me,
I suddenly see them come true.

Buenas noches, Señorita.

7. As JOLIO sings, you may wish him to stare off into space; or he may sing to JENNIFER.

8. JOLIO sings directly to JENNIFER, his arms embracing her. She looks into JOLIO's eyes.

(He bows low. She tries to curtsy in response, but the curtsy comes out a squat. He starts to walk off, then suddenly turns back to her)

You see how I walk? That's Castillian.

(He exits. She stands looking after him in a daze, then she suddenly notices his laundry bag. She runs to him and is about to call after him when she stops. A thought comes to her. Clutching the laundry bag as if it were her most cherished possession, which it probably is, she goes to Salem's store and knocks)

JENNIFER. Salem!

I Talk to the Trees

Lyrics by
ALAN JAY LERNER

Music by
FREDERICK LOEWE

With expression and not fast

I talk to the trees,_____ but they don't lis - ten to me,_____ I talk to the stars,_____ but they nev - er hear me._____ The breeze has - n't time_____ to stop and hear what I say,_____ I talk to them all_____ in vain.____ ____ But sud-den - ly my words____ reach some - one el - se's ear; ____ Touch some-one el - se's heart - strings too._____ I tell you my dreams_____ And while you're list - 'ning to me,_____ ____ I sud - den - ly see them_____ come true._____

Performing with Sets, Props, and Costumes

CHAPTER 13

Giving Your Performance

A performance may be the embodiment of the playwright's intentions, or it may be an entirely new conception of the script as interpreted by the director. This difference has often created unpleasant debates about which approach is the right one. Theater production is a cooperative art. Neither the members of the cast and crew nor the director is compelled to give a play the playwright's interpretation.

NERVES

As the day draws near for the opening performance, excitement seems to attack you. There are mental and emotional reactions which will occur after all lines, actions, and reactions are ready and waiting. Your mind keeps darting from one aspect of production to another; emotions of the average actor-in-training won't behave. The excitement grows as the hour draws nearer. You can probably forget some of your nervousness while applying makeup and dressing, but when you are ready and waiting, tension increases in spite of your will to control it. A similar feeling, to a lesser degree, is felt by seasoned actors, but they know better how to control it.

To *relieve tension*, keep your mind off your lines and try to think of other things than the play: your town or city, the weather, another interest of yours, or some of your neglected responsibilities. While you stand waiting for your first entrance, your heart will beat fastest. However, this nerve tension will slide down and almost disappear thirty seconds after you are on stage and acting your part.

Make nerves work for you. You will not want your nervousness to disappear completely. You need to be nervous, as mentioned in an earlier chapter. Stimulated nerves help you think faster and remain alert, and stimulate brightness of eyes, and alertness of facial and bodily muscles. A healthy, alert feeling of nervousness is desirable, but not nervousness to the extent of having stage fright.

THE AUDIENCE

The audience helps or hinders your acting. You probably don't realize how much effect they are sending your way, but it's true that those out front can undermine what otherwise would be a good performance. They become participants in the performance rather than merely viewers. Few members of an audience realize how much their empathic responses affect members of the cast.

Every individual in the house reacts differently to the same emotion. You cannot adjust your performance to satisfy everyone; it is the *overall* reaction that you are concerned with. However, you should try to sense audience reactions during the show.

Try as actors will to make all performances identical, they cannot be! *Audience reactions* affect actors, and their acting shows it. We have all attended performances of different kinds: football, and other sports, live theater, concerts. When the audience cheers wildly, as at a football game after a good play, the "actors" are inspired to strive to their limit.

If a city has a reputation for showing deep appreciation of visiting concert groups, the groups often hear of that reputation before their concerts; but it is after the audience responds to musical numbers with loud and prolonged applause that musicians become stimulated to reach beyond the peak of excellence of which they thought themselves capable.

The same is also true of live theater. The listeners respond, even if quietly, and their empathic feeling reaches the players, helping them to do their best. At times, somebody in the audience laughs heartily, and the contagion soon spreads over the whole audience. You, as an actor, will find yourself building to the limit of your performing power. However, the audience response need not be something you can hear. It is often an inner feeling; empathic waves of emotion, whether fear, anger, sorrow, or sympathy, that reach you.

However, there are *dangers* that result from both audible and inaudible audience responses. If you cannot sense the appreciation of the audience, you may decide that they are not appreciative, that they seem to be sluggish, disinterested. Such negative feeling is not justified. Some people are less demonstrative than others but enjoy a play more than those who respond noisily. The fact that one audience is less demonstrative than another does not mean that they appreciate your acting less. You *must not let them down*, even though you think they are a bad audience. They have come to see a good show, and it is up to you to give them what they deserve.

Another danger appears when the audience is highly emotional. They laugh, clap, and seem to enjoy the play tremendously. Somebody in your cast may decide that this is the time to throw in extra unrehearsed actions. They *begin to overact*, even clowning. This is *very* bad taste and bad acting, like a seven-year-old child who insists upon holding the floor while his elders watch. He thinks himself a big hit and so goes through ridiculous antics. Don't be guilty of such childishness. Remember Shakespeare's teaching, ". . . now this o'erdone, or come tardy of, though it make the unskilled laugh, cannot but make the judicious grieve. . . ."

LAUGHTER

Actors need training to handle audience laughter. The audience helps you throughout the play; without an audience you would have no interest in working up a part. It is only when audience members are stirred by the play that you enjoy the job of acting.

You are to help your audience when they laugh. You should hear them and *pause for the laughter* until it begins to subside before you go on with your lines. This is hard for inexperienced actors to do.

Your lines have been memorized; you have spoken them through many rehearsals; you have never been interrupted by laughter because you have had no audience. You have not been conscious of possible interruptions. Now you are before an audience. When you begin a speech you have a compulsion to continue to the end, even before an audience. However, those out front do not want you to go on speaking while they are laughing, because they are then unable to hear. When they see you speaking, they must stop laughing so they can hear. To prevent this, you will wish to hold up your lines until the laughter is subsiding.

You may go on with action without worrying your listeners, or you can "hold the picture." However, holding quietly will not look natural if the laugh continues for a while. Stay in character and use some minor action such as turning away, dropping into a chair, shaking your head, waving a hand, or some other simple movement that seems appropriate.

It will be helpful if you can have some *training* in *listening for laughter*. (Your fellow actors won't help; the lines don't seem funny to them any more!) Here is a simple training exercise that will cause you to be alert and help make you conscious of audience reaction.

If another actor or your director will *give you a signal* at any point in your lines, you can become aware of the need to pause and hold for laughter. He or she may use a small bell or a whistle or clap hands loudly *anywhere in your speech*, which you will accept as a signal to hold. This signal need not be where the laugh is expected. It is merely a training device to help you learn to listen to audience responses.

When the signal comes, hold but stay in character; otherwise, a wait may occur. There is *no place* in theater acting *for waits*. Your pause must be filled with your character's thoughts and/or actions. Do not wait for the laughter to stop completely before you pick up your lines. Instead, when it is dying away, continue your lines. Laughter will stop immediately so that the audience can hear what you say.

RESPONSIBILITIES

Onstage. It is frequently true that beginning actors do not realize the importance of their continuing to act when they have no part in the dialogue. Perhaps they are members of a background chorus in front of which four characters are talking. In most scenes, the chorus members are supposed to be listening. If they are, they should *show some feeling* for what is being said. It may be appropriate for some of them to comment to each other, their eyes indicating that their comments relate to the dialogue taking place. It should be news to them, as if they are hearing it for the first time. Try to project this "illusion of the first time" to the listeners.

Perhaps there are only four or five characters on stage, two of them in conversation. If you are one who is not speaking, it is very necessary to listen carefully to the lines—to hear them *with your mind*. You will then really be acting by responding with facial expressions, actions, or perhaps by the way you stand or sit. But be careful—guard against reacting so much that members of the audience notice you. Remember you are merely background.

Offstage. *Keep quiet!* Sometimes a number of characters are waiting in the wings. Backstage may be the only place available for crews and free members of the cast to stay when offstage. The temptation is to talk to each other, paying no attention to the lines of the play because you have heard them many times.

When talking to each other you may want to use an undertone of your natural tone of voice. *Don't!* An undertone (vocalized whisper) carries, even when its volume is low. Members of the audience are sure to hear these tones, which draw their attention away from the play. A voiceless whisper, however, *does not carry.* So remember, do not reveal your immaturity by speaking in an undertone when offstage during the play.

Between scenes, actors should hurry off to dressing rooms or other available space, so that they do not handicap the stage and prop crews, who have an important job to do in a short time. Always strive to help the play go smoothly by trying to do your part to help the production as best you can.

You are all magically weaving the many threads of a beautiful production into an ensemble work of theater art.

You have now completed your study of the many basic principles of acting on the stage. However, your use of these principles has only begun. You will continue enjoying their use for many years as you take your place in theater activities near your home.

Love of theater has kept Americans active wherever players live, as they continue to combine their efforts with those of others, whether in amateur or professional theater. As you complete this study of acting, some of you will begin to plan to join other acting groups in your communities or in new locations, where you may work professionally. But you will probably always look back with pleasure to your first learning days in the theater.

As you near the end of this phase of your study, you may wonder what type of work is available to let you carry on the theater activities you enjoy. There are many possible opportunities. You'll read about them in the pages of the following chapter. Don't be discouraged by the difficulties—you can continue rewardingly for many years if you find that you love to work in theater.

Excerpts for Practice

DARK OF THE MOON, by Howard Richardson and William Berney, is a folk drama based on the mountain ballad "Barbara Allen." JOHN, a witch-boy, has become human to marry the beautiful BARBARA. But when she is forced to be unfaithful to JOHN, the spell that keeps him human is broken. This is the final scene of the play, in which BARBARA is told she must die and in which JOHN turns back into a witch.

*CONJUR MAN   BARBARA
JOHN   *DARK WITCH
                  *FAIR WITCH
                  *CONJUR WOMAN

SUGGESTIONS AND
STAGE DIRECTIONS

FAIR WITCH. Remember, John boy, can't you remember? Remember those nights up thar in the sky, you in my arms on the screamin' wind—how free we all was then. Can't you remember? 1.

JOHN. But hit's over. Hit's finished!

DARK WITCH. Hit's jes' the beginnin'. When you a witch agin, you'll see things different.

JOHN. But I'll allus remember, and I'll allus love her.

FAIR WITCH. You'll change yore mind. (*She disappears over the rock.*)

DARK WITCH. We'll be a-waitin'. (*She too disappears.*)

JOHN. If Barbara die, let me die with her.

CONJUR MAN. You a witch, and you gotta live out yer time.

CONJUR WOMAN. Are you ready, John boy, ready fer the changin'? Hit time to be turned back to a witch.

JOHN. Give me jes' a little longer.

CONJUR WOMAN. The year up to-night. She got to be dead afore the new day.

JOHN. Don't let her see me wunst I'm a witch.

CONJUR MAN (*exits into cave*). You turn to a witch the minute she die.

JOHN. I'll see her agin. I'll fly to her on my eagle. (*He starts off.*)

CONJUR WOMAN. Not yit you can't fly. You still a human.

BARBARA (*offstage*). John!

CONJUR WOMAN. The moon, witch boy! When the moon break through the clouds, you'll be a witch agin. (*She too vanishes in the blackness.*)

BARBARA (*as she comes onstage*). John!
     (*She sees him and stops.*) 2.
     John.

Work to get used to the backwoods American dialect. Find appropriate vocal and physical contrasts to distinguish the various characters. BARBARA is the only normal human. JOHN, though he begins as human, must show in voice and body when he is transformed again into a witch.

1. Entice him by relishing these words and images.

2. The tempo and tone of this scene is slower and more intimate—a marked contrast to the preceding scene.

JOHN. We met afore, Barbara Allen. The night the wind came up and the moon went dark. Remember?

BARBARA. I remember.

JOHN. And thar ain't no moon to-night.

BARBARA. And thar a wind.

JOHN. Remember yer ballad? You said hit wouldn't be sad. You allus like the gay ones best.

BARBARA. I'm sorry. I'm sorry I spiled the ballad.

JOHN. Hit ain't spiled. Hit jes' ends sad. What matters is the singin', and hit still a good song.

BARBARA. All about a witch boy who tried to be human.

JOHN. And the gal he witched, who was untrue.

BARBARA. I couldn't hep it. They made me do hit. They said hit were the will a Gawd.

JOHN. The will of Gawd. I don't know that. I ain't no Christian.

BARBARA. Take me with you, John, take me with you. Hit don't matter whar you go, hit don't matter how fur hit be. Take me out a the valley. I want to be with you. 3.

3. She goes to him. He takes her hand.

JOHN. Hit wouldn't hep none. Not now hit won't.

BARBARA. What you mean, John?

JOHN. You gotta die, Barbara Allen.

BARBARA. I gotta die?

JOHN. Jes' like the ballad, the song you was singin'. Someone gotta die when the song ends sad.

BARBARA. Ain't thar nothin' I kin do to change hit?

JOHN. Ain't nothin' now. Song almost sung.

BARBARA. Not yit. Hit ain't time yit.

JOHN. We ain't got much longer. When the moon breaks through I'll be a witch agin.

BARBARA. Promise you'll find me. Promise you'll come.

JOHN. I can't promise that. A witch got no soul. Three hundred years, then jes' fog on the mountain.

BARBARA. Ain't nothin' else?

JOHN. Ain't nothin' else.

BARBARA (*taking off her wedding ring*).   Take my ring, John, the ring you gave me. Hit got a green stone that shine in the dark.

JOHN.   Our weddin' ring, from the day we was married. (*He looks at the ring.*)

BARBARA.   Promise you'll wear hit, you'll wear hit always.

JOHN.   Somethin' from the time when I warn't no witch, from the days I worked in the burnin' sun, from the nights I held you here in my arms. (*He takes her in his arms.*) (4) and we talked of the baby we was gonna have. We said he'd have blue eyes.

BARBARA.   Fergive me, John. Fergive me.

JOHN.   Hit the last night I kin look at you jes' like you are now, the last time I kin reach out and take yer hand, the last time I kin hold you in my arms and feel yer breath warm against my cheek——

BARBARA (*startled*).   What that I hear, John? High overhead, like the flappin' a wings?   5.

JOHN.   Hit my eagle! He comin' with the moonlight. He comin' down to git me!

BARBARA.   Hit come so quick! Hit come so quick!

JOHN.   The moon! The moon, Barbara! I kin almost see hit.

BARBARA.   I'm skeerd! I'm skeerd a dyin'. (*She almost falls.*)

JOHN.   Barbara! (*He kisses her.*)

BARBARA (*faintly*).   Hold me, John.

JOHN (*he picks her up in his arms and gradually her head and arms relax and hang lifeless. Slowly he carries her over to a ledge of the rock and gently puts her down. The moon begins to show through the clouds*).   Hit the end a the singin'. Ain't nothin' left. None a the words.

(*Suddenly, as the moonlight brightens around him his body stiffens and with a wild alertness he looks slowly around him. As he sees the moon, now full and*

4. If there is a full embrace, either here or later, be sure that the speaker's face is not covered for any length of time.

5. This rapidly changes the tone and tempo of the scene.

bright, he leaps away from BARBARA, *unaware of her.*) 6.

DARK WITCH (*running in*). Witch boy. (*She catches his hand.*)

FAIR WITCH (*catching the other hand*). We come fer you, witch boy.

DARK WITCH. Yer eagle waitin' fer you. He here to take you back.

(*The three start offstage,* JOHN *still fascinated by the moon. He stops to gaze at it again and the* WITCHES *notice the ring.*)

DARK WITCH. What you git that ring, boy?

FAIR WITCH. Hit got a green stone, and hit shine in the dark.

(JOHN *slips the ring off and looks at it a moment.*)

JOHN. I got hit—I got hit from the grave a Agnes Riddle. I cut it off the finger of her cold, dead hand.

(*The three laugh.*)

FAIR WITCH. Let me wear hit, witch boy. Let me keep hit fer you.

JOHN *holds it a moment as if to refuse, then hands it to her.*)

JOHN. All right, I reckon.

(*The* FAIR WITCH *runs offstage.*)

DARK WITCH (*starting off after her*). Come, witch boy. Time to go. (*She goes offstage.*)

(JOHN *starts to follow, then again looks at the moon.*)

JOHN. Look at the moon!

(*Turning back, he sees* BARBARA *lying on the rocks. He runs over to her. Slowly he picks up her hair and lets it fall through his fingers. Turning quickly, he pushes her body with his foot.*)

DARK WITCH (*offstage*). John

FAIR WITCH (*offstage*). Witch boy!

(*The scream of the eagle is heard.* JOHN *runs toward it.*)

6. His changed muscle tone and body attitudes must register the complex transformation back to a witch, as must his voice when he speaks below.

In MAJOR BARBARA, by George Bernard Shaw, Andrew Undershaft, *the millionaire head of a huge munitions factory, was absent while his children were growing. Now that they are adults (or near-adults),* Lady Britomart, *their mother, has arranged for them to meet their father. One of the children,* Barbara, *has become a Major in the Salvation Army. The family is now beginning to assemble itself.*

CHARLES LOMAX (SARAH's friend
ADOLPHUS CUSINS (BARBARA's friend)
* MORRISON (the butler)
ANDREW UNDERSHAFT
* STEPHEN UNDERSHAFT (the son)

LADY BRITOMART
BARBARA UNDERSHAFT (daughter)
* SARAH UNDERSHAFT (daughter)

SUGGESTIONS AND STAGE DIRECTIONS

This scene provides excellent opportunities for working with set pieces with several people onstage. Visible reactions to what is said are extremely important in establishing the comic tone. The action takes place in January 1906, in the home of an upper-class English family.

Barbara.   Are Cholly and Dolly to come in?   1.

Lady Britomart (*forcibly*).   Barbara: I will not have Charles called Cholly: the vulgarity of it positively makes me ill.

Barbara.   It's all right, mother: Cholly is quite correct nowadays. Are they to come in?

1. Peeking her head in through the door; LADY BRITOMART and STEPHEN are already in the room.

Lady Britomart.   Yes, if they will behave themselves.

Barbara (*through the door*).   Come in, Dolly; and behave yourself.

Barbara *comes to her mother's writing table.* Cusins *enters smiling,* (2) *and wanders towards* Lady Britomart.

Sarah (*calling*).   Come in, Cholly. (Lomax *enters, controlling his features very imperfectly,* (2) *and places himself vaguely between* Sarah *and* Barbara).

2. They have all been laughing uproariously in the other room. LOMAX (Cholly) is always on the verge of breaking into laughter.

Lady Britomart (*peremptorily*).   Sit down, all of you. (*They sit.* Cusins *crosses to the window and seats himself there.* Lomax *takes a chair.* Barbara *sits at the writing table and* Sarah *on the settee*). (3) I don't in the least know what you are laughing at, Adolphus. I am surprised at you, though I expected nothing better from Charles Lomax.

3. It is imperative that a group ground plan be set before rehearsals begin. This will ease the blocking immensely.

Cusins (*in a remarkably gentle voice*).   Barbara has been trying to teach me the West Ham Salvation March.

LADY BRITOMART.   I see nothing to laugh at in that; nor should you if you are really converted.

CUSINS (*sweetly*).   You were not present. It was really funny, I believe.

LOMAX.   Ripping.

LADY BRITOMART.   Be quiet, Charles. Now listen to me, children. Your father is coming here this evening.

General stupefaction. LOMAX, SARAH, *and* BARBARA *rise:* SARAH *scared, and* BARBARA *amused and expectant.* 4.

4. They are caught off guard, shocked.

LOMAX (*remonstrating*).   Oh I say!

LADY BRITOMART.   You are not called on to say anything, Charles.

SARAH.   Are you serious, mother?

LADY BRITOMART.   Of course I am serious. It is on your account, Sarah, and also on Charles's. (*Silence.* SARAH *sits, with a shrug.* CHARLES *looks painfully unworthy*). I hope you are not going to object, Barbara.

BARBARA.   I! why should I? My father has a soul to be saved like anybody else. He's quite welcome as far as I am concerned. (*She sits on the table, and softly whistles 'Onward, Christian Soldiers'*).

LOMAX (*still remonstrant*).   But really, dont you know! Oh I say!

LADY BRITOMART (*frigidly*).   What do you wish to convey, Charles?

LOMAX.   Well, you must admit that this is a bit thick.

LADY BRITOMART (*turning with ominous suavity to* CUSINS).   Adolphus: you are a professor of Greek. Can you translate Charles Lomax's remarks into reputable English for us?

CUSINS (*cautiously*).   If I may say so, Lady Brit, I think Charles has rather happily expressed what we all feel. Homer, speaking of Autolycus, uses the same phrase. πυκινὸν δόμον ἐλθεῖν means a bit thick.   5.

5. The Greek here is pronounced (puckinòn dahmin elthane).

LOMAX (*handsomely*).   Not that I mind, you know, if Sarah dont. (*He sits*).

LADY BRITOMART (*crushingly*).   Thank you. Have I your permission, Adolphus, to invite my own husband to my own house?

CUSINS (*gallantly*).   You have my unhesitating support in everything you do.

LADY BRITOMART.   Tush! Sarah: have you nothing to say?

SARAH.   Do you mean that he is coming regularly to live here?

LADY BRITOMART.   Certainly not. The spare room is ready for him if he likes to stay for a day or two and see a little more of you; but there are limits.

SARAH.   Well, he cant eat us, I suppose. *I* dont mind.

LOMAX (*chuckling*).   I wonder how the old man will take it.

LADY BRITOMART.   Much as the old woman will, no doubt, Charles.

LOMAX (*abashed*).   I didnt mean—at least—

LADY BRITOMART.   You didnt think, Charles. You never do; and the result is, you never mean anything. (6) And now please attend to me, children. Your father will be quite a stranger to us.

LOMAX.   I suppose he hasnt seen Sarah since she was a little kid.

LADY BRITOMART.   Not since she was a little kid, Charles, as you express it with that elegance of diction and refinement of thought that seem never to desert you. Accordingly—er—(*impatiently*) Now I have forgotten what I was going to say. That comes of your provoking me to be sarcastic, Charles. Adolphus: will you kindly tell me where I was.

COUSINS (*sweetly*).   You were saying that as Mr Undershaft has not seen his children since they were babies, he will form his opinion of the way you have brought them up from their behavior tonight, and that therefore you wish us all to be particularly careful to conduct ourselves well, especially Charles.

LADY BRITOMART (*with emphatic approval*).   Precisely.

LOMAX.   Look here, Dolly: Lady Brit didnt say that.

6. Be alert to all character clues as these.

LADY BRITOMART (*vehemently*).   I did, Charles. Adolphus's recollection is perfectly correct. It is most important that you should be good; and I do beg you for once not to pair off into opposite corners and giggle and whisper while I am speaking to your father.

BARBARA.   All right, mother. We'll do you credit. (*She comes off the table, and sits in her chair with lady-like elegance*).   7.

7. Exaggerate this move.

LADY BRITOMART.   Remember, Charles, that Sarah will want to feel proud of you instead of ashamed of you.

LOMAX.   Oh I say! theres nothing to be exactly proud of, dont you know.

LADY BRITOMART.   Well, try and look as if there was.

MORRISON, *pale and dismayed, breaks into the room in unconcealed disorder.*

MORRISON.   Might I speak a word to you, my lady?

LADY BRITOMART.   Nonsense! Shew him up.

MORRISON.   (8) Yes, my lady. (*He goes*).

8. Pause a moment, shocked, before the line.

LOMAX.   Does Morrison know who it is?

LADY BRITOMART.   Of course. Morrison has always been with us.

LOMAX.   It must be a regular corker for him, dont you know.

LADY BRITOMART.   Is this a moment to get on my nerves, Charles, with your outrageous expressions?

LOMAX.   But this is something out of the ordinary, really—

MORRISON (*at the door*).   The—er—Mr Undershaft. (*He retreats in confusion*).

In *Robert Bolt's A MAN FOR ALL SEASONS*, SIR THOMAS MORE, *Chancellor to* HENRY VIII, *has been divested of his office and put into jail for the sake of his conscience—he has refused to swear to the Act of Succession, by which* HENRY *pronounced himself head of the Church of England and was then able to divorce his wife Catherine. In this scene* MORE's *daughter, wife, and son-in-law visit him in prison after a long, difficult separation.*

MORE   ALICE (MORE's wife)
ROPER   MARGARET (MORE's daughter
JAILER   and ROPER's wife)

ALICE (*hostile*).   (1) You're content, then, to be shut up here with mice and rats when you might be home with us!

MORE (*flinching*).   Content? If they'd open a crack that wide (*between finger and thumb*) I'd be through it. (*To* MARGARET) Well, has Eve run out of apples?

MARGARET.   I've not yet told you what the house is like, without you.

MORE.   Don't Meg.

MARGARET.   What we do in the evenings, now that you're not there.

MORE.   Meg, have done!

MARGARET.   We sit in the dark because we've no candles. And we've no talk because we're wondering what they're doing to you here.

MORE.   The King's more merciful than you. He doesn't use the rack.

     (*Enter* JAILER)   2.

JAILER.   Two minutes to go, sir. I thought you'd like to know.

MORE.   Two minutes!

JAILER.   Till seven o'clock, sir. Sorry. Two minutes.

     (*Exit* JAILER)

MORE.   Jailer! (*Seizes* ROPER *by the arm*) Will—go to him, talk to him, keep him occupied—

     (*Propelling him after* JAILER)

ROPER.   How sir?

MORE.   Anyhow! Have you got any money?

ROPER (*eagerly*).   Yes!

MORE.   No, don't try and bribe him! Let him play for it; he's got a pair of dice. And talk to him, you understand! And take this—(*He hands him the wine*) and mind you share it—do it properly, Will! (ROPER *nods vigorously and exits*) Now listen, you must leave the country. All of you must leave the country.

Be sensitive to the range of emotions expressed in this scene, from anger to genuine love. Note how the time element lends pressure to the emotions.

1. ALICE and MARGARET have been trying to persuade MORE to compromise his conscience so that he can be set free.

2. Note how the JAILER changes the whole tone and tempo of the scene when he enters.

MARGARET.   And leave you here?

MORE.   It makes no difference, Meg; they won't let you see me again. (*Breathlessly, a prepared speech under pressure*) You must all go on the same day, but not on the same boat; different boats from different ports—

MARGARET.   After the trial, then.

MORE.   There'll be no trial, they have no case. Do this for me, I beseech you?

MARGARET.   Yes.

MORE.   Alice? (*She turns her back*) Alice, I command you!

ALICE (*harshly*).   Right!

MORE (*looks into the basket*).   Oh, this is splendid; I know who packed this.

ALICE (*harshly*).   I packed it.

MORE.   Yes. (*He eats a morsel*) You still make superlative custard, Alice.

ALICE.   Do I?

MORE.   That's a nice dress you have on.

ALICE.   It's my cooking dress.

MORE.   It's very nice anyway. Nice color.

ALICE (*turns. Quietly*).   You think very little of me. (*Mounting bitterness*) I know I'm a fool. But I'm no such fool as at this time to be lamenting for my dresses! Or to relish complimenting on my custard!

MORE (*regarding her with frozen attention. He nods once or twice*).   I am well rebuked. (*He holds out his hands*) Al—

ALICE.   No!

(*She remains where she is, glaring at him*)   3.

MORE (*he is in great fear of her*).   I am faint when I think of the worst that they may do to me. But worse than that would be to go with you not understanding why I go.

ALICE.   I don't!

MORE (*just hanging on to his self-possession*).   Alice, if you can tell me that you understand, I think I can make a good death, if I have to.

3. We are approaching the emotional climax of the scene. ALICE's glare speaks volumes with its heavy silence. MORE responds slowly and with emotional difficulty.

ALICE. Your death's no "good" to me!

MORE. Alice, you must tell me that you understand!

ALICE. I don't! (*She throws it straight at his head*) I don't believe this had to happen.

MORE (*his face is drawn*). If you say that, Alice, I don't see how I'm to face it.

ALICE. It's the truth!

MORE (*gasping*). You're an honest woman.

ALICE. Much good may it do me! I'll tell you what I'm afraid of: that when you've gone, I shall hate you for it.

MORE (*turns from her, his face working*). Well, you mustn't, Alice, that's all. (*Swiftly she crosses the stage to him; he turns and they clasp each other fiercely.*) You mustn't, you—

ALICE (*covers his mouth with her hand*). (4) S-s-sh . . . As for understanding, I understand you're the best man that I ever met or am likely to; and if you go— well, God knows why I suppose—though as God's my witness God's kept deadly quiet about it! And if anyone wants my opinion of the King and his Council they've only to ask for it!

MORE. Why, it's a lion I married! A lion! A lion! (*He breaks away from her, his face shining*) Say what you may—this custard's very good. It's very, very good.

(*He puts his face in his hands;* ALICE *and* MARGARET *comfort him;* ROPER *and* JAILER *erupt onto the stage above, wrangling fiercely*) 5.

JAILER. It's no good, sir! I know what you're up to! And it can't be done!

ROPER. Another minute, man!

JAILER (*descending: to* MORE). Sorry, sir, time's up!

ROPER (*gripping his shoulder from behind*). For pity's sake!

JAILER (*shaking him off*). Now don't do that, sir! Sir Thomas, the ladies will have to go now!

MORE. You said seven o'clock!

JAILER. It's seven now. You must understand my position, sir.

4. This action and the embrace are important actions and must be handled carefully. Take time with them.

5. If you cannot get a platform and a few steps for the higher level, play the action on one side of the stage (the entrance side). The JAILER'S entrance again triggers a new tone and tempo.

MORE. But one more minute!

MARGARET. Only a little while—give us a little while!

JAILER (*reprovingly*). Now, miss, you don't want to get me into trouble.

ALICE. Do as you're told. Be off at once!

(*The first stroke of seven is heard on a heavy, deliberate bell, which continues, reducing what follows to a babble*)

JAILER (*taking* MARGARET *firmly by the upper arm*). Now come along, miss; you'll get your father into trouble as well as me. (ROPER *descends and grabs him*) Are you obstructing me, sir? (MARGARET *embraces* MORE *and dashes up the stairs and exits, followed by* ROPER. *Taking* ALICE *gingerly by the arm*) Now, my lady, no trouble!

ALICE (*throwing him off as she rises*). Don't put your muddy hand on me!

JAILER. Am I to call the guard then? Then come on!

ALICE, *facing him, puts foot on bottom stair and so retreats before him, backwards*)

In the musical play H.M.S. PINAFORE, by W. S. Gilbert and Arthur Sullivan, JOSEPHINE, *daughter of the* CAPTAIN, *is the subject of much speculation and anxiety. She has her own ideas about different suitors. However, the* CAPTAIN *and* SAILORS *are all eager to help her choose a husband. There is much talk about possible choices.*

CAPTAIN CORCORAN	LITTLE BUTTERCUP	SUGGESTIONS AND
BOATSWAIN	SAILORS	STAGE DIRECTIONS
DICK DEADEYE		
RALPH RACKSTRAW		
SAILORS		

SUGGESTIONS AND STAGE DIRECTIONS

There can be women sailors if desirable. All may sway and act with the music.

BOAT. Ah, my poor lad, you've climbed too high: our worthy captain's child won't have nothin' to say to a poor chap like you. Will she, lads?

ALL. No, no. 1.

1. Girls may take the parts of sailors along with the men.

DICK. No, no, captains' daughters don't marry foremast hands.

ALL (*reconciling from him*). Shame! shame! 2.

2. DECK HANDS have been busy at various tasks, polishing brass rails, pulling ropes, cleaning deck, folding deck chairs.

BOAT. Dick Deadeye, them sentiments o' yourn are a disgrace to our common natur'.

RALPH.   But it's a strange anomaly, that the daughter of
a man who hails from the quarter-deck may not love
another who lays out on the fore-yard arm. For a man
is but a man, whether he hoists his flag at the main-
truck or his slacks on the main-deck.

DICK.   Ah, it's a queer world!

RALPH.   Dick Deadeye, I have no desire to press hardly
on you, but such a revolutionary sentiment is enough
to make an honest sailor shudder.

BOAT.   My lads, our gallant captain has come on deck;
let us greet him as so brave an officer and so gallant
a seaman deserves.   3.

> 3. DECK HANDS jump to attention, wherever they are.

Enter CAPTAIN CORCORAN.   4.

RECITATIVE—CAPT. *and* CREW

> 4. SAILORS salute from their various positions.

CAPT.   My gallant crew, good morning.

ALL (*saluting*).   Sir, good morning!

CAPT.   I hope you're all quite well.

ALL (*as before*).   Quite well; and you, sir?

CAPT.   I am in reasonable health, and happy
To meet you all once more.

ALL (*as before*).   You do us proud, sir!

SONG—CAPT.

CAPT.   I am the Captain of the *Pinafore*;

ALL.   And a right good captain, too!

CAPT.   You're very, very good,
And be it understood,
I command a right good crew,

ALL.   We're very, very good,   5.
And be it understood,
He commands a right good crew.

> 5. CREW may move into formation as they sing and dance.

CAPT.   Though related to a peer,
I can hand, reef, and steer,
And ship a selvagee;
I am never known to quail
At the fury of a gale,
And I'm never, never sick at sea!

ALL.   What, never?

CAPT.   No, never!

ALL.   What, *never?*

CAPT.   Hardly ever!

ALL.   He's hardly ever sick at sea!
   Then give three cheers, and one cheer more,   6.
   For the hardy Captain of the *Pinafore!*

CAPT.   I do my best to satisfy you all—

ALL.   And with you we're quite content.

CAPT.   You're exceedingly polite,
   And I think it only right
   To return the compliment.

ALL.   We're exceedingly polite,
   And he thinks it's only right
   To return the compliment.

CAPT.   Bad language or abuse,
   I never, never use,
   Whatever the emergency;
   Though "Bother it" I may   7.
   Occasionally say,
   I never use a big, big D—

ALL.   What, never?

CAPT.   No, never!

ALL.   What, *never?*

CAPT.   Hardly ever!

ALL.   Hardly ever swears a big, big D—
   Then give three cheers, and one cheer more,
   For the well-bred Captain of the *Pinafore!*

(After song exeunt all but CAPTAIN.)

Enter LITTLE BUTTERCUP

RECITATIVE—BUTTERCUP *and* CAPT.   8.

BUT.   Sir, you are sad! The silent eloquence
   Of yonder tear that trembles on your eyelash
   Proclaims a sorrow far more deep than common;
   Confide in me—fear not—I am a mother!

CAPT.   Yes, Little Buttercup, I'm sad and sorry—
   My daughter, Josephine, the fairest flower
   That ever blossomed on ancestral timber,
   Is sought in marriage by Sir Joseph Porter,
   Our Admiralty's First Lord, but for some reason
   She does not seem to tackle kindly to it.

6. The cheers may be given with a wave of one hand, all chorus's actions same.

7. All SAILORS may saunter back to their several jobs, but all turn to CAPTAIN abruptly on his ". . . big D—."

8. LITTLE BUTTERCUP is often pictured as a very plump, short, middle-aged lady.

9. CAPTAIN speaks slowly, seems down-hearted.

Bu⊤. (*with emotion*).   Ah, poor Sir Joseph! Ah, I know
    too well
    The anguish of a heart that lives but vainly.
    But see, here comes your most attractive daughter.
    I go.—Farewell.

Cᴀᴘᴛ. (*looking after her*).   A plump and pleasing per-
    son. (*Exit.*)

I Am the Captain of the Pinafore

Words by
W. S. GILBERT

Music by
ARTHUR SULLIVAN

CAPTAIN   MEN _____ *f*

cresc.

nev-er?___   Hard-ly   ev- er!   He's   hard-ly   ev - er sick   at   sea! Then
nev-er?___   Hard-ly   ev- er!   Hard-ly   ev -er swears a   big,   big   D! Then

p a tempo

give   three   cheers,   and   one   cheer   more,   For   the   har - dy   Cap - tain   of   the
give   three   cheers,   and   one   cheer   more,   For   the   well - bred   Cap - tain   of   the

f

Pin - a - fore!   Then   give   three   cheers,   and   one   cheer   more,   For   the
Pin - a - fore!   Then   give   three   cheers,   and   one   cheer   more,   For   the

a tempo   1.   *p*   2.

Cap - tain   of   the   Pin - a -   fore!   2. I
Cap - tain   of   the   Pin - a-   fore!___

CHAPTER 14

Acting in Your Future

READING PLAYS FOR PLEASURE

The art of the theater offers a very broad field of interest, so you may pick and choose the area that most appeals to you. You may enjoy theater and plays even if you do not participate in productions. Reading plays for pure *enjoyment* may be a great pastime that helps you slip away from reality and carries you into the absorbing situations of the characters. Stage work can help you relax from the day's work and problems.

Notice how you begin to identify more closely with the *characters*, seeing their motives and the reasons for the conflicts they are in. You'll see how the dramatist has put certain traits, dispositions, and peculiarities into the characters; how he or she opens the *plot* bit by bit; how problems seem to sneak in and grow. Some of you may prefer to let the play move as it will without examining the dramatist's technique. If this is your choice, close your mind to questions of writing and read just for the fun of it.

Some of you may find yourself wanting to *make changes*, mentally adding problems or even setting characters down in different times and places and then regulating their actions. You may find different crises possible. You may find yourself unconsciously criticizing the dramatist. As you do this you are developing, growing, learning the dramatist's art—an interesting challenge for theater-minded people.

Your pleasure may reach beyond reading scripts to *books* and *articles* written about theater people, backgrounds of plays, and leading actors. Theater magazines are full of absorbing articles about actors and their careers. Books and magazines discuss compositions, acting, theater construction, and many kinds of crew work.

All that you read will give you increased pleasure in watching theater productions. You'll find yourself becoming even more of a theater fan.

CAREER OPPORTUNITIES

There are always career opportunities available to a determined person who seeks them. However, so many *ifs* stand in the way of people who wish to work in any fine art that we dare not urge young people to face the difficulties they will encounter. To try to make a living by acting you need to know, ahead of trying, the problems you will face. Good luck—others have become professional actors, and you may too.

If you have strong *qualifications*, you may succeed. One quality that is a must is *inborn talent*, which is a necessity for all fine arts. You should also have a *physical appearance* that will fit you into different and varied parts. An unusual physical appearance can be an asset such as a fleshy, tall or very thin body, a homely face, a deformity. A very small person might be needed to play the role of a fairy; a very tall man would be needed to play Abe Lincoln.

An actor needs *good health*. There will be long, grueling hours of rehearsals, weeks and months without money coming in, and perhaps very poor housing and food. If you try to go into this business, you will need stability in your mental, moral, and physical life. You will also need an abundance of *self-discipline* to control yourself during the hardships you will face. You will probably experience many frustrations, repeated disappointments, and unjust criticisms.

Television makes use of many actors but, because competition is fierce in both TV and motion picture acting, you should have especially good training before trying to enter Hollywood.

If you are imbued with the qualities mentioned above and, in addition, have schooled yourself to face additional, unforeseen difficulties, you can become a *professional stage actor*.

There are opportunities in related fields that are less difficult to attain, such as that of *director* of a little theater group. The present trend is to produce good plays in a great many communities, many of them in dinner theaters. You may need to help organize such a group and face its financial difficulties until the theater becomes established. Needs other than the building to be used as a theater may be donated by the community.

You can train and become a *teacher* in public schools or, with advanced degrees and training, you may teach at the college and university level. Here, as well as directing plays, you will probably teach classes in theater, speech, or English; but you will always have the joy of preparing a new play.

LEISURE ACTING OPPORTUNITIES

Community plays are now popular all over the country. The public is becoming more and more theater-minded. No matter how small or how large your home community is, there is probably room for another theater group. In such a group you will have an opportunity to act—perhaps not in every play unless you belong to a *repertory* theater group, in which the few players act in all productions.

Another theater opportunity is in *religious groups,* which present plays of one kind or another on occasion throughout the year. Good plays are usually presented, and production is satisfactory. Few churches have good space in which to act, but a modern trend is to fit a play onto any kind of stage. Most churches have a dining room that can be adjusted to function as a theater.

Barter theater, started long ago, is another kind of theater that may interest you. Because of expenses, acting groups are often no longer able to go from town to town with their plays. However, a group that merely wants an audience for its plays might like the old Barter Theater plan.

Suppose that your group works up two plays. Two or three actors go out to book the productions in small towns. They must secure permission to come, although there is no exchange of monies or written agreement. After permission is secured for the group to bring clean plays suitable for family viewing, a makeshift theater space must be found: behind a store building, on the school grounds, or on somebody's porch.

Your next task is to put posters in stores giving the price of admission. The price may be a home-cooked meal, overnight lodging for one or two actors, or a plate of sandwiches, coffee, pop, or tea—anything the group needs to live on while in town. If you use royalty plays, you need some cash. Instead of barter, some members of the audience may pay $1.50 or some other amount to help pay royalty.

After having played the first town, you move on to the next, and after several towns you should have new plays and be ready to make the rounds again.

If your group is eager and determined enough, they may work up *radio* and *television plays*. More difficult and also more interesting would be either writing or using prepared plays for television production. Working on radio would not demand memorization. Scripts can be used so convincingly that radio listeners cannot detect the difference between productions which result from reading a script and those recited and enacted spontaneously.

If you are using a royalty play, the expense must be arranged with the radio or TV station before presentation. Another problem in giving media shows is *timing*. You must play the broadcast so that it comes out on the half-minute of time allotted; not an easy matter.

If your group should become proficient in carefully timing scenes, in creating sound effects, in shifting from scene to scene, and in fitting all into an allotted time, the program committee of a local or nearby television station may be happy to give you air time.

VICARIOUS INVOLVEMENT

You can enjoy theater that comes to you *in pictures*. For many years Americans have spent their spare time before *TV* screens, while others have lined up to buy tickets to *movies*. Both TV and movies give viewers satisfaction and pleasure. In many communities, there is opportunity for amateurs to *participate in* these forms of *media*.

The demand for *play readings* has grown because of the great increase in leisure time. Many people give delightful play reviews to various groups. More and more Americans are joining with groups to form game days, reading clubs, philanthropic groups.

Volunteer visitors call on lonely, sick, and imprisoned people who are unhappy and perhaps full of self-pity. When a visitor calls, he or she tries to bring pleasant thoughts; something for the lonely to enjoy or recall for at least a few days. The visitor can bring scenes from a play to read aloud, the reader taking all parts and telling bits of the story to tie the scenes together. The same play cuttings can be presented to organized groups, who are always looking for inexpensive entertainment by people who do not expect payment.

The work of *stage crews* lacks the glamor of acting, but it yields just as much, if not more, challenge and pleasure. With experimentation rampant in modern theater, new designs challenge scenery and light crews to try anything. Symbolic trees, furniture, a river, or a bridge are readily accepted by theater audiences. A single pole with high-hung pulley can represent a ship; steps and levels in fantastic arrangements that represent nothing at all, but supply interesting playing space, are delightful pictorial possibilities.

Few plays have received such high praise as Thornton Wilder's *Our Town*, which was played on an empty stage. Staff members are constantly planning new types of staging and then creating what the theater public has never seen before.

The appeal of the theater is an almost universal one. We all like to imagine, to watch, or enact. This is a healthy feeling and, in troubled times, the more fantasy that anguished people can see or take part in, the less real tragedy will bear down on them.

Nothing can take the place of live theater, for either the viewer or the actor. As an actor, you need the inspiration of the live audience; the audience also needs and enjoys that indescribable bond with the actors. The need for intercommunication will always exist in every human mind and heart.

May you never become so busy, so involved in business and the workaday world, that you push aside your interest in and enjoyment of theater until you have "plenty of time" to go back to it. That leisure time may never come.

Theater holds a world of enjoyment of various kinds, ready to be grasped when your mind and hands reach out. If you have perseverance you can progress through observation and practice linked with continual striving, and will have the satisfaction of reaching your goal. After your theater years you will always enjoy recalling the experiences you had.

INDEXES

Indexes

INDEX OF PHOTOGRAPHS

INDEX OF AUTHORS

INDEX OF TITLES

INDEX OF TOPICS

Globe Theater, 21
Glossary, stage, 164
Group, 181
    action, 176, 181

Hamlet, advice to players, 60
Hands:
    for action, 63
    for laughs, 63, 64, 254
    for telephone talk, 64
Humor, pointing up, 68
    exercises, 68
    personality, 112

Ibsen, Henrik, 23
Illusion of first time, 36
Imagery, 115
    examples, 115
    kinds, 115
    pantomimes, 116
    sensing, 115
Imagination, 85, 86, 138
    exercises, 85, 86
Improvisation, 9
    exercises, 10, 141, 143
Indefinite business, 37, 184
Inflection:
    in Marullus' speech, 62
    use of, 61
Interpretation, 213

James-Lange Theory, 36
Jonson, Ben, 21

Kabuki, 18
Kneeling, 186

Language, body, 34
Laughter, 13, 60, 63, 161, 253
    body creates, 112
    feed, 111
    pause, 63, 253
Listening:
    action of, 40
    character study through, 135
Locating, action of, 41

"Magic If," 23
Marlowe, Christopher, 21

Marullus, speech of, 62
Melody, 61
Memorization, 88
    exercises, 88
Menander, 19
Mimes, 5, 30
    exercises, 6
Mind, relaxation, 81
    concentration, 82
        exercises, 82
    control, 83–86
        exercises, 81
    imagination, 85
        exercises, 85
    searches, 80
Miracle plays, 20
Molière, 21
Morality plays, 20
Movement:
    do's and don'ts, 173
    principles, 175
    purpose of, 173
Music, 15
Mystery plays, 20

Nerves, actors', 251
Nineteenth-century theater, 21

Occasional action, 185
    examples, 186
Off-stage behavior, 254
Opportunities for recreational acting:
    barter theater, 25, 275
    career, 274
    community plays, 275
    director, 274
    leisure reading, 273
    listening, media, 276
    public play reading, 276
    radio reading, 276
    reading to shut-ins, 276
    religious groups, 275
    stage crews, 276
    TV acting, 276
Overacting, 112

Pace, 61
Pantomime, 4, 116
    exercises, 4, 30, 143
Pause, 63
    for comedy effect, 68
    for emphasis, 64
    to express emotions, 65
        examples, 65